HAYDN: A DOCUMENTARY STUDY

FRONTISPIECE
Joseph Haydn, engraving by J. E. Mansfeld, published by
Artaria & Co., Vienna 1781.

H. C. ROBBINS LANDON

A DOCUMENTARY STUDY

with 220 illustrations, 44 in color,
and 1 map

RIZZOLI
NEW YORK

To Alun and Rhiannon Hoddinott,
with affection

First published in the United States of America in 1981 by

*R*IZZOLI INTERNATIONAL PUBLICATIONS, INC.
712 Fifth Avenue/New York 10019

© 1981 H. C. Robbins Landon

Library of Congress Catalog Card Number: 81–50279

ISBN: 0–8478–0388–0

Printed in Spain

D.L.T.O–456–81

CONTENTS

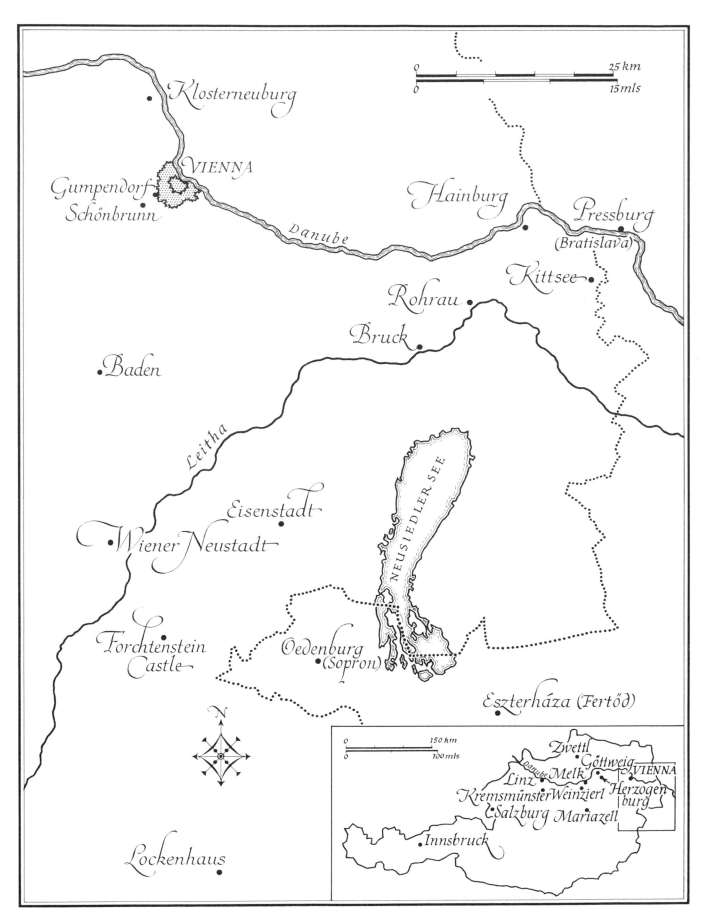

Map showing the area of Austria/Hungary in which Haydn lived and worked for most of his life. The broken line indicates the present-day boundaries between Hungary and the Austrian province of Burgenland and – north of the Danube – between Czechoslovakia and Lower Austria; modern place names are shown in parentheses. The inset shows the locations of other places in Austria with which Haydn was directly or indirectly associated.

PREFACE

IN 1957, the late Professor O. E. Deutsch and I conceived the idea of a pictorial documentary biography of Haydn, to be based on Deutsch's own magnificent documentary studies (on Schubert, Handel and Mozart); the plan was accepted for publication by Bärenreiter Verlag, and the book announced as being in preparation. Then, on a trip to Hungary, I learned that Dr László Somfai was planning a similar publication with Corvina Press in Budapest; Professor Deutsch and I therefore renounced our plans and made available to Dr Somfai the photographs we had already collected. Dr Somfai's book appeared in 1966 simultaneously in German (Bärenreiter) and English (Faber), and later also in Hungarian.

Since the publication of Dr Somfai's scholarly book, many authentic documents and portraits have come to light – including a lost Haydn portrait by James Tassie (1792; ill. 99), rediscovered by the present writer in 1978 and published in 1980), an authentic repetition (or the original?) of the Guttenbrunn Haydn portrait (London, 1792; ill. 33) and a whole series of Esterházy portraits (e.g. ill. 26) given by the princely family to the Hospitallers Order in Eisenstadt. It has not been the purpose of this study to duplicate the pioneer work of Dr Somfai. Our idea, rather, was to present a literary and pictorial view of Haydn's world from contemporary documents and illustrations, the scope of which we have extended to include some present-day photographs of extant buildings and places that Haydn knew – especially several of the justly famous 'historical reconstructions' by Erich Lessing, studies originally taken for an article he did together with my old friend Joseph Wechsberg. In this book the reader will also find many hitherto unknown pictorial documents, including a letter written by Haydn in (broken) English, discovered in 1980 and published here for the first time.

The documents (see note below concerning bibliographical sources) and some of the text have been taken from the present writer's biography *Haydn: Chronicle and Works* (five volumes, 1976–80), and some recently discovered pictorial material was in fact first published there (e.g. the portrait of Princess Maria Anna Esterházy; cf. ill. 68). In selecting representative samples of Haydn's autograph scores as illustrations – a separate section has been included at the end of the chronologically arranged pictorial and literary documents – we have tried to show the characteristic changes in Haydn's handwriting from *c.* 1755 to 1803 and to make the selection from lesser-known and in part recently discovered autographs, some in private possession (e.g. the 'March for the Prince of Wales', London 1792 [?]).

We are immensely indebted to the many owners, private and public, who supplied the illustrations for this book: a detailed list may be found on p. 221. We should like particularly to thank Her Majesty the Queen for permission to reproduce the great Hoppner portrait of Haydn (1791); Mr and Mrs Paul Mellon for some of the beautiful views of *fin-de-siècle* England in their collection (now at Yale University); the Royal College of Music in London for several beautiful portraits, not least the George Dance drawing of Haydn which the composer considered the best likeness of himself; the Albertina, the Kunsthistorisches Museum and the Historisches Museum der Stadt Wien, Vienna, from the collections of which many interesting and largely unknown views derive; as well as the Burgenländisches Landesmuseum (Eisenstadt) and the Gesellschaft der Musikfreunde (Vienna) for their many treasures of Haydniana. The Hungarian National Libraries and Archives (Országos Széchényi Könyvtár, and Magyar Országos Léveltár, Budapest) were, as always, of great assistance.

The work of selecting the documents and illustrations for inclusion – and indeed the entire planning of the book – has been a collaborative effort, and I am greatly indebted both to Else Radant Landon and to the editorial staff of Thames and Hudson for their help. It must be emphasized that the material finally chosen for inclusion represents no more than a selection – many other items could have been included with equal validity. Within the limitations of the available space we have also preferred not to attempt to achieve a degree of comprehensiveness that would, at best, remain an elusive goal; we have instead tried to present a thoroughly representative, lively and interesting choice of material giving an overall view of the life and times of Joseph Haydn.

BIBLIOGRAPHICAL SOURCES

The principal sources of contemporary documents quoted are:

(a) the 'authentic' biographies of Haydn (all published shortly after the composer's death) by G. Carpani, A. C. Dies, N. Framery and G. A. Griesinger – for details see Bibliography p. 220; and the comments made by Haydn's former composition pupil Sigismund (von) Neukomm on Dies's account (published as 'Bermerkungen Neukomms zu den biogr. Nachrichten von Dies', in *Beiträge zur Musikwissenschaft*, 1959/3).

(b) MS. diaries, correspondence, contracts etc., especially Haydn's own letters and London Notebooks (ed. Landon), the diaries of J. C. Rosenbaum in the Österreichische Nationalbibliothek (ed. Else Radant, published in translation in *Haydn Yearbook* V, 1968, and also available as a separate publication in the original German), and documents in the Esterházy Archives (now Budapest, Eisenstadt or Forchtenstein).

(c) newspaper accounts and announcements, especially in: (German) the *Wienerisches Diarium*, and *Wiener Zeitung*, the *Preßburger Zeitung*, and the *Allgemeine Musikalische Zeitung* (Leipzig); and (English) the *Gazetteer, Oracle, Morning Chronicle* and *Public Advertiser* (all London).

Other sources include memoirs and biographical publications, notably: R. Lonsdale, *Dr. Charles Burney, a literary Biography*, Oxford 1965; W.T. Parke, *Musical Memoirs*, London 1830 (2 vols.); Percy Scholes, *The Great Dr. Burney*, London 1948 (2 vols.); C.-G. Stellan Mörner, *Johan Wikmanson und die Brüder Silverstolpe*, Stockholm 1952, and Martha Wilmot's letters (ed. Marchioness of Londonderry and W. M. Hyde), published as *More Letters from Martha Wilmot: Impressions of Vienna 1819–29*, London 1935.

Hirschbach im Waldviertel,
Christmas 1980   H.C.R.L.

JOSEPH HAYDN used to say that he was the typical case of 'something coming out of nothing', or as we would put it today, his is the quintessential story of 'rags to riches'. Even though his origins were not quite so obscure as some nineteenth-century writers imagined – Haydn's father was a village magistrate as well as a respected master-wheelwright and a successful farmer – Joseph lived perilously close to starvation as an adolescent. From being an unknown and ill-trained musician (he later acknowledged, 'I wrote diligently but not quite correctly'), Haydn rose to become the most popular composer the world had ever seen, and one of the wealthiest. His was a success story rivalling that of Abraham Lincoln.

This book tells that story, largely through contemporary documents and pictures, from the composer's birth in the village of Rohrau in 1732 to his death in Vienna, at the ripe age of seventy-seven, in 1809. Before examining Haydn's extraordinary career, however, we must first consider the even more extraordinary ups and downs of his posthumous reputation. For, paradoxically, Haydn was also to become the most neglected of all great composers. Lauded and loved throughout Europe in the second half of the eighteenth century, Haydn's music fell almost completely out of favour in the nineteenth. Patronized as Papa Haydn, he was dismissed as a genial but placid and old-fashioned artist. Since then, of course, Haydn's reputation has enjoyed a spectacular renaissance. The way back to the present level of interest in his music has been long and hard, and the renaissance has, curiously, taken place primarily in the Anglo-Saxon world (though the scholarship has been largely German and Hungarian).

When Haydn's first symphonies, trios and quartets began to be circulated within the Austrian monarchy towards the end of the 1750s they achieved a phenomenal and immediate success. To be sure, symphonies by his contemporaries were already numerous, but within a few years Haydn's had almost totally replaced them in the public's affection. His early quartets, which were actually divertimenti in five movements (including two minuets), were at once played the length and breadth of Europe – even in Italy, where the composer's works were largely ignored.

There were several factors that contributed to this enormous early popularity. The first was undoubtedly the open, winning charm of Haydn's music, his folk-tune-like melodies, the Italianate serenades of his slow movements and especially the beguiling minuets and trios so evocative of his native Austria. Secondly, and of more lasting influence, was the strict discipline and meticulous craftsmanship with which these early instrumental works were informed. Haydn soon displayed a striking ability to marshal his forces; to achieve a climax, or series of climaxes, in the development sections; to infuse outwardly simple music with a sense of urgency and even dramatic force. This systematic exploitation of his existing material was to become the hallmark of Haydn's music, and in the years to come the process would be deepened and enriched. Finally, a third important factor was Haydn's introduction of wit into music. In earlier times, one could find humour, imitational effects from nature (e.g. a dog barking in Vivaldi's *Four Seasons*), but hardly wit. This was also the contribution most characteristic of the eighteenth century that Haydn made to the art of music. Earlier periods had displayed the other characteristics that made Haydn's art popular – charm, discipline, dramatic effects, and so on, but with the introduction of wit on a broad scale (and sometimes of a highly intellectual bent), the face of Western music was permanently changed.

Haydn's early music also included some religious works which became popular, but on the whole it was his instrumental music which, in the 1760s, established his European fame. It was not until the 1770s that his vocal music had anything more than local distribution.

Until about 1758, Haydn had only occasional patrons, such as the Fürnberg family, but from that date until his death in 1809, he was attached to two aristocratic houses – first (1758–60?), to that of Count Morzin, and (from May 1761) to the great Hungarian magnates, the Princes Esterházy – Haydn served under four princes: Paul Anton (died 1762), Nicolaus I (died 1790), Anton (died 1794) and Nicolaus II, who outlived the composer. Haydn was particularly fortunate in his connections with these two houses. Both they and the Fürnbergs before them were fastidious, intelligent and generous patrons. Without Count Morzin's great orchestra, including horn players of exceptional ability (their names are unfortunately not known to us), it is unlikely that Haydn's symphonic style could have flowered so quickly and in such profusion.

The distribution of Haydn's music centred round the Austrian professional copyists who, in those days, fulfilled the position that music publishers would later occupy. Haydn, as soon as he was able to amass a small amount of capital, could engage the services of these copyists and sell authentic manuscripts of his works to patrons throughout the Austrian monarchy. Much of this material remained undiscovered until after the Second World War, and mostly in Hungary and Czechoslovakia. The scribes employed by Haydn soon began to do a brisk trade in Haydn's works on their own account, selling copies to such regular patrons as the Austrian monasteries, German princely houses, but – most important – also to the music publishing centre of the world at that time: Paris. All this activity was probably taking place not only without Haydn's approval but even without his knowledge.

In 1764, French editions of Haydn's symphonies and quartets began to appear and their immediate success ensured a steady stream of further Haydn publications in Paris and, later, Lyon. But when there was not enough genuine Haydn to satisfy the avid interest of French amateurs, the unscrupulous Viennese copyists began to substitute works by followers of Haydn, such as his brother Johann Michael Haydn, Leopold Hofmann, or Carl Ditters (later von Dittersdorf). These works were mixed with real Haydn and all presented as genuine. Very soon, French publishers began their own substitutions, of which the most famous was the erasure of the composer's name on the plates of some string quartets by Pater Roman Hoffstetter, a monk from Amorbach in southern Germany, and the substitution of Haydn's name. This was the origin of the so-called 'Opus 3'

Quartets incorrectly attributed to Haydn, including the celebrated Serenade from Opus 3, No. 5.

By the end of the 1760s and during the decade from 1770 to 1780, there was as much, if not more, spurious Haydn being sold in Paris as there were publications of genuine works. The confusion which arose as a result can be easily imagined, and it was no wonder that cultivated French, British or Dutch audiences must have formed a very inadequate idea of Haydn's real style, since by 1775 there were many entire *opera* of false Haydn circulating not only in Paris but soon thereafter in Amsterdam, London and Berlin. There is no record that Haydn had any connection with music publishers before 1774, and not on any large scale until 1780, when Artaria of Vienna became his principal publishers and maintained this association for the following decade. In the 1780s, Haydn also established contact with foreign publishers in London, Paris, Lyon, Speyer and Berlin; by the time he arrived in England in 1791 his published works and fame were truly international.

After becoming full *Kapellmeister* to Prince Nicolaus Esterházy in 1766 upon the death of Gregor Joseph Werner, Haydn was able to turn his attention to vocal music, and the second half of the 1760s is marked by a whole series of vocal works both sacred and secular. The religious works that now began to circulate throughout Catholic Austria included Masses, a *Salve Regina* with organ solo (many of these works include such parts for organ solo which the composer himself played), a *Stabat Mater* – the first vocal work by Haydn to achieve international fame (it was printed in Paris and London) – and many smaller religious works. In the 1760s Haydn composed a whole series of cantatas to celebrate the name-day or some other important event in Prince Nicolaus's life; these cantatas have, up to the time of present writing (1980), remained unpublished but Haydn salvaged some of the music by turning it, or causing it to be turned into, smaller pieces of music for church use. The same procedure was also applied to Haydn's final Cantata of this series, *Applausus*, composed in 1768 for Zwettl Abbey, but which became widely known in Austria in the form of several *contrafacta* (as such adaptations are termed).

The most interesting vocal works of this new period in Haydn's life are undoubtedly the operas that he wrote at regular intervals for Prince Nicolaus Esterházy's amusement from 1762 to 1784. Largely unknown outside the Esterházy household in Haydn's lifetime and for the most part unpublished until the second half of the twentieth century, these Haydn operas have been relaunched with considerable success two hundred years after their much applauded premières in the obscurity of Eisenstadt, Pressburg and Eszterháza. Haydn undoubtedly thought that these operas were his major works. In the list of compositions mentioned in his autobiographical sketch of 1776 (quoted on pp. 8of.), the only works that Haydn mentions in any detail are his operas, an oratorio, and the *Stabat Mater*. The huge upheaval that occurs in Haydn's music during the second half of the 1760s is not documented except in the actual music itself; but there, the new style was such that its effect on Haydn's contemporaries must have been overwhelming and even alarming. Musicologists have squabbled in unenlightened fashion over the choice of a term to describe this period which has been called 'Romantic Crisis', 'Sturm und Drang' (a term borrowed from a German literary movement and, in particular, a play of that title by Klinger in 1776), and so on. Whatever phrase we choose to use, Haydn's style was now marked by a new urgency, a great interest in minor keys as the vehicle of passion, a renaissance of contrapuntal forms such as the fugue, and above all an overriding sense of power and drama. It was, nevertheless, Haydn's instrumental works that spread his name not only throughout Europe but to the New World as well; and while in some quarters his new style with its juxtaposition of the comic and serious was not always appreciated (e.g. in north Germany – see the bitter remarks in Haydn's autobiographical sketch), it is no exaggeration when we state that by the time Haydn set off for England he was Europe's most celebrated and popular composer. What had led to this extraordinary state of affairs? Primarily, it was the new and so-called 'popular' style of Haydn's music in the 1770s and 1780s that had conquered the hearts of the connoisseurs. This 'popular' style was a judicious admixture of tunes which, if not directly folk melodies, sounded just like them; of a witty, droll style which took much of its language from the fashionable *opera buffa*; and of learned writing (fugues, etc.) which, combined with Haydn's impeccable sense of form and length, interested the professional musicians, such as C. P. E. Bach and Mozart. Haydn's music, in fact, appealed to amateur and professional alike, and to all classes – from the French merchant in Lyon to the Russian prince in St Petersburg. It was an entirely new phenomenon and one that Europe had never before experienced on this broad and international scale.

When Haydn went to England at the instigation of the great impresario J. P. Salomon, he escaped from a position which had become irksome and provincial, and a life-style 'in which he had become grey' (Griesinger). In the course of his two visits to England, Haydn became financially independent (he earned the equivalent of 24,000 gulden, which sum represented twenty-four years' income at the annual rate of Prince Nicolaus's pension for his *Kapellmeister*) and grew even more famous; but most important, he created a whole series of masterpieces which, even in the 'bad' period of Haydn's reputation in the nineteenth century, were regularly performed all over the civilized world – the 'Rider' Quartet, the Piano Sonata No. 62 in E flat (1794), the 'Surprise', 'Miracle', 'Military', 'Clock', 'Drum Roll' and 'London' Symphonies, the song 'My mother bids me bind my hair', the *Andante con variazioni* in F minor for piano, and the 'Gypsy Rondo' Trio. His celebrated 'popular' style was enriched, broadened and deepened by the glorious experience of London, where the audiences shouted their applause and King George III offered him lodgings in Windsor Castle.

On his return to Vienna, Haydn took back a libretto which Salomon had given him. Haydn's friend and patron, Gottfried van Swieten, collaborated with the composer in the preparation of his sublime Oratorio, *The Creation* (1798), which rapidly became its composer's most celebrated work and was translated into many languages. Van Swieten and Haydn had provided a German and English text with which the work was first published by the composer in 1800. The imposing list of subscribers at the beginning of the handsome full score showed how many friends Haydn had throughout Europe (but not in Spain, Portugal or Italy, although his music had been extremely popular in the 1780s in Spain). *The Creation* was followed by *The Seasons* (1801), also a success but nothing like that of its immediate predecessor (*The Seasons* was never performed in England during Haydn's lifetime, for instance). While these oratorios represented, as it were, the public side of Haydn's life, he was also occupied from 1796 to 1802 with a series of great Masses for the name-day of Princess Marie Hermenegild

Esterházy, the wife of Nicolaus II (who succeeded to the princely title in 1794). These Masses kept Haydn's name alive in many a parish church in Austria and Bavaria throughout the ninteenth century.

In the 1790s, Haydn attracted a new publisher, the famous house of Breitkopf & Härtel in Leizig, which issued the authentic first editions of these late Masses as well as the Oratorios, *The Seven Words* and *The Seasons*. Although composing vocal music was now Haydn's chief occupation, he continued in instrumental works with the Trumpet Concerto (now arguably his most popular work), the Quartets of Opp. 76 (including 'The Emperor'), 77 and 103 (unfinished) and the final piano trios for English publishers. In 1797 he captured the hearts of a wartime nation with his Hymn to the Emperor Franz (Francis) II, 'Gott erhalte' (or as Haydn called it, 'Volcks Lied'), which is now (1980) the national anthem of the German Federal Republic.

When Haydn died in 1809, he was without question the most celebrated composer in the world. But as often happens – the cases of Wren and Balthasar Neumann, two of the world's greatest architects, spring to mind – the pendulum swung rapidly and brutally. Mozart's music was, in the beginning of the new century, becoming widely known for the first time – only a fraction of his enormous *œuvre* had been printed during his short lifetime (1756–1791) – and together with it that of Beethoven (born in 1770), whose mighty compositions – including symphonies, quartets, sonatas, Masses and the opera *Fidelio* – soon forced into permanent oblivion such successful contemporaries in the instrumental field as Ignaz Pleyel, Adalbert Gyrowetz or Leopold Koželuch (all of whom had been more popular, in 1791, than Mozart), just as Mozart's operas gradually erased from the repertoire such stalwarts as Paisiello, Cimarosa, Sarti, Gazzaniga and Piccinni. It was soon hard-going for Haydn's music, too. Robert Schumann, in 1840, found that the 'Military' Symphony not only had 'something pig-tail about it', but the second movement's 'Turkish music' sounded to him 'childish and tasteless'. A year later he echoed general opinion that Haydn 'no longer has any deeper interest for our age.'

As the conductor Felix von Weingartner was preparing for the press the first forty symphonies by Haydn in the then new *Gesamtausgabe* (1907), he wrote that same year elsewhere:

> Much of Haydn, Mozart and Schubert, most of Weber, enjoy an artistic existence only in the light of the imperishable works of this master [Beethoven], but already belong to past history; not true of Beethoven, if we perhaps except some youthful works and *pièces d'occasion*.

No one, in 1907, could have foreseen the enormous change in Mozart's status which began in the 1920s and 1930s and was 'codified' in the big international sesquicentennial celebrations (notably in Austria and the U.S.A.) of 1941. Haydn and Mozart used to be lumped together as the superficial scullery-musicians of a heartless rococo age. 'Even their pathos went scarcely more than skin deep,' wrote Robert Haven Schauffler in 1927. Within a generation, Mozart became almost as popular as Beethoven and today it is indeed a question if Mozart does not represent for many thinking people in the West the zenith of European music. In the wake of this extraordinary Mozart renaissance, Haydn's popularity increased. It was in particular thanks to the wireless and, even more, to the long-playing gramophone record that Haydn's music was brought back into the living rooms of many people, mainly in the Anglo-Saxon world (in Austria and Germany, Haydn is no more popular than he was thirty years ago, and scholarly interest in his music or life is scarcely more than superficial). For many seasons in the period 1946–80, for example, the Vienna Philharmonic subscription concerts have included not one single work by Haydn, a situation unthinkable in similar circumstances in England. The present Haydn renaissance, in fact, must be attributed principally and at first almost exclusively to Great Britain, the only country where Haydn's popularity may have waned but never entirely died out, even in the nineteenth century and the early years of the twentieth.

Whether this present level of interest in Haydn will extend beyond the borders of the Anglo-Saxon world is something that only time will tell; but there are signs that Haydn is again becoming popular in France and this, interestingly enough, largely through the operas (Lyon is now staging a new Haydn opera production every year). Certainly the 250th anniversary of Haydn's birth in 1982 will provide a unique opportunity for reconsideration, revaluation and, perhaps, revitalization.

I
THE EARLY YEARS
1732~1765

'... Young people can see from my example that
something can still come from nothing;
but what I am is the result of dire necessity.'

DIES, 16

1 Landscape near Eisenstadt, in Burgenland, the region of Austria in which Haydn was born and spent much of his working life. This modern vineyard is part of the inheritance of Roman occupation of the area; wine growing was introduced by the Romans into the province of Pannonia, and has continued down the centuries without interruption.

2, 3 The exterior of the former home of the Haydn family in the village of Rohrau, as seen in a nineteenth-century oil sketch and a modern photograph. Even before the sketch was executed, the building in which Joseph Haydn was born in 1732 had been gutted by fire and flooded on several occasions; hence, what we see today is largely a reconstruction, both inside and out.

6 (opposite) Hainburg seen from the opposite bank of the Danube; watercolour by Ferdinand Runk (1764–1834). As a boy, Haydn entered the choir-school in Hainburg run by his cousin, Johann Mathias Franck, and here he received his first formal musical education; in addition to studying singing, he also learned to play a variety of instruments before he was sent to Vienna at the age of eight.

4 Outside the parish church in Rohrau stands a votive statue of the Saviour; Mathias Haydn, master-wheelwright and village magistrate, established a trust fund for its upkeep, and in his will, Joseph Haydn, who was baptized in this church, also made financial provision for its future care.

5 Carl Anton, Count Harrach (1692– 1758), who – at the time of Haydn's birth and during his youth – was head of the family whose descendants still occupy Rohrau Castle. Before her marriage in 1728, Haydn's mother had been in service at the castle as a cook.

7 The Cathedral of St Stephen (Stephansdom), Vienna; coloured engraving by Carl Schütz, 1792. In 1740 Georg Reutter Jr, the Cathedral *Kapellmeister*, visited Hainburg and heard Haydn sing; he subsequently arranged with the boy's father for him to be brought to the capital as a member of the large *Capelle* which fulfilled all the various musical demands of a great metropolitan church.

8 *(below)* The garden front of the imperial palace of Schönbrunn in Vienna; detail of an oil painting by Bernardo Bellotto, 1759. In addition to their participation in all manner of church ceremonies, Haydn and the other members of the *Capelle* were also required to perform at Court.

9 *(opposite)* The Empress Maria Theresa (seated, right) and her family; group portrait by Martin van Meytens including (seated, left) the Empress's consort Francis Stephen and (standing in the foreground, from left to right) the Archduchesses Maria Anna and Marie Christine, the Archduke Joseph (the Crown Prince) and the Archduke Carl. Maria Theresa, who succeeded to the throne in 1740 at the age of twenty-three, reigned for forty years.

10 The Kohlmarkt, Vienna; to the left of the church is the large building known as the Michaelerhaus, where in his youth Haydn lived in a garret on the fifth floor. Coloured engraving by Carl Schütz, 1786.

11 The Nikolaikirche, Vienna, with (right) the Convent of the Poor Clares; engraving by J. G. Ringlin after S. Kleiner. Here, Haydn's first love, Therese Keller, younger daughter of a wigmaker, took the veil in 1756.

12–15 Four of the principal figures who influenced Haydn, directly or indirectly, in his youth: (from top) Nicola Antonio Porpora (1686–1768), his employer and teacher in the 1750s; Georg Reutter, Jr (1708–72), *Kapellmeister* at St Stephen's Cathedral; Pietro Metastasio (1698–1782), the poet, who helped him learn the Italian language; and C. P. E. Bach, whose treatise *Versuch über die wahre Art das Clavier zu spielen* was avidly studied by the budding composer.

16, 17 The country seats of Haydn's first two patrons: Weinzierl Castle, home of the Fürnberg family, where Haydn wrote his first string quartet, *c.* 1757; and Lukavec Castle, where Haydn composed his earliest symphonies, *c.* 1757–60, for performance by Count Morzin's small orchestra. In both cases, the works proved immensely successful and copies were soon circulating throughout the Monarchy.

18 The Castle at Eisenstadt, principal seat of the princely Esterházy family and centre of their estates' administration. After the medieval fortress on this site came into the hands of the family, it was gradually rebuilt and modernized in the eighteenth and early nineteenth centuries. Haydn's associations with the castle began in 1761 when he became *Vice-Kapellmeister* in the princely household (cf. ill. 22).

19 The old *Capellhaus* in Eisenstadt, situated behind the Bergkirche (ill. 188); here, in his early years of service, lodgings were provided for Haydn and the other musicians employed by Prince Paul Anton. The building is under threat of demolition.

Haydn and the Esterházys

20 The Esterházy estate at Lockenhaus in Burgenland (formerly in Hungary, now in Austria) was responsible for supervising the local paper-mill which supplied the paper (with the famous stag watermark) that Haydn used for most of his compositions in the 1760s.

21 The princely carriage at the entrance to Forchtenstein Castle, which always served as the principal archives of the Esterházy family. In 1779, after the disastrous fire at Eszterháza (cf. ill. 34), in which most of the musical instruments used by the orchestra were destroyed, Haydn asked for the timpani then at Forchtenstein to be made available as replacements.

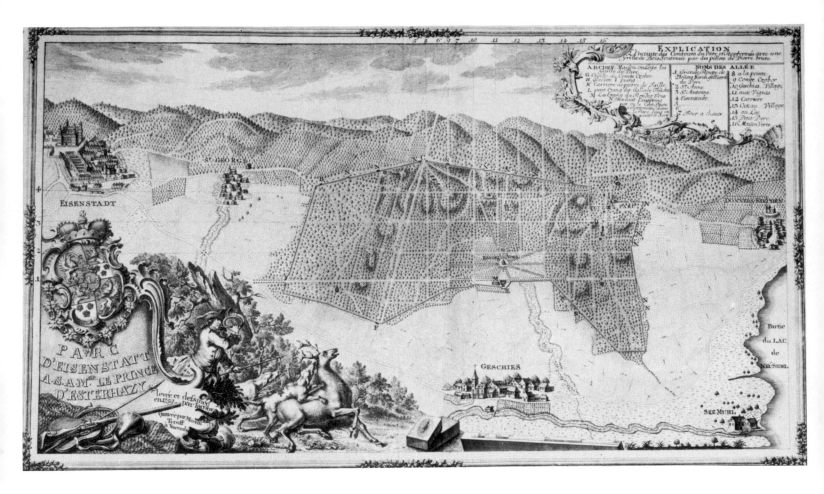

EISENSTADT

St. GEORGE

DONNERSKIRCHEN

GESCHIES

Partie du LAC de NEUSIDEL

See MÜHL

PARC D'EISENSTATT A S.A.M.re LE PRINCE D'ESTERHAZY

Palatium Principis Pauli Antonii ab Esterhazy de Galantha in platea, quae Wallerstrass dicitur. Das Majorat Hauß des Fürstens Paul Anthonn von Esterhaß de Galantha in der Waller Straß.

22 The Esterházy Castle at Eisenstadt and the hunting park as Haydn would have known them when he entered princely service in 1761: hunting was one of the composer's favourite pastimes. Engraving by Martin Tyroff after a drawing executed in 1759 by the Princely Architect, Nicolaus Jacoby.

23 The Esterházy Palace in the Wallnerstraße, Vienna; it was probably in the great hall of this building that Haydn conducted the first orchestral compositions that he wrote in 1761 for Prince Paul Anton, the Symphonies (Nos. 6–8) known as 'Le Matin', 'Le Midi' and 'Le Soir'. Engraving by J. G. Ringlin after Salomon Kleiner.

24 The earliest portrait of Haydn dates from *c*. 1762–3. The painting, which was destroyed in 1945, is probably by Johann Basilius Grundmann (1726–98) who was also in Esterházy service at the time; it shows the composer wearing the blue uniform with silver trimmings of the *Vice-Kapellmeister* in the Esterházy household.

25 A stage design, dated 1762, attributed to Girolamo Bon, whose troupe was engaged by Prince Nicolaus I Esterházy to give theatrical performances at Eisenstadt. Haydn composed his first music for an Italian comedy – *La Marchesa Nespola* (1763?) – for performance by Bon (who was engaged on a permanent basis in July 1762) and the *Capelle*.

26 Prince Paul Anton, the first of the Esterházy princes whom Haydn served as *Kapellmeister*; both Paul Anton and his younger brother Nicolaus (ill. 42), who succeeded him in 1762, were accomplished amateur musicians and were fluent in several languages. This oil painting, together with a matching portrait of Princess Maria Anna, who outlived her husband by more than two decades, were presented to the Hospitallers Order in Eisenstadt, of which the prince and princess were patrons.

27 A reconstruction, at the Castle at Eisenstadt, of the seating arrangements for a concert in the great hall in Haydn's day. The seats at the far end would be occupied by the Prince and Princess and their honoured guests.

Monastic associations

28–31 Haydn maintained close connections with several of the great monastic foundations in Austria. For the pilgrimage church at Mariazell in Styria *(left)* he composed two votive Masses (1766 and 1782), having previously made a pilgrimage there in the 1750s.

Kremsmünster *(opposite, above)* owns an important collection of works by Haydn, the earliest being a series of early string quartets dated 1762.

Göttweig *(opposite)* began acquiring works by Michael Haydn in 1759 and those by Joseph in 1762, and eventually amassed a formidable collection of compositions by both brothers; the works by Joseph in contemporary MS. copies owned by Melk *(below)* include eighty symphonies, and the Violin Concerto in A (of which only one other copy is known).

32 The church (now cathedral) of St Martin, Eisenstadt; here Haydn's friend, the school teacher Carl Kraus, was *Regens chori*. The archives of the church include many unique MSS. of Haydn's compositions, among them the late *Libera me* (*c.* 1782 or 1790), which was discovered in the organ loft there in 1966 (cf. ill. 197).

THE HOME of the Haydn family was in Rohrau, an old market town on the River Leitha in Lower Austria. In the period of Joseph Haydn's youth the Leitha formed part of the border between Austria and Hungary, and Rohrau itself is now situated not far from a third border, that of Slovakia (part of Czechoslovakia). The villages in this part of Austria have among their inhabitants Croatian-, Hungarian-, Slovakian- and German-speaking peoples, but in Rohrau almost all the population in Haydn's time was of German (Austrian) descent.

In the register of the parish church in Rohrau, Joseph Haydn's baptism is recorded as follows (it is not quite certain whether the actual date of his birth was 31 March – the usually accepted date – or 1 April 1732):

Dies et mensis	Infantes	Parentes	Patrini	Baptizans	Locus
den 1. April	Franciscus Josephus fil: legit:	Mathias Haiden bürgl. Wagner-maister / zu Rohrau Vnd / Anna Maria uxor / ejus	Herr Josephus Hoffmann Herrschaftl. bestand Müllner zu Gerhaus et Catharina D[omi]na uxor ejus	ego q: [ui] supra	Rohrau

The godparents ('Patrini') were the Estate's Master Miller Johann Joseph Hoffmann from the nearby town of Gerhaus, together with his wife; the couple were evidently close friends of Haydn's parents, and the records show that they often acted as godparents to the family. It was customary in those days to make general use of only the second Christian name, and hence Haydn's first name, Franz, was not used for everyday purposes. Joseph was the eldest son in the large family of Mathias Haydn (1699–1763) and his wife Anna Maria (*née* Koller). Of the twelve children of Mathias's first marriage, five died in infancy; two of the other sons – Johann Michael (born 1737) and Johann Evangelist (born 1743) would also follow musical careers. Mathias Haydn, who was born at nearby Hainburg, was a master-wheelwright and village magistrate, while his wife served as a cook at Rohrau Castle, the seat of the Counts Harrach. Thanks to their respective positions in the community and the castle, both of Haydn's parents had associations with the local gentry, at that time Count Carl Anton Harrach and his wife Catharina (*née* Countess von Bouquoy). We hear of their interest in Haydn's music via a report from a captured Prussian officer who was quartered with the Harrachs in 1757/58; at Rohrau Castle he heard the composer playing in his own earliest string quartets, and this suggests that the local *Herrschaft* was not unaware of his

All marginal references
are to illustration
numbers

talents. Haydn's male grandparents were, respectively, master-wheelwright at Hainburg (Thomas Haydn) and village magistrate at Rohrau (Lorenz Koller). Haydn's father was musical and liked to sing of an evening, accompanying himself on the harp.

4   The village of Rohrau has changed somewhat, but not in a very basic sense, from its physical shape of 1732. The church remains; the pious statue that Mathias Haydn erected; the great Castle, now with the magnificent 2, 3 picture gallery from the Harrach Palace in Vienna; and Haydn's house, which today has only a vague resemblance to the composer's birthplace as it was in 1732; it burned down in 1899 and before that had been subjected to floods which twice (1813, 1834) almost totally destroyed everything except the outside walls. Today, Haydn's birthplace is rather a 'remembrance' than an actual relic of his youth. But that which has changed hardly at all is the mysterious, age-old countryside around Rohrau, with its ancient history of Roman legionaries, migratory peoples from the east, invading Turkish troops and revered Christian traditions, binding people to the Cross and to their country in such ceremonies as Corpus Christi (where Mother Earth was gently combined with Mother Church). And hard by there was the Danube, one of Europe's great rivers, whose endless and swift waters brought ships and men from Germany, Austria and Hungary, to faraway lands at its mouth in the Black Sea. The Danube countryside exerts a peculiar fascination: its 1 surrounding vegetation, the great vineyards which the first Roman settlers had lovingly planted, the texture of the hills and plains through which the river runs, are quite different from those of any other part of Austria. And as the great river debouches on to the great plains, we find ourselves in the former Roman province of Pannonia, on the borders of which Haydn would spend most of his adult life.

Our knowledge of Haydn's early years comes almost entirely from his first biographers, who noted down the composer's reminiscences in his old age. The most accurate of these biographers is Georg August Griesinger (pp. 8ff.):

... Of the twenty [*sic*] children from two marriages of his father Mathias, a wheelwright by profession, Joseph was the eldest [son]. As was customary in his trade, the father had seen a little of the world, and during his sojourn in Frankfurt am Mayn he had learned to strum the harp. As a master of his trade at Rohrau, he continued to practise this instrument for pleasure, after work; nature had also endowed him with a good tenor voice, and his wife, Anne Marie, accompanied his playing with her singing. The tunes of these songs were so deeply imprinted in Joseph Haydn's memory that he could recall them even in advanced old age. One day the school rector from the neighbouring little town of Haimburg [*sic*], a distant relative of the Haydn family, came to Rohrau. Master Mathias and his wife gave their usual little concert, and five-year-old Joseph sat near his parents and sawed at his left arm with a stick, as if he were accompanying on the violin. The schoolteacher noted that the boy marked the time accurately; he inferred from this a natural talent for music, and he advised the parents to send their Sepperl [an Austrian diminutive for Joseph] to Haimburg in order to help acquire an art which in time would without fail open to him the prospect 'of becoming a clergyman'. As ardent admirers of the clergy, the parents jumped at this proposal, and in his sixth year Joseph Haydn went to the school rector at Haimburg. Here he received lessons in reading and writing, in catechism, in singing, and in almost all wind and string instruments, even in playing the timpani. 'I shall owe it to that man even in my grave,' Haydn used to say frequently, 'that he taught me so many things, though in the process I received more thrashings than food.'

Hainburg was a flourishing market and border town on the Danube.   6
Here Mathias Franck, Haydn's cousin was *Regens chori* of the Parish Church
of SS. Philip and James; on feast days he performed large-scale Masses with
trumpets and kettledrums, in which young Joseph also witnessed his first big
ceremonies wherein the whole town participated, such as the Feast of Corpus
Christi and the entry, in May 1739, of the Imperial and Royal Commissioner,
Cetto von Cronstorff. Among the earliest surviving pieces by Haydn are four
Motets (XXIIIc:5a–d) written for the Corpus Christi Feast.

Griesinger continues:

Haydn, who even then wore a wig for the sake of cleanliness, had been about three years
in Haimburg when the Court Chapel Master Reutter from Vienna, who directed the music   13
at St Stephen's Cathedral, came to visit his friend the dean in Haimburg. Reutter told the
dean that his older choir-boys, whose voices were beginning to break, were about to become
useless, and that he would have to replace them with younger substitutes. The dean proposed
the eight-year-old Haydn, and both he and the schoolmaster were at once called for. The
badly nourished Sepperl cast hungry glances at the cherries that were siting on the dean's
table: Reutter tossed a few handfuls into his hat, and he seemed quite satisfied with the Latin
and Italian strophes that Haydn had to sing. 'Can you also make a trill?' asked Reutter. 'No,'
said Haydn, 'for even my cousin [Herr Vetter] can't do that.' This answer greatly
embarrassed the schoolteacher, and Reutter laughed heartily. He showed the mechanical
means by which a trill could be produced. Haydn imitated him, and succeeded at the third
attempt. 'You shall stay with me', said Reutter. The departure from Haimburg was soon
arranged, and Haydn came as a pupil to the Choir School at St Stephen's Cathedral in
Vienna, where he remained until he was in his sixteenth year.

Vienna was the great capital of a very large empire, and its spiritual
centre was, of course, St Stephen's. It is thought that Haydn arrived there in   7
1740, becoming a minute cog in the ponderous, complex machinery of a great
European cathedral. He took part in solemn Masses, short Masses, requiems,
Te Deums, *rorate* ceremonies for Advent, great processions – all the busy life of
a metropolitan church which was also the parish church for many in the
neighbourhood. Sometimes the *Capelle* made trips to the nearby monastery
and town of Klosterneuburg, or to Schönbrunn Palace. Haydn became a   8
famous soloist but soon his brother Michael joined the *Capelle* and even
outshone his brother as soprano solo. It is thought that Joseph's *Missa brevis* in
F for two soprano soloists, choir and orchestra was written for himself and his
brother.

In October 1740 the Emperor Charles VI died and his daughter, Maria
Theresa, assumed the Habsburg crown. She was an astute ruler and was
particularly adept at dealing with the temperamental Hungarians, whose
hearts she won when, at the Coronation ceremonies in Pressburg, she galloped
on her coal-black stallion up a hill and brandished her sword toward the four
quarters of the globe. Her consort was the amiable Prince Francis Stephen of
Lorraine; theirs had been a love match. On 13 March 1741, the city of
Vienna rejoiced with the Imperial and Royal couple: to Maria Theresa was   9
born a healthy boy-child who would in time become Emperor Joseph II.

One of the requiem Masses in which Haydn participated was that held on
28 July 1741 for Antonio Vivaldi, in which the records of St Stephen's show
that the six choir-boys took part. Vivaldi died a pauper and it was Haydn's
first experience of a great musician who ended his days poor and forgotten. In

the course of his long life, Haydn would see many of his brother artists dying in hideous poverty – copyists, violinists, singers, composers, among them the famous Dittersdorf and (worst shame of all) the incomparable Mozart.

Griesinger's account continues:

Apart from the scanty instruction customary at that time in Latin, religion, arithmetic and writing, Haydn had in the Choir School very capable instructors on several instruments, and particularly in the art of singing. Among the latter were Gegenbauer, a member of the Court choir, and an elegant tenor, Finsterbusch. In the Choir School there was no instruction in musical theory, and Haydn recalled having received only two such lessons from the worthy Reutter. But Reutter did encourage him to make whatever variations he liked on the motets and Salves that he had to sing in church, and this discipline soon led him to ideas of his own which Reutter corrected. He also came to know Mattheson's [*Der*] *vollkommene Kapellmeister*, and Fux's *Gradus ad Parnassum* in German and Latin – a book he still in his old age praised as a classic and of which he kept a well-used copy. With tireless exertion Haydn tried to understand Fux's theory; he worked his way right through the whole school, wrote out the exercises, put them by for several weeks and then took them up again, polishing them till he considered them perfect. 'Of course the talent was latent in me: as a result of it, and with great diligence, I made progress.' In his fevered imagination he even ventured into compositions in eight and sixteen parts. 'In those days I used to think everything is fine so long as the paper was well covered. Reutter laughed about my immature products, about movements which no throat and no instrument could have executed, and he scolded me for composing in sixteen parts before I had learned how to write in two.'

At that time many castrati were employed at Court and in the Viennese churches, and the director of the Choir School no doubt considered that he was about to make the young Haydn's fortune when he brought forth the plan to turn him into a permanent soprano, and actually asked the father for his permission. The father, who totally disapproved of this proposal, set forth at once for Vienna and, thinking that the operation might already have been performed, entered the room where his son was and asked, 'Sepperl, does anything hurt you? Can you still walk?' Delighted to find his son unharmed, he protested against any further proposals of this kind, and a castrato who happened to be there even strengthened him in his resolve.

Albert Christoph Dies, another of Haydn's early biographers, elaborates (30ff.) on the composer's experiences as a choir-boy:

As a choir-boy Haydn had many amusing adventures. Once, when the Court was building the summer castle at Schönbrunn, Haydn had to sing there in the choir during Whitsuntide. Except for the church services, he used to play with the other boys, climbing the scaffolding round the construction and making a terrible racket on the staging. What happened? The boys suddenly beheld a lady. It was the Empress Maria Theresa herself, who ordered someone to get the noisy boys off the scaffolding and to threaten them with a thrashing if they dared to be caught there again. The next day Haydn, driven by curiosity, climbed the scaffolding alone, was caught and collected the promised thrashing.

Many years later, when Haydn was in the service of Prince Esterházy, the Empress came once to Esterhaz [Eszterháza, 1773]. Haydn presented himself before her and thanked her most humbly for the reward he had received. He had to tell the whole story, which occasioned much merriment.

In nature there is no standing still. Haydn now had to discover that he was not destined to remain a choir-boy for ever. His beautiful voice, with which he had so often sung for his supper, suddenly betrayed him. It broke, and wavered between two whole notes.

The following anecdote Haydn told me at a later time, but it belongs to this period in which his voice broke. At the ceremony performed every year at Klosterneuburg in honour of St Leopold, the Empress Maria Theresa usually appeared. The Empress had already let it be said in jest to *Kapellmeister* Reutern, 'Joseph Haydn doesn't sing any more: he crows.' So Reutern had to replace Joseph with another soprano for the ceremony. His choice fell on Joseph's brother, Michael, who sang so beautifully that the Empress had him called before her and presented him with 24 ducats.

'Michael,' Reutern asked him, 'now what will you do with all that money?' Michael thought for a short moment and answered: 'One of our father's animals has just died, so I shall send him 12 ducats; I would ask you to keep the other 12 for me until my voice breaks, too.' Reutern took the money but forgot to give it back again.

Since Haydn, with his cracked voice, was unfit to be a choir-boy any more and thus had no monetary value for *Kapellmeister* Reutern, the latter found it only quite fair to discharge him.

A piece of mischief on Haydn's part hastened his dismissal. One of the other choir-boys, contrary to the usual custom of a choir-boy at that time, wore his long hair in a pigtail, and Haydn, just for the fun of it, cut if off. Reutern called him to account and sentenced him to a caning on the palm of the hand. The moment of punishment arrived. Haydn tried every way to escape it and finally declared he would rather not be a choir-boy any more and would leave at once rather than be punished. 'That won't help,' answered Reutern, 'first you'll be caned and then march!'

Reutern kept his word, and so it was that the cashiered choir-boy, helpless, without money, with three mean shirts and a worn coat, stepped into the great world that he knew nothing about. His parents were very upset. Especially the tender motherly heart showed her anxiety with tears in her eyes. She implored her son that 'he might yet accede to the parental desires and prayers and dedicate himself to the priesthood'. This wish had lain slumbering for ten years, and it now awoke, its force undiminished. The parents gave their son no peace; they were sure that they must impose their will on him, but Haydn remained unswerving in his purpose and paid no attention. It is true that he could not provide any reasons for opposing his parents' wishes; he considered that he had explained things clearly enough when he squeezed the force of genius, mysterious even to himself, into the few words, 'I don't want to be a priest'. But how could this answer satisfy his parents? How could they imagine the development of their son's talents, of the future, so fortunate and so full of fame, when Haydn himself entertained no such thoughts, and when he understood just as little as did his parents what genius was, knew nothing of the pride that usually conquers the youthful genius, and was himself blessed with no insight whatsoever?

Griesinger (11f.):

Haydn was dismissed from the Choir School in his sixteenth year because his voice had broken; he could not hope for the least support from his poor parents and thus was obliged to make his own way simply by his talents. He took lodgings in a wretched garret (in the house No. 1220 in the Michaelerplatz) in Vienna, without a stove, and where he was barely protected from the rain. Deprived of life's comforts, he divided his whole time giving lessons, studying his art and performing. He played for money in evening serenades and in the orchestras, and studied composition diligently, for 'when I was sitting at my old, worm-eaten spinet [*Klavier*] I envied no king his lot'. About this time Haydn came upon the first six sonatas of [Carl Philipp] Emanuel Bach; 'I did not leave my clavier until I had played them through, and whoever knows me thoroughly must discover that I owe a great deal to Emanuel Bach, that I understood him and have studied him with diligence. Emanuel Bach once paid me a compliment on that score himself.'

Dies (33f.):

I reminded Haydn of the garret and asked him to tell me how he escaped from it.

'It happened', Haydn began, 'that I made the acquaintance of the celebrated
12   *Kapellmeister* Porpora, who was much in demand as a teacher, but who, perhaps because of
his age, was looking for a young assistant and found one in me. Among Porpora's pupils was a
young girl between seven and nine years old. The famous Metastasio was the benefactor of
this girl and her mother; he was educating her at his own expense, and Porpora gave her
singing lessons.'

The old Porpora made use of Haydn at these lessons, and Haydn was glad to undertake
the task, regardless of the distance; he was now lucky enough to earn two gulden a month.
While Porpora taught the girl singing, Haydn, who had to accompany on the keyboard
[*Klavier*], found it a useful opportunity to gain a perfect knowledge of, and practice in, the
Italian method of singing and accompanying.

Porpora was a man who was severe with Haydn who, for his part, was happy to put up
with it all and bore the pokes in the ribs and epithets 'Bestia! – C[oglione]!' with submission;
he even cleaned the shoes when he had to accompany Porpora to the country during the
summer months. Haydn was glad to suffer all this because he learned so much from the man.

Haydn's fortunes now seemed to be taking a turn for the better. He was introduced to
14   Metastasio, who gave him much useful advice and in whose house he soon learned the Italian
language. About this time he also made the acquaintance of an honest bourgeois family in the
stocking business who, without being well-to-do or even protected from want themselves,
nevertheless did their best to help Haydn. Haydn told the mother about the holes in the roof
under which he slept and joked about the snow on his bedclothes. But although he had only
intended to laugh at his troubles, the good woman took a more serious view; she was touched,
and offered the young Haydn her own bedroom to sleep in during the winters. Haydn was
pleased to accept, with the secret hope that he would soon be in a position to return this great
service.

Since the poor woman had only the most essential furnishings, however, the floor had to
take the place of a bed; and thus it was that Haydn found at least a warm place ready for him
on any winter evening.

The family's name was Buchhol(t)z. When Haydn made his first Will in
1801 he left 100 gulden 'For Miss Anna Buchholz . . . because her grandfather
lent me 150 fl. without interest when I was young and in great need; which
money, however, I repaid 50 years ago.' Anna's father was Anton, a judge,
who was a witness at Haydn's marriage in 1760. It is the first of many cases in
which Haydn's capacity for making friends is touchingly documented.

Griesinger (12):

. . . the following, purely coincidental circumstance led him to try his hand at the
16   composition of quartets. A Baron Fürnberg had an estate in Weinzierl, several stages from
Vienna; and from time to time he invited his parish priest, his estates' manager, Haydn and
Albrechtsberger (a brother of the well-known contrapuntist, who played the violoncello) in
order to have a little music. Fürnberg asked Haydn to write something that could be played
by these four friends of the Art. Haydn, who was then eighteen years old, accepted the
proposal, and so originated his first Quartet which, immediately upon its appearance,
received such uncommon applause as to encourage him to continue in this genre.

It was about 1757 or 1758 that Haydn was invited to Weinzierl Castle, the
pretty estate a few miles away from the old town of Wieselburg in Lower

Austria. He was a guest of Carl Joseph, Edler von Fürnberg, an official in the Lower Austrian Government, married at that time to his second wife, Marie Antonie (*née* von Germetten). Fürnberg's eldest son, Joseph, was an army man but also a passionate music-lover, whose Haydn collection, discovered at a Hungarian castle after World War II, contains authentic copies (with corrections by Haydn himself) of the early quartets, the symphonies for Morzin, some divertimentos and two string trios.

There were two Albrechtsbergers: the composer, contrapuntist and teacher of Beethoven was Johann Georg (born Klosterneuburg 1732, died Vienna 1809), who was a famous organist and is reported to have played the 'cello. The brother was Anton Johann, born at Klosterneuburg on 20 November 1729, and also a composer (later in the service of the Bishop of Wiener Neustadt). It is not clear which of them was actually the 'cellist in Haydn's early quartets.

These quartets – ten have survived – proved to be immensely popular. They were circulating in the Austrian monasteries (Göttweig, Kremsmün-ster) by 1762 and in 1764 four were published in Paris (all these early French editions of Haydn's works appeared without his participation and were pirated from Austrian MSS. by professional copyists).

30, 31

Griesinger (14f.):

In the year 1759 Haydn was engaged as Music Director to Count Morzin in Vienna at a salary of two hundred gulden, free lodging and board at the officers' table. Here he was finally able to enjoy the happiness of a carefree existence; he was quite contented. He spent the winter in Vienna and the summer in Bohemia near Pilsen. He used to like to relate, in later years, how one day he was seated at the harpsichord [*Klavier*] when the beautiful Countess Morzin leaned over him in order to see the notes and her neckerchief came undone. 'It was the first time I had ever seen such a sight; I became confused, my playing faltered, my fingers became glued to the keys. – What is that, Haydn, what are you doing? cried the Countess; most respectfully I answered: But, Countess, your grace, who would not be undone at such a sight?'

17

... As Music Director in the service of Count Morzin Haydn composed his First Symphony.

Dies (45):

Haydn was now *Kapellmeister*, he had a certain income and was satisfied with his life with one exception, that he was still unmarried. It was not to be expected of a fiery young man that he would continue to heed the ban [on marriage, imposed by Count Morzin on his musicians] for very long. His natural urges grew stronger because of the ban, and Haydn could withstand it no longer. Since he lived with a wig-maker in his home where there were two daughters, and this man had said jokingly to him: 'Haydn, you ought to marry my eldest daughter,' Haydn did so (against his instincts, in fact, for the younger was the real object of his love), just to get a wife for himself quickly.

Haydn, says Griesinger, 'had often received assistance in the home of a hairdresser in Vienna (in the Landstraße) named Keller; he also gave music lessons to their eldest daughter, and with closer acquaintance he grew increasingly fond of her.' Haydn's first love was in fact not the eldest but the youngest daughter, Therese; but she was destined for the church and in May 1756 she took her solemn vows as Sister Josepha. Haydn composed an organ

11

concerto (C major; XVIII:1) and the *Salve Regina* in E (XXIIIb:1) for this – to him – sad occasion. Wig-maker Keller, to whom Haydn was patently very much indebted, persuaded the composer to marry his eldest daughter, Maria Anna (1729–1800), and the ceremony took place at St Stephen's Cathedral on 26 November 1760. Their marriage contract stipulated that Haydn provide the sum of 1,000 gulden (to 'match', as was the custom, her dowry of 350 gulden in goods and 500 in cash), which shows that he was now financially successful. He had undoubtedly made that large sum of money by selling authentic copies of his early quartets, trios, sonatas and symphonies to wealthy patrons in Vienna and the Austrian provinces: for example Prince Schwarzenberg acquired a Haydn symphony in 1758 for Krumau (Česky Krumlov) Castle and Bishop Leopold Egk von Hungersbach of Olmütz (Olomouc) acquired Haydn's Symphony No. 1 at Vienna before November 1759. Griesinger (15):

> Haydn had no children by this marriage. 'My wife was incapable of having children, and thus I was less indifferent to the charms of other women.' Altogether his choice was not a happy one, for his wife had a domineering, unfriendly character; and he had carefully to hide his income from her since she was a spendthrift. She was also bigoted, and was always inviting clergymen to dinner; she had many Masses said and was rather more liberal in her support of charity than her financial situation allowed. Once, when Haydn had done someone a favour for which he would take no recompense, it was suggested that I [Griesinger] offer something to his wife instead; he answered me: 'She doesn't deserve anything, for it is a matter of indifference to her whether her husband is a cobbler or an artist.'

Haydn's marriage was not a success, but Maria Anna had many grounds for protesting against her husband's conduct in the marriage, at least as far as his fidelity to her bed was concerned; and no doubt the black picture usually painted of Frau Haydn is a very one-sided one.

26 Dies tells us (49) of Haydn's momentous engagement by Prince Paul Anton Esterházy:

> A year passed without Count Morzin's learning of his *Kapellmeister*'s marriage; but it happened that Haydn's situation took a different turn. The Count found it necessary to reduce his hitherto great expenses. He dismissed his virtuosi and Haydn thus lost his post as *Kapellmeister*.
>
> Meanwhile, public opinion proved to be a great recommendation for Haydn. His attractive character was known. Count Morzin was at pains to be of service. Three circumstances which fortunately occurred simultaneously enabled Haydn, when he ceased being (in the year 1760) *Kapellmeister* to Count Morzin, to become *Vizekapellmeister*, under the direction of *Kapellmeister* Gregorius Werner, in the service of Prince Anton Esterházy de Galantha at Eisenstadt with a salary of 400 fl.

20–22 The Esterházy family was one of Hungary's richest, owning vast lands with dozens of castles (some in what is now Burgenland in Austria). They were renowned for their love for and understanding of music, and one of their illustrious members, Prince Paul (1635–1715), who became Palatine of Hungary, was the composer of a beautiful series of church music pieces entitled 'Harmonia caelestis' (published 1711), which have recently been revived with great success.

Haydn was engaged by Prince Paul Anton who, like all the Esterházys, had faithfully served the Habsburgs, first on the field and later as Ambassador. He was married to a handsome and vivacious Italian aristocrat, Marchesa Maria Anna di Lunati-Visconti, for whose name-day in 1773   68 Haydn composed his brilliant opera *L'infedeltà delusa*. Paul Anton's brother, Nicolaus, lived quietly in a hunting lodge in Hungary named Süttör (the site of what would be later Eszterháza Castle), he too was a great musician and music-lover (Paul Anton played the violin, flute and lute; Nicolaus viola da gamba, violoncello and baryton).

The princely establishment was run from Eisenstadt Castle, where the   22, 27 court lived in summer; in winters they lived in a roomy palace on the Wallnerstraße in Vienna. Haydn's first three symphonies for Prince Paul   23 Anton were composed in 1761 and were entitled 'Le Matin', 'Le Midi' and 'Le Soir'; they were first performed in the great hall of the Wallnerstraße Palace. Together with Haydn's own engagement, several other musicians for the orchestra were added and others dismissed; Haydn had at his disposal one flute, two oboes, two bassoons, two horns and a small string orchestra (after 1 June 1761: five violins and viola players, including Haydn, one violoncello, one double bass). The church music continued to be in the hands of the full *Kapellmeister*, Gregor Joseph Werner, while Haydn, as his deputy, directed the orchestra.

Haydn's contract with the Esterházys, signed on 1 May 1761, has been the subject of widespread comment, but the astonishment expressed at its phrasing and the tone of its language and supposedly demeaning contents is perhaps unwarranted. Many of the 'demeaning' clauses were simply used as standard for all house officers' contracts with the family. It is certainly not true that Haydn was treated like a servant. On the contrary, there was a vast difference between a real servant (and they, too, were subdivided into classes) and a house officer. The language in which a prince of the Holy Roman Empire expected to be addressed, either *viva voce* or in writing, is to be found throughout this study. The fawning, flattering tone of formal addresses and good wishes for name-days and birthdays strike oddly on the twentieth-century ear, but they were common all over Europe. As a contract, Haydn's was as fair and proper as would have been possible anywhere on the Continent, and there can be no doubt that Haydn signed it with relief, joy and high hopes.

CONVENTION AND RULES FOR BEHAVIOUR

OF THE *Vice-Capel-Meister* [*sic*]

This day, according to the date hereto appended, Joseph Heÿden [*sic*], native of [blank] in Austria, is accepted and appointed a *Vice-Capel-Meister* in the service of his Serene Princely Highness, Herr Paul Anton, Prince of the Holy Roman Empire, of Esterházÿ and Galantha Tit. etc. etc. in this manner; that whereas

1mo. There is at Eÿsenstadt a *Capel-Meister* named Gregorius Werner who, having devoted many years of true and faithful service to the Princely house, is now, on account of his great age and the resulting infirmities that this often entails, unfit to perform the duties incumbent on him, it is hereby declared that said Gregorious Werner, in consideration of his long service, shall continue to retain the post of *Ober-Cael-Meister*, while the said Joseph Heÿden, as *Vice-Capel-Meister* at Eÿsenstadt, shall in regard to the choir music depend upon and be subordinate to said Gregorio [!] Werner, *quà Ober-Capel-Meister*; but in everything else, whenever there shall be a musical performance, and in all required for the same in general and in particular, said *Vice-Capel-Meister* shall be responsible. And whereas

2do. The said Joseph Heÿden shall be considered and treated as a house officer. Therefore his Serene Princely Highness is graciously pleased to place confidence in him [Haydn], that as may be expected from an honourable house officer in a princely court, he will be temperate, and will know that he must treat the musicians placed under him not overbearingly, but with mildness and leniency, modestly, quietly and honestly. This is especially the case when music will be performed before the high *Herrschafft*, at which time said *Vice-Capel-Meister* and his subordinates shall always appear in uniform; and said Joseph Heÿden shall take care that not only he but all those dependent upon him shall follow the instructions which have been given to them, appearing neatly in white stockings, white linen, powdered, and either with pigtail or hair-bag, but otherwise of identical appearance. Therefore

3^tio. The other Musici are responsible to said *Vice-Capel-Meister*, thus he shall the more take care to conduct himself in an exemplary manner, so that the subordinates may follow the example of his good qualities; consequently said Joseph Heÿden shall abstain from undue familiarity, from eating and drinking, and from other intercourse with them so that they will not lose the respect which is his due but on the contrary preserve it; for these subordinates should the more remember their respectful duties if it be considered how unpleasant to the *Herrschafft* must be the consequences of any discord or dispute.

4to. The said *Vice-Capel-Meister* shall be under permanent obligation to compose such pieces of music as his Serene Princely Highness may command, and neither to communicate such new compositions to anyone, nor to allow them to be copied, but to retain them wholly for the exclusive use of his Highness; nor shall he compose for any other person without the knowledge and gracious permission [of his Highness].

5to. The said Joseph Heÿden shall appear daily (whether here in Vienna or on the estates) in the *antichambre* before and after midday, and inquire whether a high princely *ordre* for a musical performance has been given; to wait for this order and upon its receipt to communicate its contents to the other *Musici*; and not only himself to appear punctually at the required time but to take serious care that the others do so as well, specifically noting those who either arrive later or absent themselves entirely. If nevertheless.

6to. Contrary to rightful expectations there should arise between the *Musici* quarrels, disputes or complaints, said *Vice-Capel-Meister* shall endeavour himself to arrange matters, so that the high *Herrschafft* be not incommoded with every trifle and *bagatelle*; but should a more serious matter occur, which the said Joseph Heÿden is not able himself to set right or in which he can not act as intermediary, then his Serene Princely Highness must be respectfully informed.

7mo. The said *Vice-Capel-Meister* shall take careful charge of all the music and musical instruments, and shall be responsible for ensuring that they are not ruined and rendered useless through carelessness or neglect.

8°. The said Joseph Heÿden shall be obliged to instruct the female vocalists, in order that they may not again forget (when staying in the country) that which they have been taught with much effort and at great expense in Vienna, and inasmuch as the said *Vice-Capel-Meister* is proficient on various instruments, he shall take care to practice on all those with which he is acquainted.

9mo. A copy of this *Convention* and Rules for Behaviour shall be given to the said *Vice-Capel-Meister* and to all the *Musiquanten* subordinate to him, in order that he may hold them to all their obligations therein established. Moreover,

10mo. It is considered unnecessary to set forth on paper all the duties required of the said Joseph Heÿden, more particularly since the Serene *Herrschafft* is pleased to hope that he shall of his own free will strictly observe not only the above-mentioned regulations but any others – in whatever circumstances – which the high *Herrschafft* might issue in the future; and that he

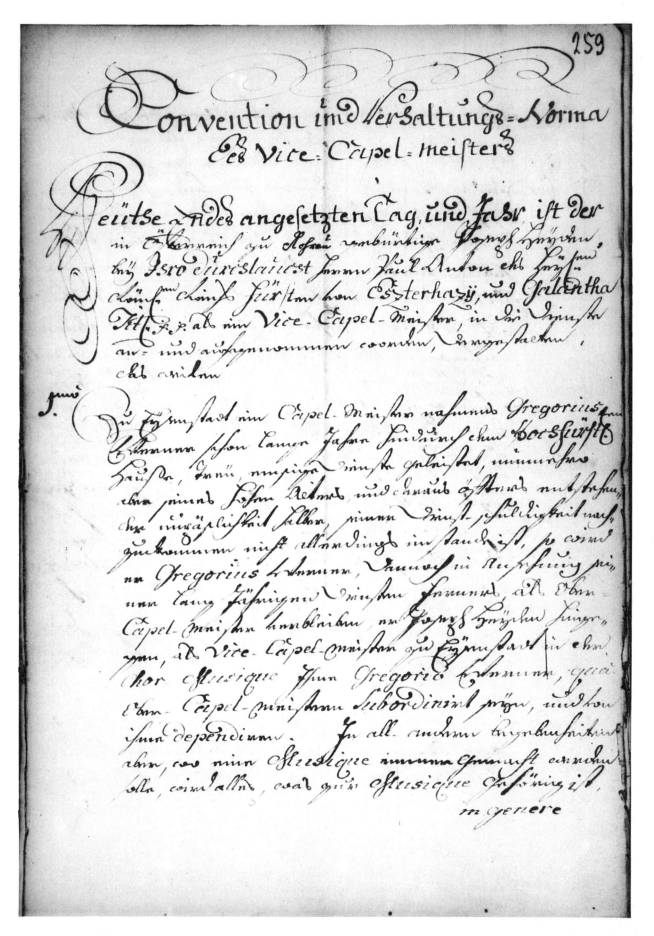

The first page of Haydn's copy of the contract, signed on 1 May 1761, appointing him *Vice-Kapellmeister* in the household of Prince Paul Anton Esterházy.

shall place the *Musique* on such a footing, and in such good order, that he shall bring honour upon himself and thereby deserve further princely favour; to which end his discretion and zeal are relied upon. In confidence of which

11mo. A yearly salary of 400 frn. [florin] Rhine value to be received from the Office of the Chief Collector [Cashier] in quarterly payments is hereby agreed. In addition,

12mo. When on the estates, said Joseph Heÿden shall board at the officers' table or receive half-a-gulden in lieu therefor. Finally

13mo. This *Convention* with the said *Vice-Capel-Meister* is agreed to on 1st May 1761 and is to hold good for at least three years, in such manner that if the said Joseph Heÿden at the end of that period wishes to seek his fortune elsewhere, he shall inform the *Herrschafft* of his intention by half-a-year's previous notice. Similarly,

14mo. The *Herrschafft* undertakes not only to retain the said Joseph Heÿden in his service during this period, but should he provide complete satisfaction, he may look forward to the position of *Ober-Capel-Meister*. On the other hand, his Highness is free at all times to dismiss him from his service, also during the period in question. In witness whereof, two identical copies of this document have been prepared and exchanged. Given at Vienna this 1st of Maÿ 1761.

[signed:] Joseph Haydn mpria.

What do we know of Haydn's life as a house officer with Prince Paul Anton, apart from the documents in the Esterházy Archives (which, however revealing in their details, tell us nothing of the composer before the first surviving autograph letter of 1765)? As it happens, we have, probably transmitted by Haydn's pupil Ignaz Pleyel, a curious anecdote from Framery's *Notice sur Joseph Haydn* (Paris 1810). After noting that a 'riche seigneur de la cour' (probably Morzin is meant) assisted the composer in gaining 'une réputation si brillante', and that Haydn entered the service of the Esterházys, Framery continues:

... In the first days when he [Haydn] was admitted to the household officers' table, the major domo was absent due to illness and the Secretary had him sit next to him, in the place normally occupied by the major domo himself. Some days later this man, now recovered, came to take his customary seat at table; he found it occupied by the place of the new member. 'Who dared', he said, 'have this young man placed here?' 'I did', replied the Secretary. 'You, is it possible? How does a mere composer, only just arrived in this household, come to enjoy such a distinction, to the detriment of the man who has been in the Prince's service for many years?' Haydn replied: 'Wherever there is a *Kapellmeister*, he must occupy the first place; this one was given to me and I shall keep it.' The major domo, greatly annoyed, gathered up the composer's place setting to take it to the far end of the table and returned to the place which he was claiming for himself; without saying a word, the Secretary went and sat next to the place where Haydn's setting had just been moved; the officers followed him, each according to his rank, in such a way that the major domo naturally found himself last; he left in a fury to complain to the Prince.

This quarrel – which, in a country so hidebound by etiquette, must have taken on an importance much greater than it would have done here – was treated quite seriously by the Prince. The next day he summoned our young maestro in order to reprimand him. 'You have offended an old servant whom I value', he said, 'and one who has been with me for a long time. I desire that peace shall reign in my household; you should not have caused an upset as soon as you arrived. The *Kapellmeister* repeated first of all what he had said the previous night concerning the prerogative and rights attached to his title; then he added, 'My Prince, on more than one occasion I have had the honour of being invited to the table of great lords, and I have never seen any major domo present, unless to serve. ... I had no intention of offending your man, but his pretensions and his manner of upholding them were an insult which your *Kapellmeister* could not possibly tolerate.' The Prince smiled, and promised to settle matters. ...

In March 1762, Prince Paul Anton died, to be succeeded by his younger brother Nicolaus, whose passion for music was only equalled by his passion for the theatre. On 12 May 1762, he engaged strolling players to come to Eisenstadt, an Italian operatic troupe under Hieronymus (Girolamo) Bon or Le Bon, from Pressburg. Nicolaus liked them so much that he engaged several of their members on the spot, Bon in July 1762 and two of the singers (Leopold Dichtler and Auguste Houdière) in 1763. Nicolaus was particularly fond of opera and encouraged Haydn to compose operas, which met with great princely approval.

42, 27

25

In the middle of the Italian company's guest appearance, Prince Nicolaus performed his first official act for a member of the *Capelle*. A document in the Esterházy Archives (Forchtenstein) states:

According to princely Decretation dd° 25ᵗᵉⁿ Junÿ (which is attached to the General Cassa Statements of the year 762) [*Vice-Capel-Meister* Haydn] is to receive an annual increase of ... 200f.

In other words, Haydn's salary had been raised by fifty per cent. A more dramatic way of showing princely approbation and encouragement could hardly be imagined.

If Haydn's position was acknowledged, there were other members of the Esterházy musical establishment who were treated quite differently. Consider the following letter by the regular copyist, Anton Adolph:

Most Serene Highness and Noble Prince of Holy Roman Empire Gracious and Dread Lord!

It will be known to Your Serene Princely Highness in your infinite grace that I, a poor copyist, Anton Adolph, have often submissively requested Your Princely Highness in your gracious mercy to improve my yearly salary; for I, a poor man, who is also married, have no more each month than twelve gulden in cash, together with the livery like other servants, and from this my meagre salary I must not only pay for my lodgings but also for wood, candles, and must support myself, miserably, even though I am crushed with work, so that as copyist I work day and night to supply the operas and comedies, as the enclosed list [of work done between May and August 1763; here omitted] will attest. And not only must I copy all this but even supply my own ink.

Considering that for all this I receive only 12 fl. and the livery (but without coat), it is difficult especially when it rains or snows, which is bad for the paper I take back and forth; that I have to pay for lodgings, wood and especially candles because I have to write so much at night; that my yearly salary, which is anyway not large, is stretched to the utmost; therefore I beg Your Serene Princely Highness on my knees, in humility and submissiveness, that in your graciousness (known to the whole world) you grant me some improvement in my monthly salary, or something towards lodgings, wood or candles; for which act of grace God the Almighty will reward you richly, but I with my poor wife will pray to God every day in our prayers to grant rich blessings on Your Serene Prince Highness. And so I comfort myself that you will heed this my request, and remain, Your Serene Princely Highness's

Humble and Submissive Servant,
Anton Adolph

The request was refused and in May 1764 Anton Adolph secretly fled from Eisenstadt.

In January 1763 the eldest son of Prince Nicolaus Esterházy was married to Marie Therese, Countess Erdödy. A splendid three-day festival was held in their honour at Eisenstadt, during which Haydn's first opera, *Acide*, was performed. A report in the *Wienerisches Diarium*:

113

Eisenstadt, 20 January.

We have never seen so many distinguished guests, and such joyous festivities, as during the last week on the occasion of the marriage of the Lord Son of his Princely Grace, Fürst Niclas [*sic*] Esterházy of Galantha, our gracious Sire, with the Demoiselle Countess von Erdödy, I.R. Maid of the Chamber. After the noble bridal pair had been joined in matrimony, with the usual ceremonies, on the 10th inst. by the Lord Archbishop of Colocza at the Court in Vienna, they enjoyed the favour of being invited, together with their nearest noble relatives, to lunch at the table of both their Majesties and Serene *Herrschafften*. We then had the pleasure of seeing them here, with a large number of distinguished guests, that very same evening. The road from Windpaßing [Wimpassing] to Eisenstadt, which is a three-hours' drive, was illuminated, and the same with our suburb and the ghetto, through which the procession passed. But the magnificent illumination of the princely castle outshone all else and was generally admired. In the middle of the square in front of the castle, a portal of honour had been erected, whereupon trumpets and kettledrums were heard. The Princely Guard, consisting of a Grenadier's Company of selected men, stood to attention. After the happy arrival of the noble Count and Countess, with their company, the Te Deum was celebrated in the Castle Chapel. Then, at two tables, each containing more than sixty couverts, the evening meal was taken; during which the guns were fired, a well trained exercise performed by the Princely Guard, and grenades were exploded, for the amusement of the spectators.

The next day, after solemn Mass, His Serene Princely Grace had arranged for a tribune in the manner of a Neapolitan *cocagna* to be put up, on which were roast hams, *Würste*, smoked meats and bread, and these were then distributed to the population which had assembled in very great numbers. Wine flowed from two great vats. And not the least disorder was to be observed. The midday meal in the Castle was most excellent, and afterwards there was a beautiful Italian Opera entitled *Acide*, performed by the virtuosi in the actual service of His Princely Grace: the princely musicians were all in identical, dark-red uniforms trimmed with gold. Thereafter, in the incomparable, and for this purpose marvellously decorated, great hall of the Castle was a masked ball, to which anyone possessing an entrance ticket was freely admitted: the number of masks was exceptionally large, and refreshments of all kinds were provided in abundance.

On the 12th the midday meal was even more largely attended. In the evening, part of the time was devoted to a pleasant spectacle of tightrope-walkers, acrobats, jugglers and balancing artists; and part to a ball which lasted until the early morning: 600 masks were counted, and many of them changed costumes several times.

On the third day an opera buffa was given with exceptional applause, and afterwards a ball began, during which the entire castle garden was magnificently illuminated and the number of masks even greater than before. And with this, these marvellous three-day festivities were at an end, distinguished not only by their magnificence and opulence, but also by the exceptional hospitality to the many lunch and dinner guests, and also by the excellent taste and most fitting sense of order that obtained throughout: but most especially by the delightful and condescending fashion which His Princely Grace showed to every man, and which was generally admired. In the reflection of the host's honour, and in a universal enjoyment, the events thus concluded.

In 1764 Haydn was ill; no details are known, but the matter was serious enough for the *Vice-Kapellmeister* to seek the Prince's help, as the reply (which survives in the Esterházy Archives, Forchtenstein) indicates. Here, we see one example of the many instances of Prince Nicolaus's personal kindnesses towards Haydn:

Petition of *Capell-Meister* Heyden.
The subject of this petition is hereby graciously permitted to purchase the necessary medicines at our expense, but without setting a precedent; for the other musicians, since they are in any case well paid, are to secure the necessary medicines on their own.

Vienna, 27th Xber [Dec.] 1764.
Nicolaus Fürst Esterhazy mpria

In the pyramid-shaped system of administration adopted by Prince Nicolaus Esterházy, the *Regent* (after the Prince himself head of the household) was a former military man, Peter Ludwig von Rahier, who tended to treat employees of the Esterházy household as if they were recalcitrant foot-soldiers. Haydn often had to act as a diplomatic go-between in Rahier's outbursts of temper with the musicians. In one such episode in 1765, the flute player, Franz Sigl, was shooting birds at Eisenstadt and set the roof of a house on fire. With great presence of mind, the fire brigade at once removed the roof of the neighbouring house to stop the blaze from spreading; it was a close thing, however, and in a fury Prince Nicolaus summarily dismissed the flautist (Rahier performing the task on his behalf). The earliest complete letter in Haydn's own hand to have survived concerns these events and his own attempt to intercede:

SERENE HIGHNESS AND NOBLE PRINCE OF THE HOLY ROMAN EMPIRE, GRACIOUS AND DREAD LORD!
I have received with every submissive and dutiful respect YOUR ILLUSTRIOUS AND SERENE HIGHNESS' letter of the 8th inst. addressed to me, and I see from it that your Highness has taken it very amiss that I protested against the detention of the flauto traverso player Frantz Sigl to Herr von Rahier, whose commands I am now admonished to follow, in order that I may behave better in the future, on penalty of the dread displeasure of my SERENE HIGHNESS.
MOST SERENE HIGHNESS! GRACIOUS LORD! On behalf of the above-named flauto traverso player, because of whom the fire started, I went with the whole band to Herr von Rahier, and it was not on account of the detention, but only on account of the rude detention and the harsh treatment of the subject that I protested, but with all proper respect, to Herr von Rahier. But we could not get anywhere with the administrator, and I even had to put up with his slamming the door in my face, he addressed all the others in the 'Ihr' form and threatened everyone with detention. Similarly, this very day Friberth fled excitedly from the *Regent*'s passion (on account of not doffing his hat, which must have been an oversight), and does not dare to come home, because this same *Regent* pretends that the first-mentioned Friberth was rude to him, and that therfore he will mete out his own punishment. But I testify, as do all the other musicians, that Friberth did nothing else except that, when the Regent threatened all of us with detention – and without any reason – he said he had no other master but HIS SERENE HIGHNESS, PRINCE ESTERHÁZY. I myself told the *Regent* to complain to YOUR SERENE AND ILLUSTRIOUS HIGHNESS if he felt his own person to have been insulted, but I was given the answer that the *Regent* is his own judge and will mete out the punishment himself. Everyone is very upset on this account, these honourable men find this treatment very unfair and hope that YOUR SERENE AND GRACIOUS HIGHNESS' intentions certainly do not

extend this far, and that for this reason you will graciously put a stop to such exercises of power whereby anyone can be his own judge without differentiating between guilty or not guilty.

The orders of the oft-mentioned *Regent* (as YOUR SERENE AND GRACIOUS HIGHNESS knows anyway) have been correctly carried out at all times, and as often as I receive through him an order of YOUR SERENE AND GRACIOUS HIGHNESS, I shall always execute it to the best of my ability; if therefore the *Regent* has complained in this regard, it must be the result of his angry pen. But moreover YOUR SERENE AND ILLUSTRIOUS HIGHNESS must yourself remember, in your graciousness, that I cannot serve two masters, and cannot accept the commands of, and subordinate myself to, the administrator, for YOUR SERENE AND ILLUSTRIOUS HIGHNESS once said to me: COME FIRST TO ME, BECAUSE I AM HIS MASTER.

I am therefore confident that YOUR SERENE AND ILLUSTRIOUS HIGHNESS will not receive ungraciously this my most submissive and obedient letter, but will regard me and the whole *Musique* with gracious eyes, and, since everyone is desirous of this grace, that you will watch over us in fatherly protection. I hope for further marks of favour and grace from YOUR HIGHNESS and I remain ever, with every mark of profound respect,

YOUR SERENE AND GRACIOUS HIGHNESS'
most humble and obedient
Josephus Haydn.

Eisenstadt, 9th September 1765

Haydn's intervention on all these levels seems to have had its wished-for effect; perhaps Rahier's anger had died down in the intervening four days, and possibly Prince Nicolaus put in a word to calm the irate spirits, but in any case Rahier's next letter is in a more civilized tone ('as', might have thought Esterházy, 'befits the language of an honourable princely court'). Unfortunately there was no way to save Sigl.

Relations between Haydn and his nominal head, *Kapellmeister* Werner, had deteriorated; no doubt Werner was jealous of the enormous success of his *Vice-Kapellmeister*; but Haydn, it seems, always respected Werner's music and as an old man took the trouble to edit a whole series of Werner's instrumental pieces for Artaria & Co., in Vienna (Haydn's principal Austrian publishers). Towards the end of October 1765, Werner – now a sick and embittered old man – wrote the following letter to Prince Nicolaus at Süttör:

HIGH BORN PRINCE OF THE HOLY ROMAN EMPIRE,
GRACIOUS AND DREAD LORD!
I am forced to draw attention to the gross negligence in the local castle chapel [i.e. Eisenstadt], the unnecessarily high princely expenses, and the lazy idleness of the whole band, the principal responsibility for which must be laid at the door of the present director, who lets them all get away with everything, so as to receive the name of a good Heyden [*sic*]; for as God is my witness, things are much more disorderly than if the 7 children were about; it seems that there are only libertines among the chorus people, who according to their fancy take their recreation for 5 or even 6 weeks at a time: the poor chapel thus has only 5 or six at a pinch, also not one of them pays attention to what his neighbour is playing. Over half the choir's instruments are lost, and they were collected only seven years ago, after many requests, from the late lamented Prince. Apart from all that, now most of the church music itself goes out to all the world; before, the late organist took care of it, but after his death it had to happen that I gave the key to the present *Capell Meister* to care for; but with the proviso that he should draw up a proper catalogue of the items in the choir-loft, and this should have been copied three times. One for Your Highness; the second for the princely book-

keepers; the third deposited in the actual choir-loft. Herr Heyden most willingly agreed, also with the preparation of the catalogues, which he was to bring to my sick bed; but up to now nothing has been done.

The cabinet with the music, however, as true Christian men report to me, has been considerably depleted, which is the more easily credible if one considers that on my sick bed I have already had requests from three parties, asking if I could supply church music for them advantageously, since Vienna at present has a considerable lack of church composers.

I, however, left such letters unanswered. But it is easy to presume that they will have addressed their request to Heyden. Thus the church choir will be meanwhile depleted completely unless Heyden is seriously ordered to prepare a catalogue at least of what pieces remain.

Incidentally, it is humbly requested: Your Princely Highness should give him a severe order that he must issue the strictest command to the princely musicians that they appear in the future, all of them without exception, at their duties. And because it is likely that he, Heyden, will try to lie his way out of it, the order must come from on high, that the extent choir instruments be examined, among which there must be 12 old and new violins.

Of the violas, 2 old and 2 new, but 2 Passetel [violoncellos] and 2 good large double basses: all too soon it will be seen where the truth lies.

Under the late lamented Prince, apart from the usual summer *fatigue*, it was ordered that in winter time we were to give two academies [concerts] a week in the princely officers' room, Tuesdays and Thursdays, for which two hours each was required. If this were to be reinstated now, the injurious laziness would be removed, and no longer would such bad practices obtain as, alas, experience has shown to have occurred.

Because today, as a very old man who has borne the title of *Capellmeister* here for 37 years, and because the price of wood has risen considerably, and I as a sick man cannot deal with the heating myself and am forced as a result to get outside people, who do not forget to look after their own interests, to come and do it.

Thus I must humbly beg your Princely Highness only out of pity to add two cords of wood to my emoluments [in kind], for my constitution is so weakened by loss-of-weight, that my sick body consists of almost nothing except skin and bones. For such a stroke of generosity I will earnestly pray to God, not only as long as I am alive but also when I am dead, for your long and happy reign and for an increase of your rents and income.

With which I most humbly recommend myself to Your Highness' grace and favour, and remain,

Your Serene Highness'
most obedient servant
Gregorius Werner

1765 in 8^{ber} [October]

Prince Nicolaus, busy supervising the building of the new Castle of Eszterháza in Süttör, seems to have taken this outburst with a grain of salt, for when he returned it to Rahier, it was accompanied by the following laconic note: 'Moreover, I attach the document of *Kapellmeister* Werner here; as concerns his laments, you will be in the best position to act on them'.

On 3 March 1766 Werner died. In Haydn's contract of 1761, clause 14 had provided for an initial three-year period of service and the eventual prospect of being appointed full *Kapellmeister*. Although that contract had been drawn up in the days of Prince Paul Anton, his successor was certainly satisfied with Haydn – notwithstanding the flurry of events in the autumn of 1765 – and his promotion following Werner's death seems to have been so automatic that there is no known written record of it in the Esterházy Archives.

We know almost nothing of Haydn's personal life at Eisenstadt. He lived in an apartment in the 'Old Apothecary' next to the Bergkirche, and he seems to have employed a boy servant. At least that would seem to be the explanation for an unedifying legal wrangle recorded in the Eisenstadt Town Books, in which Haydn's 'Godless boy' (*gottlosem Buben*) is mentioned, one Ludwig Hänl.

Joseph Haydn, 1762.5.10 / Minute

On the application of the Music Director to the Prince Esterházy, Joseph Haydn, a further examination is to be undertaken of the case of the weaver Mathias Strobel, who is in custody under suspicion of conspiracy [with Ludwig Hähnl in respect of a theft of money]: but since, according to the written report received from Ferdinand Petzelbauer, Master Weaver residing at Wandorf near Ödenburg [Sopron, Hungary], the aforesaid conducts himself at all times with honesty, and since the impious knave ['Godless boy'] Ludwig Hähnl has confessed before a Justice to having withdrawn his previous evidence and has further stated that he did not give any of the stolen money to Strobel, Strobel is not only freed from arrest but it is ordered that a confirmation of his innocence in this instance as well as a judicial attestation shall be made available in the determination of the examination.

Apart from these things, however, being the typical manifestations of life in a small town during the period, Haydn had consolidated his position, both financially and in other ways. Haydn enjoyed the greatest confidence of his patron, and all things considered, the history of Joseph Haydn and Nicolaus Esterházy is one that reflects the greatest credit on both sides. The two (for Esterházy's role cannot be underestimated) made cultural and musical history. Haydn was now sufficiently well situated to ask Prince Nicolaus if his brother Johann might come to Eisenstadt as an unpaid tenor in the *Chor Musique*. The Prince agreed and in 1765, Johann joined the *Capelle* in an honorary capacity, being supported by his elder brother. About 1765, Haydn began to use the permanent services of a copyist in princely employ named Joseph Elssler. Haydn became a kind of protector to the whole Elssler family, being present at their marriages and christenings, and finally engaging the son Johann as a permanent valet, factotum and copyist (Johann went with Haydn to England in 1794). Joseph Elssler's hand was clear and precise, and Haydn used him for the most important tasks, though of course there had to be many other copyists as well to cope with the enormous amount of scores and parts to be produced.

In 1765, Haydn is known to have composed at least four Symphonies: Nos. 28, 29, 30 ('Alleluja') and 31 ('Hornsignal') – not necessarily in that order – and probably many other works as well which cannot be dated precisely. But even these four works reveal a sure hand technically and an inner emotional stability, a maturity, which augured well for the future of the *Capelle*, and the future of music, too, though no one could yet foresee the effect that Haydn would have on that future.

II
THE ESZTERHÁZA YEARS
1766~1790

'... [at Eszterháza] I was cut off from the world;
there was no one in my vicinity to make
me unsure of myself or to persecute me; and so I had
to become original.'

GRIESINGER, 17

33   This portrait of Haydn by Ludwig Guttenbrunn exists
in two versions. This, the second of the two (in a private
collection), dates from c. 1791–2. It is based on an original,
painted c. 1770, which was owned by Haydn's wife and,
after passing through various hands, is now owned by the
Burgenländisches Landesmuseum, Eisenstadt. The artist,
who became Frau Haydn's lover while at Eszterháza, was
also responsible for frescoes and decorative schemes while
employed there by Prince Nicolaus.

The 'Versailles of Hungary': Prince Nicolaus I Esterházy's castle of Eszterháza

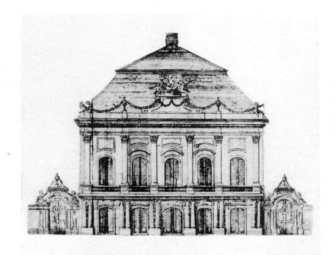

34, 35 One of the outstanding features of Eszterháza – one of the last great Rococo palaces to be built within the imperial and royal domains – was the inclusion of an opera house and a marionette theatre. Although the building work was substantially finished by the autumn of 1768 when the opera house was inaugurated, the Prince did not consider his castle complete until 1784.

In a lost oil painting *(above, right)* showing the principal buildings seen from the garden side, the opera house (which has not survived) can be seen to the left of the palace; the entrance façade *(above, left)* is seen in an engraving by Joseph von Fernstein, published in 1784. Both views show the building as it was rebuilt (1780–1) following a disastrous fire in November 1779.

36–38 In addition to facilities for opera, the castle also included a great music room *(left)*, specially designed for the purpose. Although the palace and its decorations were badly damaged during the Second World War, they have been largely restored *(opposite, below)* to their former splendour, complete with formal gardens.

After the death of Prince Nicolaus in 1790, Eszterháza was scarcely used by his successor, Prince Anton (cf. ill. 112), but the entrance courtyard was the scene of the latter's installation as Governor of the County of Oedenburg on 3 August 1791 *(opposite, above)*; in addition to military units on parade, a band of gypsy musicians can be seen in the foreground on the right.

Eszterháza today

39–41 The decorative wrought-iron gates and screen *(right)* frame the main entrance to the palace. The imposing double staircase and the curve of the low buildings enclosing the entrance courtyard *(top)* contrast with the formal symmetry of the palace seen from the garden side *(above)*.

42–44 Prince Nicolaus I Esterházy, Haydn's patron from 1762 to 1790; in addition to his wide-ranging interest in the arts and literature, the prince was a skilful performer on the baryton; the instrument made in 1732 by Stadlmann *(above, right)* may have been Haydn's own. During the Eszterháza years Haydn composed over a hundred trios (for baryton, viola and violoncello) for the prince's private pleasure, as well as other chamber works for baryton.

Haydn's devotion to Prince Nicolaus gave rise in 1772 to a setting of the Mass – the *Missa Sancti Nicolai* – written for the annual celebration of the prince's name-day (6 December). The opening of the Benedictus for soprano solo is shown *(right)* in a copy for the original performance made by Joseph Elssler, with the Latin text filled in by the composer himself.

Haydn and France: the fruits of international fame

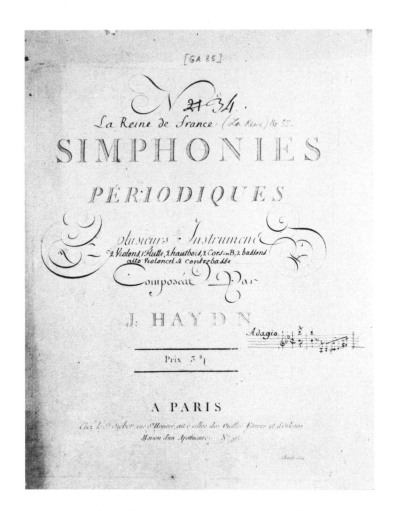

45–47 The first pirated publications of Haydn's works appeared in Paris in 1764, and his compositions rapidly achieved popularity there. The 'Paris' Symphonies (Nos. 82–87) were composed in 1785 and 1786 to a commission from the Concert de la Loge Olympique; a leading backer of this Masonic organization in Paris was Claude-François-Marie Rigoley, Comte d'Ogny *(right)*. One of the resulting works, Symphony No. 85, was the favourite of Marie Antoinette, Queen of France (formerly the Arch-duchess Maria Antonia of Austria), seen – in a portrait by F. X. Wagenschön *(above right)* – seated at a spinet. In the first French edition of the 'Paris' Symphonies (1788) No. 85 bore the inscription 'La Reine de France'; the work was immediately nicknamed 'La Reine', as the title page of this 1789 edition published by Sieber shows, and has been known by this name ever since.

48   The first page of the finale from Haydn's autograph of
Quartet, Op. 20, No. 5 (1772), marked 'Fuga a 2 Soggetti'
and 'Sempre sotto voce'. This group of six quartets is
regarded as epitomizing the full maturity of the Viennese
classical style; the works were first printed in Paris, c. 1774.

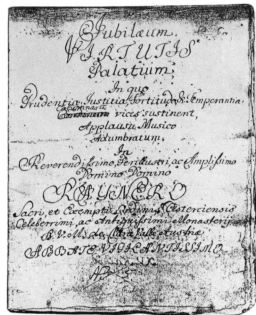

49,50 Zwettl Abbey, a Cistercian house in Lower Austria, was the source of an interesting and unusual commission. The monks wished to celebrate in 1768 the fiftieth anniversary of their Abbot's taking his vows, and for this occasion Haydn wrote a Cantata, 'Applausus', for which he received a fee of 100 gulden; the opening page of the MS. libretto is shown *(above, right)*. Haydn also wrote a letter, which accompanied the Cantata, explaining how the work should be correctly performed.

51 The house in Eisenstadt (now a museum), which Haydn purchased in 1766 after becoming full *Kapellmeister* to Prince Nicolaus I Esterházy; the building was twice ravaged by fire – in 1768 and 1776 – and reconstructed on both occasions at the Prince's expense.

52–54 *L'infedeltà delusa* (1773)

The title page and cast list *(above)* from the libretto printed for the second official performance at Eszterháza in September 1773 in honour of the visit of the Empress Maria Theresa. The Italian peasant costume *(above, right)* was typical of the region (Lucca-Pisa) in which the action is set. Later, the Empress recalled the performance, saying 'If I want to hear good opera, I must go to Eszterháza.'

The work was revived at the Holland Festival in 1963 *(right)*; in this scene the heroine Vespina sings a Duet with her angry brother Nanni outside their Tuscan farmhouse.

55,56 *Il mondo della luna* (1777): Marcello Cortis (centre) as Buonafede in the scene depicting a fantastic garden on the moon (Act II), from the first modern production of the original score, presented at the Holland Festival, 1959; and *(left)*, another scene from the production at Lyon, 1979/80.

57, 58 *Le pescatrici* (1769; first performed 1770). In a scene from Act II *(left)* – from the Holland Festival production (1965) – the as yet undiscovered princess (Eurilda) sings a duet with her foster-father Mastricco; another scene *(left, below)* – from the Bregenz production (1973) – shows Eurilda after she has been identified and is affianced to Prince Lindoro; the ship on which they will depart together can be seen in the background.

59–61 *Armida* (1783; first performance 1784), a heroic drama.
The only surviving pictorial record of a production of a Haydn opera during the composer's lifetime is a small engraving *(above)*, associated with a performance given at Pressburg in 1786; it shows the tents in the Frankish camp; two of the costume designs by Pietro Travaglia for the original 1784 production *(opposite)* have also survived.

62 (opposite) *La fedeltà premiata* (1780; first performed 1781)
This opera was successfully revived in 1970 at the Holland Festival, and was included in the 1979 Glyndebourne repertoire (and repeated in 1980), the first Haydn opera to be performed there. The scene shown *(right)* is taken from the latter production.

63, 65 *Orlando Paladino* (1782)
Design for a stage set for the first performance at Eszterháza *(above)*, from the sketch-book of Pietro Travaglia; and *(below)* the first page of the autograph score.

64 *La vera constanza* (1779)
Title page and cast (set out in the characteristic diagrammatic manner of an Eszterháza production) from the printed libretto.

66, 67 (opposite) The auditorium and stage (with a contemporary set) of the beautiful little castle theatre at Böhmisch Krumau (Český Krumlov), formerly owned by the princely Schwarzenberg family. This is one of the very few eighteenth-century theatres that have survived in Central Europe, and as such it helps us to imagine how the interior of the Eszterháza theatre may have looked; since the latter was destroyed in the nineteenth-century, our only detailed knowledge about it is confined to a few technical engravings.

68 The Dowager Princess Maria Anna Esterházy (*née* Marchesa Lunati-Visconti), widow of Prince Paul Anton (d. 1762; cf. ill. 26), depicted in a miniature portrait on ivory. A performance of Haydn's opera *L'infedeltà delusa* was given in July 1773 to celebrate the Princess's name-day.

69 Anton Walter, the greatest fortepiano builder of his age, whose instruments were favoured by Mozart, was summoned from Vienna to Eszterháza in February 1781, where he worked for twelve days carrying out repairs to the keyboard instruments.

70, 71 Joseph Haydn, anonymous portrait miniature on ivory, *c.* 1780, and *(below)* a trompe-l'œil collage dating from 1772 which incorporates a portrait of the well-known 'cellist, Joseph Weigl. Haydn and Weigl, who was engaged by Prince Esterházy in 1761, were great friends; among Haydn's works specially composed for Weigl was the 'Cello Concerto in C, composed *c.* 1765.

72–74 Three of the contemporary composers of Italian opera whose works were performed under Haydn's direction at Eszterháza: Domenico Cimarosa (oil painting by Alessandro Longhi); Tommaso Traetta; and Giovanni Paisiello (engraving after a painting by Elisabeth Vigée-Lebrun). Works by other composers often had to be adapted to suit the singers available at Eszterháza, resulting in both cuts and the addition of insertion arias.

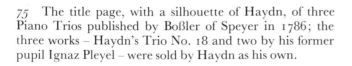

75 The title page, with a silhouette of Haydn, of three Piano Trios published by Boßler of Speyer in 1786; the three works – Haydn's Trio No. 18 and two by his former pupil Ignaz Pleyel – were sold by Haydn as his own.

76 Another prolific composer who wrote symphonies, quartets, serenades and trios in the manner of Haydn was Adalbert Gyrowetz; his Symphony in G major was published by Sieber in Paris as Haydn.

77–79 The friendship between Mozart *(centre)* and Haydn probably began in 1784; in 1785 the younger composer dedicated six string quartets – the title page of the Artaria edition is shown *(left)* – to Haydn, and he was also one of those responsible for introducing Haydn to Freemasonry; an initiation ceremony, such as the one in which Haydn was admitted to the Viennese Lodge 'Zur wahren Eintracht' in February 1785, is shown *(above)* in an anonymous painting, *c.* 1780. (In the year 1780 Prince Nicolaus I Esterházy was Master of Ceremonies at the Lodge 'Zur gekrönten Hoffnung', and it is possible that he is depicted here supervising the initiation of a new Brother.)

80 An engraving by J. de Loutherbourg after Landseer shows Haydn and Mozart as the leading figures in the hierarchy of musicians in the late eighteenth century. The group of portraits, based on cameos, is valuable for the likeness of leading performers of the day. During his first visit to England Haydn met de Loutherbourg in London.

AFTER SUCCEEDING to the princely Esterházy title in March 1762, Nicolaus I decided to erect on the site of his former home – the remote hunting lodge at Süttör – what was to be the most lavish secular building of its period within the Monarchy: Eszterháza Castle. The plans for this fairy-tale castle, the 'Hungarian Versailles', situated on the south side of the large lake – the Neusiedlersee – which today forms part of the international boundary between Austria and Hungary, were drawn up in the early 1760s, the principal architect being Melchior Hefele. However, Prince Nicolaus also played a decisive role in the building's shape – hence the great hall upstairs, which was designed *a priori* as a concert room, and in which such works as 36 Haydn's 'Farewell' Symphony would later be performed.

Construction work on a large scale began in 1766. Before the project was begun and until the completion of the opera house and musicians' quarters, Haydn and the musicians lived most of the year at Eisenstadt, making excursions to Vienna in the winter, to the Esterházy castle at Kittsee, or to Pressburg, in fact 'wherever their lordships [*Herrschaft*] so wished.' The Prince would give his *Kapellmeister* and his musicians an annual vacation at Christmastide, when he himself went to the Imperial Court in Vienna to pay his respects at the New Year. Haydn usually went to Vienna, too, so that he could see his publishers, visit friends, visit instrument makers, search for new music, and so on.

In 1768 the opera house and the musicians' building were completed, 34, 35 enabling Haydn and the members of the *Capelle* to reside there on a permanent basis; but it was not until 1784 that the building and gardens were completed in all details. Eszterháza cost 13,000,000 gulden and contained one hundred and twenty-six rooms. The castle contained a marionette theatre (completed 1773) where Haydn conducted his own and other marionette operas in German. The opera house was reserved for operas in Italian, though it was also used by the strolling players whom Nicolaus Esterházy engaged every year to come for several months and give German-language comedies, tragedies and pantomimes. Ballet companies and children's groups were also engaged.

At first, operas were given at Eszterháza for special occasions, such as the marriage of an Esterházy son or niece; Nicolaus would use such a marriage celebration, or the visit of an archduke, as a pretext to arrange an elaborate festival that usually lasted several days, and of which the performance of an opera (generally composed for the occasion by Haydn) was a central feature. For such *feste*, Haydn composed *Lo speziale* (1768), *Le pescatrici* (1769, performed 1770), *L'infedeltà delusa* (1773), and so on. After 1775, in which year Esterházy arranged a huge festival to mark the visit of Archduke Ferdinand and his consort, a new epoch began at Eszterháza. Starting in 1776 there were regular performances of opera at the Castle, including works by

72, 74   such popular composers of the time as Paisiello, Anfossi or Cimarosa. The Prince's preference was for *opera buffa*, and Haydn was expected to prepare works in this *genre* for the particular ensemble at his disposal (this entailed transpositions, removal of clarinet parts because he had these instruments only for limited periods, etc.), coach the singers and conduct the

52–64   performance. Gradually, this operatic activity came to dwarf every other type of music making, including Haydn's own composing (which had somehow to be squeezed into a busy operatic season). In 1786, the year in which Haydn delivered his 'Paris' Symphonies to the Concert de la Loge Olympique, he had to prepare and conduct 125 performances of eight 'new' operas and nine other works already in the Eszterháza repertoire; this scarcely believable feat was repeated in 1788, when seventeen operas (seven 'new' works and ten repeats) were also staged.

As time went on, Prince Nicolaus stayed longer and longer at his beloved 'Hungarian Versailles'. These lengthy stays gave rise to the famous 'Farewell' Symphony, when Haydn's compositional talents were organized to persuade his Prince to allow the musicians to go home (they were not allowed to take their wives with them to Eszterháza because there was not enough room in the musicians' quarters, especially since there were also actors and actresses in residence for months at a time). Haydn's season at Eszterháza gradually came to be almost ten, and often eleven, months in each year, and operas were usually given from the end of April to Christmas.

After Prince Nicolaus died in 1790, Eszterháza was never used as the principal residence of the family. It suffered heavy damage during the Second World War and has since been lovingly rebuilt by the Hungarian

39–41   government; it is now a museum and one of the country's great tourist attractions. The magnificence of the castle and its gardens can be gauged from the following vivid description by Baron Riesbeck translated from the version adapted for and published in Cramer's *Magazin der Musik* in 1784:

... With the exception of Versailles, there is perhaps in the whole of France no place to compare with it for magnificence. The castle is very large and filled to bursting with luxurious things. The garden contains everything that human fantasy can conceive to improve or, if you will, undo the work of nature. Pavilions of all kinds stand like the dwellings of voluptuous fairies, and everything is so far removed from the usual human operations that one looks at it as if in the middle of a marvellous dream. I will not enter into a description of all this magnificence, but I must say that, at least in the eyes of one non-connoisseur, I found some of it very offensive because too much art prevails. I remember the walls of the sala terrena, which has painted figures that are at least twelve feet [*12 Schuhe*] high, and since the sala is not big enough for a human eye to take them in, an earthbound figure such as myself felt acutely dwarfed. I know that you are for the grand style, and when viewing these monster figures I remembered everything you told my profane ears about the theory of the Roman school, their large designs, etc., but I am sure that had you seen these fantastical figures you would have readily admitted that the grand style was misplaced here.

What increases the magnificence of the place is the contrast with the surrounding countryside. Anything more dull or depressing can hardly be imagined. The Neusiedler See, from which the castle is not far removed, makes miles of swamp and threatens in time to swallow up all the land right up to the Prince's dwelling, just as it has already swallowed up huge fields containing the most fertile land which had been laid out. The inhabitants of this country look for the most part like ghosts, and in Spring they almost always get cold fever. One has figured out that with half the money the Prince spent on his garden, he could not only have dried out the swamp but regained as much land again from the lake. Since the water flowing into the lake is always more than that which flows out, the danger with which these low-lying lands are threatened is really very acute. What would be necessary would be to construct a canal which would take the superfluous water and pour it into the Danube, an operation which would not strain the Prince's capabilities and would in the eyes of certain persons make him more honourable than by the presence of his magnificent garden. On the other side of the castle one doesn't need to make a day's journey to see Tartars, Hottentots, Iroquois and people from Tierra del Fuego living together and going about their various businesses.

Unhealthy as is the country, especially in Spring and Autumn, and although the Prince himself is attacked by cold fever, he is firmly persuaded that in the whole wide world there is no more healthy and pleasant place. His castle is quite isolated, and he has no one about him except his servants and the strangers who come to admire his beautiful things. He keeps a marionette theatre which is certainly unique of its kind. The biggest operas are given in it. One doesn't know whether to laugh or cry when one sees *Alceste, Alcide al Bivio*, etc., given by marionettes all finely costumed. His orchestra is one of the best I ever heard, and the great **Haydn** is his court and theatre composer. For his curious theatre he keeps a poet whose ability to fit large subjects into the theatre, and whose parodies of serious pieces, are often very successful. His theatrical painter and decorator is an excellent artist, although he can display his talents only on a small scale. In short the operation is small, but the outward trappings are on a very large scale. He often engages a troupe of players for several months at a time, and apart from some servants he is the whole audience. They have his permission to appear uncombed, drunk, and dishevelled. The Prince is not one for the tragic and serious, and he likes it when the characters, like Sancho Panza, lay on the humour with a trowel. Apart from ... servants, he also keeps a bodyguard which consists of handsome people ....

Although Haydn shared some of the writer's reservations about Eszterháza, life there had its compensations in both work and leisure opportunities, as Griesinger observes in his biography:

Prince Nikolaus Esterhazy was an educated connoisseur and passionate lover of music, and also a good violin player. He had his own opera, spoken theatre, marionette theatre, church music and chamber music. Haydn had his hands full; he composed, he had to conduct all the music, help with the rehearsals, give lessons and even tune his own piano [*Klavier*] in the orchestra. He often wondered how it had been possible for him to compose as much as he did when he was forced to lose so many hours in purely mechanical tasks. ...

Although it must be said that Haydn's outward circumstance was anything but brilliant, it nevertheless provided him with the best opportunity for the development of his many-sided talents. 'My Prince was satisfied with all my works; I received approval; as head of an orchestra, I could undertake experiments, could observe that which enhanced an effect and that which weakened it, thus improving, adding to it, taking away from it, taking risks. I was cut off from the world; there was no one in my vicinity to make me unsure of myself or to persecute me; and so I had to become original.' [17]

Hunting and fishing were Haydn's favourite pastimes during his sojourn in Hungary, and he could never forget that once he brought down with a single shot three hazel-hens, which arrived on the table of the Empress Maria Theresa. Another time he aimed at a hare but only shot off its tail, but the same shot killed a pheasant that happened to be nearby; while his dog, chasing the hare, strangled itself in a snare. In riding Haydn never developed any skill, because ever since he had fallen from a horse on the Morzin estates [at Lukavec in Bohemia], he never trusted himself to mount a horse again; Mozart too, who liked horseback riding for exercise, was always terrified when doing so. [19]

43 Prince Nicolaus's favourite instrument, on which he played with considerable skill, was the baryton, a kind of viola da gamba with a series of sympathetic vibrating strings behind the fingerboard which could be plucked. The Prince expected Haydn to write new music for this instrument, which has a rather sombre and melancholic sound, and Haydn obliged with, *inter alia*, 125 divertimentos for baryton, viola and 'cello, as well as numerous kinds of solos, duets and concerted music which feature the instrument (sometimes two). Prince Nicolaus also commissioned other composers 'from outside' to provide new music for his well-nigh insatiable demands. Dies (58) relates:

The Prince loved music and he himself played the baryton, which in his opinion should be limited to one key only. Haydn could not be certain of that because he had only a very superificial knowledge of the instrument. Nevertheless, he thought it must be playable in several keys. Unknown to the Prince, Haydn conducted an investigation into the instrument's capabilities, and he acquired a liking for it; he practised it late at night because he had no other time, with a view to becoming a good player. He was, of course, often interrupted in his nocturnal studies by the scolding and quarrelling of his wife, but he did not lose his patience and in six months he had attained his goal.

The Prince still knew nothing. Haydn could not resist a touch of vanity any longer. He played in public before the Prince in a number of keys, expecting to reap enthusiastic applause. But the Prince was not in the least surprised and took the whole thing in his stride; he merely remarked: 'You are supposed to know about such things, Haydn!'

'I quite understood the Prince,' said Haydn to me, 'and though I was at first hurt by his indifference, nevertheless I owe to his curt rejoinder the fact that I gave up my intention of becoming a good baryton player. I remembered that I had already gained some reputation as a *Kapellmeister* and not as a practising virtuoso. I reproached myself for half a year's neglect of composition, and I returned to it with renewed vigour.

The Prince's name-day was celebrated by the household at Eisenstadt on 6 December 1766. Haydn took the occasion to write the following letter to Nicolaus; it was probably delivered to him by a courier at Eszterháza.

Most Serene Highness [etc.]

The most joyous occasion of your name-day (may Your Highness celebrate it in divine Grace and enjoy it in complete well-being and felicity!) obliges me not only to deliver to you in profound submission 6 new Divertimenti [for baryton, viola and 'cello; unidentified], but also to say that we were delighted to receive, a few days ago, our new Winter clothes – and submissively to kiss the hem of your robe for this especial act of grace: adding that, despite Your Highness' much regretted absence, we shall nevertheless venture to wear these new clothes for the first time during the celebration of High Mass on Your Highness' name-day. I have received Your Highness' order to have the Divertimenti I wrote (twelve pieces in all) bound. But since Your Highness has returned some of them to me to be altered, and I have not noted the changes in my score, I would respectfully ask you to let me have the first twelve you have at hand for three days, and then the others one after the other, so that apart from the required changes, they may be all neatly and correctly copied and bound: in this connection I would like to ask respectfully in which way Your Highness would like to have them bound?

Incidentally, the two oboe players report (and I myself must agree with them) that their oboes are so old that they are collapsing, and no longer keep the proper pitch [*Tonum*]; for this reason I would humbly point out to Your Highness that there is a master Rockobauer in

Vienna, who in my opinion is the most skilful for this sort of work. But because this master is continually busy with work of this kind, and since it requires an exceptionally long time to complete a pair of good and durable oboes with an extra length of reed pipe (as a result of which, however, all the necessary notes can be produced) – for these reasons the cheapest price is 8 ducats. I therefore await YOUR HIGHNESS' gracious consent whether the above-mentioned and most urgently needed two oboes may be constructed for the price indicated. I hope for your favour and grace,

YOUR SERENE AND GRACIOUS HIGHNESS'

most humble

Joseph Haydn.

In 1766, when Haydn had become full *Kapellmeister*, he decided to move away from the old *Capellhaus* behind the Bergkirche in Eisenstadt and to purchase his own house. He found an attractive little Baroque house near the Franciscan Monastery and, although he had to borrow money from his wife's relatives to make the purchase, he must have been glad of the relative peace and quiet (free, for example, of the sounds of musicians' practising next door, as had been the case in the *Capellhaus*). Haydn seems to have lived in comfortable rooms on the first floor (American: second storey), and today the house is a museum, filled with souvenirs, portraits and manuscripts. When the house was almost totally destroyed by fire, first in 1768 and a second time in 1776, Prince Nicolaus had it rebuilt at his own expense. He also helped Haydn in 1771 by advancing the necessary capital when repayment of the loan from his in-laws was demanded. Haydn's request to the Prince and the latter's reply read as follows:

SERENE HIGHNESS [etc.]

In order to purchase my house, I had to borrow 400 gulden in cash some years ago, and now this capital has been recalled. Since I do not have the sum, I wanted to take out another loan in this amount (on which I would pay interest) to repay the debt. But I could not find any creditors here in Eisenstadt, and inasmuch as I have to repay this loan soon, I would humbly ask Your Highness graciously to allow me to have these 400 gulden, against a receipt from the cashier's office, whereby the 50 gulden I receive quarterly from that source (of which the first payment is due to me by the end of January 1771) would be withheld until such time as the whole debt is repayed. I most humbly commend myself to your favour and grace,

YOUR SERENE HIGHNESS'

most humble

Josephus Haydn.

[Prince Nicolaus Esterházy to his Chief Cashier Zoller. *German*]

The *Capeln Meister* Haÿden [*sic*] has asked us to advance him four hundred Gulden, for the repayment of which he will turn over to us his quarterly salary of fifty Gulden (of which the first falls due already at the end of this month), so that the whole debt should be paid in two years; and since we agree to this, he will advance to him the said four hundred Gulden and accordingly enter them in the books.

Vienna, 6th January 771.

Nicolaus Fürst Esterhazy.

Evidence of Haydn's growing reputation had begun to show itself by 1766. One of the first public references to it appeared in an article entitled

'On the Viennese Taste in Music', published in the *Wienerisches Diarium* of 18 October:

> **Herr Joseph Hayden**, the darling of our nation, whose gentle character impresses itself on each of his pieces. His movements have beauty, order, clarity, a fine and noble expression which will be felt sooner than the listener is prepared for it. In his cassatios, quartets and trios he is a pure and clean water, over which a southerly wind occasionally ripples, and sometimes rises to waves without, however, losing its bed and course. The art of writing the outer parts in parallel octaves is his invention, and one cannot deny that this is attractive, even if it appears rarely and in a Haydnisch fashion. In symphonies he is as masculinely strong as he is inventive. In cantatas charming, fetching, flattering; and in minuets natural, playful, alluring. In short, **Hayden** is that in the music which **Gellert** is in poetry.

Prince Nicolaus had clearly decided that his *Capelle* should also perform a Haydn opera in the capital; to this end he secured, in the spring of 1770, the loan of Baron von Sumerau's palace in the suburb of Mariahilf, for the Prince apparently did not have quarters in his own palace in the Wallnerstraße large enough to mount a whole opera, in this case *Lo speziale*. The *Wienerisches Diarium* reports:

> Vienna, 24 March 1770. Yesterday at about noon her I. R. Majest. our most gracious Empress arrived back from Preßburg safely.
>
> As an especially pleasant piece of news which we did not wish to overlook, we would report that last Wednesday the 21st inst. in the quarters of Herr Baron von Sumerau near Maria Hilf an opera entitled The Apothecary by the Princely Esterhasi [*sic*] Kapellmeister, Herr Joseph Hayden [*sic*], was performed by the assembled Chamber Virtuosi of Prince Esterhasi on that day, and upon the request of high personages it was repeated with quite exceptional applause upon the following Thursday in the form of a musical academy and in the presence of many high persons; a fact that reflects exceptional honour on the aforesaid Herr Kapellmeister Hayden, whose great talents are sufficiently known to all lovers of music, and no less upon the aforesaid assembled virtuosi.

The social event of the year 1770 was the marriage of Prince Nicolaus's 'dear niece', Countess Lamberg, with Count Poggi (*recte*: Pocci). Identically worded reports appeared in the *Preßburger Zeitung* and *Wienerisches Diarium*, which suggests that both journals were given what we would now call a 'Press release' by someone at Eszterháza. They read as follows:

[Extract of a letter from Oedenburg in Hungary, 20th September]

At the moment, everyone is talking only about the magnificent fêtes given by Prince Esterházy on the 16th, 17th and 18th inst. at his splendid castle, Esterház, a few miles distant from this town, on the occasion of the wedding of his niece, Countess von Lamberg, to Count von Poggi. Our readers are therefore due a short account of them.

At 5 o'clock in the afternoon of Sunday the 16th, the bridal couple betook themselves to the princely chapel, accompanied by Prince and Princess Esterházy and a large company of invited cavaliers and ladies, to receive the blessing of the church. Then the whole company repaired to the theatre, where a comic opera in Italian, *le Pescatrici* (or The Fisher-Women), was performed with all possible skill and art by the princely singers and instrumentalists, to universal and well-deserved applause. The princely *Kapellmeister*, Herr Hayden [*sic*], whose many beautiful works have already spread his fame far and wide, and whose flaming and creative genius was responsible for the music to the *Singspiel*, had the honour ro receive the most flattering praise from all the illustrious guests.

About this time Haydn seems to have become seriously ill. Griesinger (18) relates:

> About the year 1770, Haydn succumbed to a fever [*hitziges Fieber*], and the doctor had strictly forbidden him, during his slow recovery, to occupy himself with music. Soon afterwards, Haydn's wife went to church, and before she left the house she gave strict instructions to the maid not to let her master go near the piano. Haydn was in bed and pretended to have heard nothing of this order, and hardly had his wife left than he sent the maid out of the house on some errand. Then he rushed to his piano. At the first touch the idea for a whole sonata came to him, and the first section was finished while his wife was still in church. When he heard her returning, he hastily retreated to his bed, and there he wrote the rest of the Sonata, which he could not identify for me more precisely than that it had five sharps.

Ordinarily the season at Eszterháza closed at the end of October. In 1772, however, the Prince decided to stay on in his Hungarian castle. The musicians were eager to return to their wives and appealed to Haydn for help. The result was the celebrated 'Farewell' Symphony (No. 45). Griesinger (19) described the episode thus:

> Among Prince Esterházy's *Kapelle* there were several vigorous young married men who in summer, when the Prince stayed at Esterhazy [*sic*], were obliged to leave their wives behind in Eisenstadt. Contrary to his custom, the Prince once extended his sojourn in Esterhaz by several weeks: the loving husbands, thoroughly dismayed over this news, went to Haydn and asked for his advice.
>
> Haydn had the inspiration of writing a symphony (which is known under the title of 'Farewell' Symphony), in which one instrument after the other is silent. This Symphony was performed as soon as possible in front of the Prince, and each of the musicians was instructed, as soon as his part was finished, to blow out his candle and to leave with his instrument under his arm. The Prince and the company understood the point of this pantomime at once, and the next day came the order to leave Esterhaz.

A page from the Breitkopf catalogue of 1769, in which several Symphonies by Haydn were advertised for sale in MS. copies (the *incipits* shown are those of No. 24, 38, 36 and 27).

The following year saw the three-day visit of the Empress Maria Theresa and her entourage to Eszterháza. The *Preßburger Zeitung* (No. 73, 11 September 1773) reports:

> ... On Sept. 1st, Her Imperial and Royal Apostolic Majesty arrived at Esterház after a five-hour journey from Vienna, accompanied by the Archduchesses Marianna and Elisabeth, and by the Archduke Maximilian. His Serene Princely Highness arranged various entertainments for the diversion of his Royal guests. After luncheon, Her Majesty went driving in the gardens, the Archduke and Archduchesses promenading on foot beside the carriage. Then Haydn's marionette operetta *Philemon und Baucis* or *Jupiters Reise auf die Erde* was performed in the new theatre. This was followed by a festive masked ball. The forenoon of the 2nd was spent strolling in the castle park, and after lunch the little operetta was presented again.... After this, the rear of the new theatre began to sink before all eyes, and in its stead the illustrious audience saw the splendid illumination in the princely garden, and the fireworks began....

Another proof of Haydn's growing fame is the autobiographical sketch of 1776, which he was requested to write for a publication entitled 'Das gelehrte Oesterreich.' The editor appears to have applied for it in a very roundabout manner to a 'Mons. Zoller' (Chief Cashier in the Prince's service), who in turn asked 'Mademoiselle Leonore'. Although it repeats much that we already know (as well as containing some factual errors), Haydn's sketch is of such interest and importance that it is reproduced here *in toto*. Note what Haydn considered to be his most successful works. There is not a word about his symphonies (more than 60 in all by 1776), sonatas, or trios, and only a brief mention of chamber music altogether.

Estoras, 6th July 1776.

Mademoiselle!

You will not take it amiss if I hand you a hotchpotch of all sorts of things as an answer to your request: to describe such things properly takes time, and that I don't have; for this reason, I do not dare write to Mons. Zoller personally, and therefore ask for forgiveness.

I send you only a rough draft, for neither pride, nor fame, but solely the great kindness and marked satisfaction that so learned a national institution has shown towards my previous compositions, have induced me to comply with their demand.

I was born on the last day of March 1733 [*sic*] in the market town of Rohrau, Lower Austria, near Prugg on the Leythä. My late father was a wheelwright by profession, and served Count Harrach, a great lover of music by nature. He [my father] played the harp without knowing a note of music, and as a boy of 5, I correctly sang all his simple little pieces: this induced my father to entrust me to the care of my relative, the schoolmaster in Haimburg [*sic*] in order that I might learn the rudiments of music and the other juvenile requirements. Almighty God (to Whom alone I owe the most profound gratitude) endowed me, especially in music, with such proficiency that even in my 6th year I was able to sing some Masses in the choir-loft, and to play a little on the harpsichord and violin.

When I was 7, the late *Capellmeister* von Reutter passed through Haimburg and quite accidentally heard my weak but pleasant voice. He forthwith took me to the choir house [of St Stephen's Cathedral in Vienna] where, apart from my studies, I learnt the art of singing, the harpsichord, and the violin, from very good masters. Until my 18th year I sang soprano with great success, not only at St Stephen's but also at the Court. Finally I lost my voice, and then had to eke out a wretched existence for eight whole years, by teaching young pupils (many geniuses are ruined by their having to earn their daily bread, because they have no time to study): I experienced this, too, and would have never learnt what little I did, had I not, in my zeal for composition, composed well into the night; I wrote diligently, but not quite correctly, until at last I had the good fortune to learn the true fundamentals of composition from the celebrated Herr Porpora (who was at that time in Vienna): finally, by the recommendation of the late Herr von Fürnberg (from whom I received many marks of favour), I was engaged as *Directeur* at Herr Count von Morzin's, and from there as *Capellmeister* of His Highness the Prince [Esterházy], in whose service I wish to live and die.

Inter alia the following compositions of mine have received the most approbation:

	Le Pescatrici [1769: perf. 1770]
	L'incontro improvizo [*sic*] [1775]
The operas	*L'infedeltà delusa*, performed in the presence of Her Imperial and Royal Majesty [Maria Theresa, in 1773].
The oratorio	*Il Ritorno di Tobia*, performed in Vienna [in 1775]
The *Stabat Mater*	[1767], about which I received (through a good friend) a testimonial of our great composer Hasse, containing quite undeserved eulogiums. I shall treasure this testimonial all my life, as if it were gold; not for its contents, but for the sake of so admirable a man.

In the chamber-musical style I have been fortunate enough to please almost all nations except the Berliners; this is shown by the public newspapers and letters addressed to me. I

52

only wonder that the Berlin gentlemen, who are otherwise so reasonable, preserve no medium in their criticism of my music, for in one weekly paper they praise me to the skies, whilst in another they dash me sixty fathoms deep into the earth, and this without explaining why; I know very well why: because they are incapable of performing some of my works, and are too conceited to take the trouble to understand them properly, and for other reasons which, with God's help, I will answer in good time. *Herr Capellmeister* von Dittersdorf, in Silesia, wrote to me recently and asked me to defend myself against their hard words, but I answered that one swallow doesn't make the Summer; and that perhaps one of these days some unprejudiced person would stop their tongues, as happened to them once before when they accused me of monotony. Despite this, they try very hard to get all my works, as Herr Baron von Sviten [van Swieten], the Imperial and Royal Ambassador at Berlin, told me only last winter, when he was in Vienna: but enough of this.

Dear *Mademoiselle* Leonore: You will be good enough to give this present letter, and my compliments, to Mons. Zoller for his consideration: my highest ambition is only that all the world regard me as the honest man I am.

I offer all my praises to Almighty God, for I owe them to Him alone: my sole wish is to offend neither my neighbour, nor my gracious Prince, nor above all our merciful God.

Meanwhile I remain, *Mademoiselle*, with high esteem,

Your most sincere friend and servant

Josephus Haydn [m.p.] ria

On 17 July 1776, a terrible holocaust ravaged Eisenstadt, destroying within two hours the town hall, the Franciscan church and monastery, the brewery and this time the Parish Church; 104 houses were destroyed and sixteen people died. The Prince rebuilt Haydn's house and altogether paid out more than 7,000 gulden to owners of damaged or destroyed property. Haydn's house was more badly damaged in this than in the previous (1768) fire, and it cost Esterházy 450 gulden to repair it. Now that Haydn was living most of the year in Eszterháza, he may have thought it a disadvantage to have almost his entire capital tied up in a house at Eisenstadt that he hardly used, and on 27 October 1778, Haydn sold his property to the princely book-keeper Anton Liechtscheidl, who paid 2,000 gulden; on that same day, Haydn took 1,000 gulden to the princely disbursar, who thereafter paid him five per cent interest p.a., or 50 gulden, in semi-annual payments, the last made on 13 December 1808. This was the first capital Haydn had ever invested, and he referred to it when, many years later, he told his biographers Dies and Griesinger that he had 'barely 2,000 gulden capital' when he left Austria for England in 1790.

A new contract between Prince Nicolaus Esterházy and Haydn, dated 1 January 1779, now replaced the original one of 1761 (see pp. 41ff.). The document, now in the Esterházy Archives (Forchtenstein), is very modern in its terse tone:

This day, according to the day, month and year hereto appended, is ratified between H. Highness, Prince of the Holy Roman Empire, Lord and Master Nicolai Eszterházy v. Gallantha, Hereditary Count of Forchtenstein, Knight of the Golden Fleece, Comendeur [*sic*] of the Military Maria Theresia Order, Chamberlain and Acting Privy Councillor of Her Imp. Royal and Apostolic Maj., General Field Marshal, Colonel and owner of a Hung: Infantry Regiment, Captain of the Noble Hungarian Body-Guard, and likewise Acting Hereditary *Ober-Gespanns* of the *Oedenburg Gespanschafft*; and *Capelmeister* [*sic*] Herr Joseph Haydn, to be considered an Officer, the following contract agreed between them.

Primo: Herr Heydn is to conduct himself in a manner which is edifying, Christian and God-fearing.

Secundo: *Herr Capell-Meister* is to treat his subordinates at all times with great goodness and forbearance.

Tertio: The party of the second part agrees to perform any music of one kind or another in all the places, and at all the times, to which and when H. Highness is pleased to command.

Quarto: The party of the second part should not, without special permission, absent himself from his duties, nor from the place to which H. Highness has ordered the musicians.

Quinto: Both contractual parties reserve the right to cancel the agreement.

Sexto: *Herr Capell-Meister* will receive every two years one winter and one summer uniform, alternately, according to H. Highness's discretion; and he will receive the following (but apart from these items he will receive nothing further either in money or in kind), to wit:

As *Capellmeister*

In cash	782	f 30 Xr
Officer's wine in Eszterház	9	*Eimer* [kegs]
Good genuine firewood in Eszterház	6	*Klafter* [fathom cords; each 'cord' = 6 ft or 1·90 m]

As Organist

Waitz [wheat]	4	*Metzen* [3·44 litre, miller's dry measure]
Kohrn [rye]	12	
Greißl [i.e. 'Grieß' = semolina or grits]	3/4	
Rindtfleisch [beef]	300	*Pfundt* [pound = 56 dkg.]
Saltz	50	
Schmaltz [lard] .... alles in	30	
Kertzen [candles] .... Eszterház	36	
Weinn [wine]	9	*Eimer*
Krauth und Rueben zusamen [cabbage & beets together]	1	
Schwein [pig]	1	*Stuck* [one whole pig]
Good firewood	6	*Klafter*

Then the necessary forage for 2 horses. Finally two identical copies of this contract are to be prepared and exchanged one with the other, and all previous *Resolutions*, *Conventiones* and Contracts are declared null and void. Schloß Eszterház the 1st of January 779.

[signed:] Josephus Haydn mpria

Concerning the above payment in kind and the 100 fl. (which latter are not listed in the above contract) which are to be paid in Eisenstadt, there is the following condition that, when I am not able to play the organ myself in Eisenstadt, I herewith agree myself to provide, to install and to recompense an organist.

[signed:] Josephus Haydn mpria

In March 1779, the Esterházy musical establishment was enlarged by the arrival of a new couple from Italy, Antonio and Luigia Polzelli, respectively violinist and soprano. They received the smallest salary of the whole troupe and were probably not exceptionally talented; on Christmas Day 1780 they and a pair of trumpeters were dismissed, before their respective contracts had expired, with two months' salary. Suddenly, however, we find the Polzellis re-engaged, no doubt at Haydn's insistence. Luigia, who was then about thirty (not ten years younger as is usually asserted – she died in 1832 at the age of eighty-two), had become Haydn's mistress. He lovingly rewrote the parts she was to sing and composed a whole series of arias for her to replace others less suited to her voice (many of these arias were discovered in the Esterházy Archives by Dénes Bartha and László Somfai in the 1950s). The arrival of Signora Polzelli cannot have been welcomed by Frau Haydn, even if she had herself enjoyed an affair with the Esterházy painter Ludwig Guttenbrunn ten years before.

That same year a fire at Eszterháza did much damage. We have the following contemporary description of it from the *Preßburger Zeitung*:

Wednesday, 24 November 1779.

From Eszterház we receive the unpleasant news that last Thursday the 18th at 3:30 a.m. a dreadful fire broke out in the world-famous Chinese ball-room, which because of its magnificence, taste and comfort was so admired by all visitors. As a result, the adjoining water works with the tower, and the theatre, which was so excellently appointed and which contained not only a grand box for the Prince but also two comfortable side-boxes for the other guests, were entirely destroyed. The fire was dreadful to behold and glowed now and again the next day, because the ball-room was mostly painted with varnish and in the theatre was stored a large quantity of wax lights. The fire must have burned in the roof for some hours, because the whole of the valuable roof was in flames, and also the beautiful walls were almost consumed by the time the fire was discovered. – The origin of this unexpected occurrence was as follows: as is well known, the 21st inst. was the day set for the exalted marriage of Count Forgátsch with the noble Countess Miss Graschalkowitz. For this celebration the stoves in the ball-room were to be previously lit. There were also two Chinese stoves therein which were more for show than for actual use. They were nevertheless lit despite all previous warnings. They probably exploded from the heat and thus the fire spread. It would have spread even further if not for the wise order to remove the roofs of the nearby buildings, and for the fact that heavy rains and strong winds lessened the fire's effect and finally extinguished it. The damage, according to several eye-witnesses, is estimated to be more than 100,000 gulden. Two beautiful clocks; the magnificent theatrical costumes; all the music collected at great effort and expense; the musical instruments, including the beautiful harpsichord [*Flieg*] of the famous *Kapellmeister* Haiden [*sic*] and the concert violin of the virtuoso Lotsch [Luigi Tomasini] – all were lost to the flames, which reached their height at 8:00 a.m. His Highness the Prince, despite the inclement weather, was at once present at a time when a speedy rescue seemed distant.

Since various high persons had already arrived for the festivities, a brand new opera [*L'amore soldato*] was given in the marionette theatre on the 21st.

Haydn composed a whole series of marionette operas for the marionette theatre at Eszterháza, but of these only two have survived complete: *Philemon und Baucis* (1773) and *Die Feuersbrunst* (1776). Haydn was fascinated with the possibilities of these puppet operas and for a while he actually organized his own puppet theatre at Eszterháza during Carnival time. After the terrible fire of 1779, the operatic troupe had to move into the marionette theatre, and it was there that Haydn conducted the première of his new opera, *L'isola disabitata* (with libretto by Metastasio), on Prince Nicolaus's name-day, 6 December.

On 18 December (the Prince's birthday) – precisely one month after the fire – Nicolaus laid the cornerstone for the new theatre; for that occasion Haydn composed a new symphony, the extraordinary and dramatic No. 70 in D, which has as its last movement a magnificent triple fugue in D minor but ends, in proper *settecento* fashion, in D major (as befits the Age of

Enlightenment). The construction of the new building was hampered by all manner of vicissitudes – bad weather, hasty plans, etc. – and the opening originally planned for December 1780, had to be postponed. Finally, all was ready, and the opening took place on 25 February 1781 with the first performance of *La fedeltà premiata*. Haydn referred to his new opera in the course of a letter to the Viennese music publisher Artaria:

... Now something from Paris. Monsieur Le Gros, *Directeur* of the Concert Spirituel, wrote me the most flattering things about my *Stabat Mater*, which was performed there four times with the greatest applause; the gentlemen asked permission to have it engraved. They made me an offer to engrave all my future works on the most favourable terms for myself, and were most surprised that I was so singularly successful in my vocal compositions; but I wasn't at all surprised, for they have not yet heard anything. If they only could hear my operetta *L'isola disabitata* and my most recent opera, *La fedeltà premiata*, I assure you that no such work has been heard in Paris up to now, nor perhaps in Vienna either; my misfortune is that I live in the country. ...

At some point in the first half of 1781, Haydn sent a score of *L'isola disabitata* to the Prince of Asturias, later Carlos IV of Spain. The *Wiener Zeitung* of 6 October reports:

His Catholic Majesty, the King of Spain, unexpectedly rewarded the princely Esterhazi *Herr Kapellmeister* Joseph Hayden [*sic*], long celebrated through his original compositions, for some music sent [to Spain]; the reward was a golden, jewel-studded tabatière and that which must far outweigh gold and jewels in the eye of a great artist, namely the flattering way it was presented. The Secretary of Legation of the Spanish Court, accredited to the I.R. Court, had, upon the explicit order of his monarch, to bring the present personally to Esterhaz and, apart from presenting the gift in person, he was to report to Madrit [*sic*] upon the box's delivery and also to assure [Haydn] of the ever well disposed wishes of his Catholic Majesty.

On 26 January 1782 there appeared in Berlin No. IV of the *Literatur- und Theater-Zeitung* bearing the *impressum* 'bei Arnold Weber'. In it we have the following report:

News of the princely castle Esterhaz in Hungary
... The Prince ... always divides a part of his entertainment with everyone. Whenever friends of some standing come to Esterhaz and take up quarters in the *Gasthaus*, he sends his carriage, has them taken to his castle and invites them to dine with him. Every day there is theatre, three times a week Italian opera and the same for German plays. The entrance is free for everyone. When new pieces are given, he has the libretti printed in Oedenburg and distributed to the audience. His wish that in this magnificent castle there should always reign happiness and politeness, is followed explicitly by his personnel. ... Most rooms in the castle are designed for great rulers who from time to time come here. The Prince and dowager Princess live on the rez-de-chaussée. ... The Prince has some four hundred clocks, each one of different and beautiful workmanship. Among the most remarkable that I saw was one with a stuffed canary which every hour sings an aria [*sic*] like a real bird, and the beak, breast and the whole body move like a real bird ... and [there are] various clocks with all sorts of music. A similar musical plaything is an armchair which, when you sit in it, begins to play various pieces and continues with new ones. ... From the garden one arrives at the theatre. It burned to the ground some 1½ years ago ... and now it is there again with renewed brilliance. Everything is larger. ... his chamber musicians wear a uniform (green coats with red and

gold), and at their head is Haydn, a man whose music is admired in Italy, England and France. . . .

In the course of the twenty years since Haydn's first works had been (illegally, as it were) published in France in 1764, the distribution of music within the Austrian monarchy had changed radically. In 1764, hardly any music was printed in Vienna and ninety per cent of the sonatas, symphonies, trios and so on played by amateur and professional alike were copied in manuscript. By 1784, the function of the copyists was slowly but very surely being assumed by Austrian music publishers, foremost among them the Viennese firms, Artaria and Torricella; both published Haydn's latest works. But in the early 1780s Haydn also secured valuable contacts with foreign publishers: Guéra of Lyon, Sieber of Paris, Hummel of Amsterdam and Berlin (which firm had been pirating Haydn's works for twenty years), and Forster in London. Haydn tried, and often with success, to sell the same set of symphonies simultaneously to London, Paris, Berlin, Lyon and Vienna; and in the case of Nos. 76–78 (1782) he seems to have done precisely that. As a result of all this publishing activity, Haydn's fame increased with a sudden bound. Even the recalcitrant Italians, whose interest in and love of music north of the Alps was always limited, managed to publish Haydn, first in Venice (geographically nearest to Austria) but later in Naples, too.

Haydn's symphonies, sonatas, and quartets of the 1780s were in the new 'popular' style – folk-like tunes alternating with learned contrapuntal developments and pert Austrian minuets leading to finales in the new sonata rondo form (basically: rondo form with a development section in the manner of sonata form). Soon Haydn created a huge school of followers who in part were as successful, if not more so, than their model: Haydn's pupil Ignaz Pleyel, Leopold Koželuch (whose markedly successful Haydnesque symphonies were published during the 1780s), and Adalbert Gyrowetz (one of whose symphonies was published, with wide applause, as Haydn's in Paris). The Haydn school had conquered Europe.

76

Haydn had developed a Symphony (No. 73, 'La Chasse') from the hunting Overture to *La fedeltà premiata* and had given it to Christoph Torricella, who published it in July 1782. We find it reviewed in Cramer's *Magazin der Musik* (1783, pp. 491f.):

This symphony is quite as worthy of its author as the newest Op. 18 . . . [Hummel ed.], and in no way needs our praise. In listening to it, the very beginning and the wonderful workmanship of the following parts reveal the hand of the great master, who seems to be inexhaustible in new ideas. It goes without saying, of course, that there are in this, as in all his symphonies, difficulties and unexpected progressions which require trained and correct players, and cannot be entrusted merely to good luck, without the closest study of the key-signatures, and without knowing the work. So let this be a warning to amateurs and hesitant players, who dare not essay this work without knowing it exactly beforehand, else they shame themselves. We hope, indeed, that Heydn [*sic*] will crown this great epoch of the symphony with more such wonderful pieces, and thereby reduce all bad writers of symphonies to silence, or to improving their superficial products, through which none but themselves can derive any pleasure.

On 1 May 1784 the famous Italian composer Giovanni Paisiello arrived in Vienna to oversee the production of his new opera *Il rè Teodoro in Venezia*. He

74

and the librettist, Abbate Casti, were present at a quartet party attended by Michael Kelly, the entertaining Irish singer who formed part of a curious and interesting English-speaking colony in Vienna during this period; in the *Reminiscences* (218), Kelly writes:

[... Storace gave a 'quartet party' to his friends.] The players were tolerable; not one of them excelled on the instrument he played, but there was a little science among them, which I dare say will be acknowledged when I name them:

The First Violin	HAYDN.
„ Second Violin	BARON DITTERSDORF.
„ Violoncello	VANHALL.
„ Tenor	MOZART.

The poet Casti and Paesiello formed part of the audience. I was there, and a greater treat, or a more remarkable one, cannot be imagined.

On the particular evening to which I am now specially referring, after the musical feast was over, we sat down to an excellent supper, and became joyous and lively in the extreme.

...

The Age of Enlightenment cast its healing light on Freemasonry, which flourished in the Austrian monarchy as never before. There were Lodges in Vienna and all the provincial capitals. Perhaps the most famous was the Lodge 'Zur wahren Eintracht' in Vienna, of which the celebrated natural historian, Ignaz von Born (the model for Sarastro in *Die Zauberflöte*) was the master. Prince Nicolaus Esterházy was a member of the Viennese Lodge 'Zur gekrönten Hoffnung' and in 1780 was Master of Ceremonies. Since many of Haydn's Viennese friends already belonged to the Brotherhood, he naturally considered the possibility of joining their society, and at the end of December 1784, he officially applied to Franz Philipp von Weber, *Hofsecretaire* and Master of Ceremonies at the lodge 'Zur wahren Eintracht'.

Nobly born,
Most highly respected *Herr Hoff Secretaire*,
The highly advantageous impression which Freemasonry has made on me has long awakened in my breast the sincerest wish to become a member of the Order, with its humanitarian and wise principles. I turn to you, Sir, with the most urgent request that you have the great kindness to intervene on my behalf with the Lodge of the Order, in order to implement this my petition, as indicated above.
I have the honour to remain, with profound esteem,

Your obedient servant,
Josephus Haydn,
CapellMeister to Prince Esterházy.

Vienna, the 29th of the Christmas Month
1784.

Haydn's initiation took place on 11 February 1785. He never attended another meeting, however, and in 1786 his name was removed from the membership list. On the day of Haydn's initiation Leopold Mozart arrived in Vienna to visit his son and daughter-in-law in their large flat in the Domgasse, in the shadow of the Cathedral of St Stephen, so full of memories and sentiment for every Viennese. Next day, Wolfgang gave a quartet party in honour of his new Masonic Brother; two members of Haydn's own Lodge, the Barons Tinti, were also present. The report which Leopold wrote to his daughter contains what has become perhaps the most quoted remark that Haydn ever made.

Saturday Evening Herr Joseph Haydn and the two Barons Tindi [*sic*] were here; the new Quartets were played, the three new ones that he [Wolfgang] wrote to go with the other three which we already own; they are a little easier than the others but composed brilliantly. Herr Haydn said to me: 'I tell you before God, and as an honest man, that your son is the greatest composer I know, either personally or by reputation. He has taste and, apart from that, the greatest knowledge of composition [*Compositionswissenschaft*].'
[Mozart *Briefe und Aufzeichnungen*, vol. III, Kassel 1963, p. 373.]

On 1 September, Mozart wrote his famous letter of dedication to Haydn, accompanying the Artaria first edition of six of his Quartets (K.387, 421, 428, 458, 464, 465). The letter, written in Italian, reads: 78

To my dear friend Haydn:
A father, having resolved to send his sons into the great world, finds it advisable to entrust them to the protection and guidance of a highly celebrated man, the more so since this man, by a stroke of luck, is his best friend. – Here, then, celebrated man and my dearest friend, are my six sons. – Truly, they are the fruit of a long and laborious effort, but the hope, strengthened by several of my friends, that this effort would, at least in some small measure, be rewarded, encourages and comforts me that one day, these children may be a source of consolation to me. – You yourself, dearest friend, during your last sojourn in this capital, expressed to me your satisfaction with these works. – This, your approval, encourages me more than anything else, and thus I entrust them to your care, and hope that they are not wholly unworthy of your favour. – Do but receive them kindly, and be their father, guide, and friend! From this moment I cede to you all my rights over them: I pray you to be indulgent to their mistakes, which a father's partial eye may have overlooked, and despite this, to cloak them in the mantle of your generosity which they value so highly. From the bottom of my heart I am, dearest friend,

Your most sincere friend,
W. A. Mozart

Vienna, 1st September 1785.

In October 1784, there had appeared in the *European Magazine* 'An ACCOUNT of JOSEPH HAYDN, a CELEBRATED COMPOSER of MUSIC', which was flattering and interesting but full of inaccuracies. In the article, it is stated that Haydn's detractors had accused him of inventing 'a new musical doctrine and introducing a species of sounds totally unknown in that country.' 'In the last position they were perfectly right', continues the anonymous author, who adds, 'Amongst the number of professors who wrote against our rising author was Philip Emanuel Bach ...'. When this article appeared in German, C. P. E. Bach read it and felt constrained to write an open letter in the Hamburg *Unpartheiische Korrespondent*; it was published in the issue of September 1785: 15

My way of thought and my occupations have never allowed me to write against anyone: the more was I astonished about a passage in a recent article in The European Magazine in England, where I am accused in a mendacious, crude and shameful way of having written against the good Herr Haydn. According to my news from Vienna and even from members of the Esterhazi [*sic*] Kapelle who came to me, I must believe that this worthy man, whose works continue to give me much pleasure, is surely as much my friend as I his. According to my principles, every master has his true and certain value. Praise and criticism cannot change any of that. Only the work itself praises and criticizes the master, and therefore I leave to everyone his own value. Hamburg, 14th September 1785. C. P. E. Bach.

Even earlier, in 1782, the first plans had been made to lure Haydn to England, and preparations were sufficiently advanced for the composer to write three new symphonies (Nos. 76–78) in expectation of the London concerts. However, Prince Esterházy would not let Haydn leave, and the plan was – as Haydn thought – postponed. As the years dragged by, no Haydn arrived in England, and by the beginning of 1785, the *Gazetteer & New Daily Advertiser* (17 January) had conceived the idea of kidnapping the composer and bringing him from the slavery of the Holy Roman Empire to the freedom of Albion's shores:

There is something very distressing to a liberal mind in the history of *Haydn*. This wonderful man, who is the Shakespeare of music, and the triumph of the age in which we live, is doomed to reside in the court of a miserable German Prince, who is at once incapable of rewarding him, and unworthy of the honour. *Haydn*, the simplest as well as the greatest of men, is resigned to his condition, and in devoting his life to the rites and ceremonies of the Roman Catholic Church, which he carries even to superstition, is content to live immured in a place little better than a dungeon, subject to the domineering spirit of a petty Lord, and the clamourous temper of a scolding wife. Would it not be an achievement equal to a pilgrimage, for some aspiring youths to rescue him from his fortune and transplant him to Great Britain, the country for which his music seems to be made?

[Roscoe, 205]

But Haydn had no intention of leaving Prince Nicolaus. His biographer A. C. Dies (73f.) reminds us:

Haydn owned a little house in Eisenstadt which twice fell prey to flames. The generous Prince Nicolaus both times hurried there and found Haydn in tears, comforted him, had the house rebuilt, and provided the necessary furnishing. Haydn, much touched by the Prince's generosity, could repay him only with love, attachment, and with the products of his music. Touched to the heart, he wished to prove his gratitude. He swore to the Prince to serve him till death should bring to a close the life of one or the other, and never leave him even should he be offered millions.

During the period 1766–85 the writing of operas had dominated his composing activities. Even a bare list is impressive in itself:
La canterina (1766)
Lo speziale (1768)
Le pescatrici (1769, performed 1770)
Hexenschabbas (1773)
Philemon und Baucis (1773)
L'infedeltà delusa (1773)
Acide (revised version 1773–4)
L'incontro improvviso (1775)
Die Feuersbrunst (1776; probable date of performance)
Dido (1776)

Il mondo della luna (1777)
Die bestrafte Rachbegierde (1779)
La vera costanza (1779)
L'isola disabitata (1779)
La fedeltà premiata (1780, performed 1781)
Orlando Paladino (1782)
Armida (1784)
La vera costanza, revised version (1785)

Nowadays Haydn's stage works are taken far more seriously than ever before. He had the misfortune to produce them at the same time as Mozart's, against which no eighteenth-century operas – not even Gluck's – can stand in competition. It is, however, quite clear that these operas are full of exquisite, subtle, interesting and moving music, and are more interesting than all except a handful of his contemporary instrumental productions. Many of these operas, particularly *L'infedeltà delusa*, have been revived with outstanding success in recent years. But Haydn was a realist, and the following letter reveals that his self-knowledge was as acute as his judgement of Mozart. In a letter to Franz Roth (Rott), *Oberverpflegs-Verwalter*, Prague, he wrote:

December 1787

... You ask me for an *opera buffa*. Most willingly, if you want to have one of my vocal compositions for yourself alone. But if you intend to produce it on the stage at Prague, in that case I cannot comply with your wish, because all my operas are far too closely connected with our personal circle (Esterház, in Hungary), and moreover they would not produce the proper effect, which I calculated in accordance with the locality. It would be quite another matter if I were to have the great good fortune to compose a brand new libretto for your theatre. But even then I should be risking a good deal, for scarcely any man can brook comparison with the great Mozart.

If I could only impress on the soul of every friend of music, on high personages in particular, how inimitable are Mozart's works, how profound, how musically intelligent, how extraordinarily sensitive! (for this is how I understand them, how I feel them) – why then the nations would vie with each other to possess such a jewel within their frontiers. Prague should hold him fast – but should reward him, too; for without this, the history of great geniuses is sad indeed, and gives but little encouragement to posterity to further exertions; and unfortunately this is why so many promising intellects fall by the wayside. It enrages me to think that this incomparable Mozart is not yet engaged by some imperial or royal court! Forgive me if I lose my head: but I love the man so dearly. I am, &c.

Joseph Hayden [*sic*] ...

Haydn was now moving in circles far more elevated socially and also more stimulating intellectually that the *milieu* of musicians and actors at Eszterháza. Alas, Haydn's new circle was in Vienna, which he could visit only briefly, but we are fortunate in having a nearly complete correspondence between Haydn and one of his new (in this case, lady) friends, Maria Anna Sabina (1750–93), wife of the fashionable ladies' doctor and Physician in Ordinary to Prince Nicolaus, Peter Leopold von Genzinger. Haydn loved the Genzinger family, with its many children, and its hospitable flat in the Schottenhaus (next to the Schottenkirche); and perhaps Maria Anna Sabina meant more to him than he cared to admit (and more than she would have wished for). Here is the beginning of that correspondence, Maria Anna's first letter, with its pious three crosses:

† † †

Most respected Herr v. Hayden,

With your kind permission, I take the liberty of sending you a pianoforte arrangement of the beautiful Andante from your so admirable composition. I made this arrangement from the score quite by myself, without the least help from my teacher; please be good enough to correct any mistakes you may find in it. I hope that you are enjoying perfect health, and I wish for nothing more than to see you soon again in Vienna, so that I may demonstrate still further the esteem in which I hold you. I remain, in true friendship,

Your obedient servant,
Maria Anna *Noble v.* Gennzinger
née Noble v. Kayser.

My husband and children also
ask me to send you their
kindest regards.
Vienna, 10th June 1789.

Haydn replied:

Nobly born and gracious Lady!

In all my previous correspondence, nothing delighted me more than the surprise of seeing such a lovely handwriting, and reading so many kind expressions; but even more I admired the enclosure – the excellent arrangement of the Adagio, which is correct enough to be engraved by any publisher. I would like to know only whether Your Grace arranged the Adagio from the score, or whether you took the amazing trouble of first putting it into score from the parts and only then arranging it for the pianoforte; if the latter, such an attention would be too flattering to me, for I really don't deserve it.

Best and kindest Frau v. Gennsinger! [*sic*] I only await a hint from you as to how and in what fashion I can possibly be of service to Your Grace. Meanwhile I return the Adagio, and very much hope to receive from Your Grace some demands on my modest talents; I am, with sincere esteem and respect,

Your Grace's
most obedient servant,
Josephus Haydn [m.p] ria.

Estoras, 14th June 1789.

Their friendship developed through further correspondence and was strengthened when Haydn came to Vienna in January 1790 for his annual winter visit, during which he heard *Le nozze di Figaro* for the first time and attended the rehearsals and first performances of *Così fan tutte*. On 29 January, Haydn helped organize a quartet party at the Genzinger home. Then he was called back to Eszterháza, which gave rise to the most amusing, sad, witty and self-revealing correspondence of his career. He wrote to Maria Anna von Genzinger in Vienna as follows:

Nobly born,
Most highly respected and kindest Frau von Gennzinger,

Well, here I sit in my wilderness—forsaken—like a poor waif—almost without any human society—melancholy—full of the memories of past glorious days—yes! past alas!—

and who knows when these days shall return again? Those wonderful parties? Where the whole circle is one heart, one soul—all these beautiful musical evenings—which can only be remembered, and not described—where are all these enthusiastic moments?—all gone—and gone for a long time. Your Grace mustn't be surprised that I haven't written up to now to thank you. I found everything at home in confusion, and for 3 days I didn't know if I was *Capell*-master or *Capell*-servant. Nothing could console me, my whole house was in confusion, my pianoforte which I usually love so much was perverse and disobedient, it irritated rather than calmed me, I could only sleep very little, even my dreams persecuted me; and then, just when I was happily dreaming that I was listening to the opera, *Le nozze di Figaro*, that horrible North wind woke me and almost blew my nightcap off my head; I lost 20 lbs. in weight in 3 days, for the good Viennese food I had in me disappeared on the journey; alas! alas! I thought to myself as I was eating in the mess here, instead of that delicious slice of beef, a chunk of a cow 50 years old; instead of a ragout with little dumplings, an old sheep with carrots; instead of a Bohemian pheasant, a leathery joint; instead of those fine and delicate oranges, a *Dschabl* or so-called *gross Sallat* [*sic*]; instead of pastry, dry apple-fritters and hazelnuts—and that's what I have to eat. Alas! alas! I thought to myself, if I could only have a little bit of what I couldn't eat up in Vienna.—Here in Estoras no one asks me: Would you like some chocolate, with milk or without? Will you take some coffee, black, or with cream? What may I offer you, my dear Haydn? Would you like a vanilla or a pineapple ice? If I only had a good piece of Parmesan cheese, especially in Lent, so that I could more easily swallow those black dumplings and noodles; just today I told our porter here to send me a couple of pounds. . . .

On 25 February 1790 occurred the death of Princess Maria Elisabeth, Esterházy's wife; the consequence was a temporary interruption in Haydn's correspondence, as he explains in his next letter written over two weeks after the Princess's death:

Estoras, 14th March 1790.

Nobly born,
Most esteemed and kindest Frau von Gennzinger!

I ask Your Grace's forgiveness a million times for having so long delayed the answer to your kind 2 letters. This is not negligence (a sin from which Heaven will preserve me as long as I live) but is because of the many things I have to do for my most gracious Prince in his present melancholy condition. The death of his wife so crushed the Prince that we had to use every means in our power to pull His Highness out of this depression, and thus the first 3 days I arranged enlarged chamber music every evening with no singing; but the poor Prince, during the concert of the first evening, became so depressed when he heard my Favourite Adagio in D that we had quite a time to brighten his mood with the other pieces. . . .

In his next letter to Frau von Genzinger we hear of Haydn's increasing frustration with Eszterháza. Altogether, this is a different Haydn from the one we met at the beginning of this section – he has outgrown Eszterháza and the restricted life of a provincial opera *Kapellmeister*; he had also outgrown *la* Polzelli, whose charms, such as they were, were obviously of a strong but rather limited character. Haydn writes:

Estoras, 30th May 1790.

Nobly born,
Most highly esteemed and kindest Frau von Gennzinger!

I was just at Oedenburg when I received your last welcome letter, whence I had gone to enquire about the lost letter: the house-master there swore by all that is holy that he had seen no letter in my hand-writing at that time, and so this letter must have gone astray in Estoras. Be that as it may, this curiosity can do me no harm, much less Your Grace, for the whole contents of the letter were partly about my opera, *La vera costanza*, which was performed at the new theatre in the Landstrasse, and partly about the French teacher who was to have come to Estoras. Your Grace need have no fear, therefore, either about the past or about the future, for my friendship and the esteem in which I hold Your Grace (tender as they are) will never be reprehensible, because I always have in mind my respect for Your Grace's profound virtue, which not only I but all who know Your Grace, must admire. Therefore I beg Your Grace not to be frightened away from consoling me occasionally by your pleasant letters, for they comfort me in my wilderness, and are highly necessary for my heart, which is so often deeply hurt. Oh! If only I could be with Your Grace for a quarter of an hour, to pour forth all my troubles to you, and to hear all your comforting words. I have to put up with many annoyances from the Court here which, however, I must accept in silence. The only consolation left to me is that I am – thank God! – well, and eagerly disposed to work; I am only sorry that despite this eagerness, Your Grace has had to wait so long for the promised Symphony, but this time it's simply bare necessity which is responsible, arising from my circumstances here and the present rise in the cost of living. Your Grace therefore mustn't be angry at your Haydn who, often as his Prince absents himself from Estoras, cannot go to Vienna even for 24 hours; it's scarcely credible, and yet the refusal is always couched in such polite terms, so polite in fact that I just don't have the heart to insist on receiving the permission. Oh well! As God pleases! This time will also pass away, and the day come when I shall have the inexpressible pleasure of sitting beside Your Grace at the pianoforte, hearing Mozart's masterpieces, and kissing your hands for so many wonderful things. With this hope, I am,

> Your Grace's
> most sincere and humble servant,
> Josephus Haydn.

In the last days of August 1790, Haydn was conducting the final rehearsals of Mozart's *Le nozze di Figaro* for the Eszterháza theatre, and probably a full rehearsal with orchestra was held at the beginning of September. After two operatic evenings in September, however, Prince Nicolaus went to Vienna where, on the 18th, 'after a short illness and in his 76th year' (*Wiener Zeitung*) he died. Musical activity at Eszterháza came to a sudden halt: the copyist Johann Schellinger put down his pen in the middle of the second horn part of Paisiello's *Il rè Teodoro in Venezia* and never finished the part. News came that Prince Anton, the new head of the family, had dismissed the whole *Capelle*. Haydn and Luigi Tomasini received handsome pensions (Haydn 1,000 gulden p.a.) from Prince Nicolaus's estate. The strolling players who had been at the Castle – the Johann Mayer Troupe – were given a 'special gratuity' and dismissed. The fairy-tale of Eszterháza was at an end.

Haydn fled to Vienna, leaving behind a quantity of valuable music which he later missed (and the recovery of which took place, it seems, in 1793). There, he took rooms with Johann Nepomuk Hamberger, a government official, who lived on the Wasserkunstbastei.

Meanwhile, the German-born impresario and violinist, Johann Peter Salomon, who had settled in England, happened to be in Cologne when he read in the newspapers that Prince Nicolaus had died. He was undertaking his annual Continental trip to engage singers for the forthcoming London concert season, and forthwith determined to persuade Haydn to come to England; he set off at once for Vienna and having arrived there, he had himself announced to Haydn and, upon entering, spoke the now famous sentences: 'I am Salomon of London and have come to fetch you. Tomorrow we will arrange an *accord*' (Dies).

Haydn was at first not sure whether a man of his years should undertake such a strenuous trip, but Salomon was persuasive and, moreover, the terms for the London concerts were exceptionally generous (a total of 5,000 gulden guaranteed for a year, the Opera included; Sir John Gallini represented the latter organization and had empowered Salomon to act in his name). As soon as Haydn had signed the agreement in Vienna, Salomon sent off an open letter to John Baptist Mara, husband of the famous *prima donna*, Gertrud. This letter was printed in the *Morning Chronicle* and *St James's Chronicle or, British Evening-Post* on 1 January 1791, being preceded by a similar announcement with only slightly different word-order in the *Morning Chronicle* of 29 December 1790:

To the MUSICAL WORLD.

London, Dec. 27, 1790.

By a letter just received, on my arrival in Town, from Mr. SALOMON, I am authorised to lay before the Publick an Advertisement, written by Mr. Salomon at Vienna, which he desires may be immediately inserted in the English Newspapers.

JOHN BAPTISTA MARA.

'Mr. SALOMON having taken a Journey to Vienna purposely to engage the celebrated HAYDN, Chapel-Master to his present Highness Prince ESTERHAZY, to come to England, most respectfully acquaints the Nobility and Gentry, that he has actually signed an agreement with Mr. Haydn; in consequence, they are to set out together from Vienna in a few Days, and hope to be in London before the end of December when Mr. Salomon will have the honour of submitting to the Publick a Plan of a Subscription Concert, which he flatters himself will meet with its Approbation and Encouragement.

Vienna, Dec. 8, 1790.'

Griesinger (22) reports on the last meal that Mozart, Haydn and Salomon had together before the impresario and Haydn set off:

Mozart said, at a merry meal with Salomon, to Haydn: 'You won't stand it for long and will soon return, for you aren't young any more.' 'But I am still vigorous and in good health,' answered Haydn . . .

Ironically, it was at this meal that Salomon also arranged for Mozart to come to England when Haydn returned, and on similar terms to those for Haydn. From Dies (81, 83) we learn further that

Especially Mozart took pains to say, 'Papa!' (as he usually called him), 'You have had no education for the great world, and you speak too few languages'. – – 'Oh!' replied Haydn, 'my language is understood all over the world!' [The travellers fixed their departure] and left on December 15, 179[0] . . . Mozart, that day, never left his friend Haydn. He dined with him, and at the moment of parting, he said, 'We are probably saying our last adieu in this life.' Tears welled in both their eyes. Haydn was deeply moved, for he applied Mozart's words to himself, and the possibility never occurred to him that the thread of Mozart's life could be cut by the inexorable Parcae [Fates] the very next year.

Haydn and Salomon travelled via Munich and Bonn. Dies (84f.) tells of a surprise that awaited Haydn in the latter city:

In Bonn, the capital, he was surprised in more ways than one. He arrived there on a Saturday and intended to rest during the following day.

Salomon [a native of Bonn] took Haydn on Sunday to the court chapel to hear Mass. Hardly had they entered the church and found a good place, when the High Mass began. The first sounds announced a work of Haydn's. Our Haydn presumed this to be a flattering coincidence, but it was pleasant for him to hear his own work. Towards the end of Mass, someone approached and invited him to go into the oratory, where he was awaited. Haydn went and was no little astonished to see that the Elector Maximilian had summoned him, took him at once by the hand, and presented him to his musicians with the words, 'Now may I present to you the Haydn you admire so much.' The Elector gave them time to become acquainted and then, to show Haydn persuasive proof of his esteem, invited him to his own table. Haydn was no little embarrassed by this unexpected invitation, for he and Salomon had arranged to have a small *dîner* served in their rooms, and it was already too late to make a change. So Haydn had to make his excuses, which the Elector kindly accepted. Haydn then took his leave and returned to his quarters where he was surprised by unexpected evidence of the Elector's good will. His little *dîner* was transformed by the Elector's quiet order into a large one for twelve, and the ablest of the musicians were invited to it.

From Bonn the travellers proceeded to Calais, and from there, Haydn sent his first letter of the trip to Maria Anna von Genzinger:

Calais, 31st December 1790.

Nobly born,
Most highly respected Frau von Gennzinger!

The recent bad weather and the continual downpour of rain were responsible for my having just arrived (as I write this letter to you) at Calais this evening. Tomorrow morning at 7 we cross the sea to London. I promised Your Grace to write from Brussels, but I could not stay there more than an hour. I am well, thank God! though I am somewhat thinner, owing to fatigue, irregular sleep, and eating and drinking so many different things. In a few days I shall describe my journey in more detail to Your Grace, but I must beg you to excuse me today. I hope to God that Your Grace, your husband and the whole family are well. I am, most respectfully,

Your Grace's
most obedient servant,
Jos:Haydn.

On New Year's Day, 1791, Haydn set forth across the Channel for England and what was to prove the beginning of the greatest adventure of his life.

III
THE VISITS TO ENGLAND
1791~1795

'. . . how sweet this bit of freedom really is!

I had a kind Prince, but sometimes I was forced to be

dependent on base souls. I often sighed

for release, and now I have it in some measure.'

LETTER FROM HAYDN TO MARIA ANNA VON GENZINGER,
17 SEPTEMBER 1791

81 Joseph Haydn, portrait in oils by Thomas Hardy, 1791; this painting, now in the Royal College of Music, London, was also engraved by the artist in 1792 and became perhaps the best-known likeness of the composer in his lifetime.

82, 83 Johann Peter Salomon, the German-born violinist and impresario, portrayed by Thomas Hardy, 1791. Salomon was the moving spirit in persuading Haydn to come to London following the death of Prince Nicolaus I Esterházy; his concert series in London were notable for the inclusion of works by European composers and performances by visiting artists. The concerts were given at the Hanover Square Rooms (cf. ill. 92), and elegantly engraved tickets such as the one shown *(left)* for the evening of 16 May 1791, were prepared for each concert.

Some notable performances and composers active in the London musical scene in the 1790s

84–87 Among the leading singers of the day who appeared at the Opera and Salomon concerts were Gertrud Elisabeth Mara-Schmeling (soprano; *top, left*), Anna Selina (Nancy) Storace (soprano; *top, right*), Giacomo Davidde (David; tenor) and Brigida Banti-Giorgi (soprano), who made her London début in 1794. While in London, Haydn wrote the concert aria 'Cara, deh torna in pace' (lost) especially for David, who also took the part of Orfeo in *L'anima del filosofo* (1791), and the *Scena di Berenice* (1795) for Banti.

88, 89 Johann Nepomuk Hummel and Jan Ladislaus Dussek *(below)*, both of whom were brilliant pianists and successful composers, made regular appearances in London concerts; later, Hummel, who had been a child prodigy, was appointed *Konzertmeister* to Prince Nicolaus II Esterházy.

The London scene

91 (below) The royal residence, Buckingham House (now Palace), as seen from St James's Park; watercolour by E. Dayes, 1790. During Haydn's second visit to London he lived only a few minutes' walk away, at No. 1 Bury Street, St James's.

90 Panoramic view of the Thames, with Somerset House (left), St Paul's Cathedral and Blackfriars Bridge; pen-and-ink and watercolour by Jean-Louis Desprez, 1804.

92 Hanover Square, from the north-west; coloured engraving after E. Dayes, 1787. The Hanover Square Rooms, in which the Salomon concerts were given, stood on the corner of Hanover Street (left, background), on the east side of the square.

The Royal family

93, 94 King George III and his consort, Queen Charlotte; details from portraits by Sir Thomas Lawrence and Sir William Beechey, respectively. The king was especially fond of Handel's music and supported the 'Antient Concerts'; Haydn came to the notice of the Royal Family particularly during his second visit and in 1795 was invited to Buckingham House, where he sang German songs for the king and queen.

95 A satirical engraving by S.W. Fores, 1787, makes pointed reference to the parsimony of the king and queen in attending the 'Antient Concerts' as subscribers rather than arranging musical entertainment at Buckingham House.

The First Lord of the Treasury and Chancellor of the Exchequer, William Pitt, is shown (left) performing on whistle and rattle while the allegorical figure representing avarice keeps time by shaking money bags.

96 The view from the north terrace at Windsor Castle; watercolour by Paul Sandby (1730–1809). Haydn visited the castle in June 1792 and described the view as 'divine'.

97 One of the principal social events of the year was the annual ball held in honour of Queen Charlotte's birthday on 18 January. The formal elegance of such occasions is captured in this engraving after a drawing by R. Dodd; Haydn was present at the ball held at St James's Palace in January 1791, where he was 'recognized by all the Royal Family'.

A View of the BALL at St James's on her MAJESTY's Birth Night.

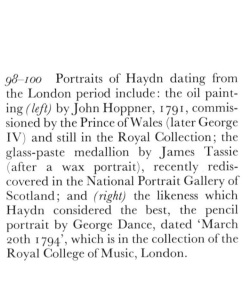

98–100 Portraits of Haydn dating from the London period include: the oil painting *(left)* by John Hoppner, 1791, commissioned by the Prince of Wales (later George IV) and still in the Royal Collection; the glass-paste medallion by James Tassie (after a wax portrait), recently rediscovered in the National Portrait Gallery of Scotland; and *(right)* the likeness which Haydn considered the best, the pencil portrait by George Dance, dated 'March 20th 1794', which is in the collection of the Royal College of Music, London.

Patrons, friends and ceremonial

101 William Shield, operatic composer and music theoretician, who was one of Haydn's most sympathetic friends in England; engraving after a pencil drawing by George Dance, 13 May 1798.

102 The Earl of Abingdon *(below)*, was a good amateur musician who also tried his hand at composition; engraving after J. F. Rigaud. Many of Haydn's social contacts with the English aristocracy and gentry were the result of his friendship with Lord Abingdon. The two figures depicted in this engraving were for long identified as Mozart (seated) and Haydn, and it is possible that the standing figure was always intended to represent Haydn.

103 Mrs Papendiek and her son *(below)*, crayon portrait by Sir Thomas Lawrence, 1789; Charlotte Papendiek, whose husband (a flautist) taught music to the Royal Family, kept a diary in which she recorded her impressions of the Haydn-Salomon concerts she attended. Her memoirs, written shortly before her death in 1839, include interesting (though not always accurate) accounts of the events she describes.

104–106 Dr Charles Burney, composer and well-known music historian, portrayed in a pencil sketch by George Dance, 1794 *(centre)*, was instrumental in arranging the award of an honorary doctorate of music to Haydn by the University of Oxford (July 1791); the scene at the degree ceremony (Encaenia) which Haydn attended in the Sheldonian Theatre can be imagined from this watercolour by S.H. Grimm *(above)* showing a similar occasion ten years earlier. When Haydn visited Oxford he also conducted a concert in the Sheldonian Theatre, on which occasion the leader of the orchestra was William Cramer *(right)*, seen here in a portrait by Thomas Hardy, 1794.

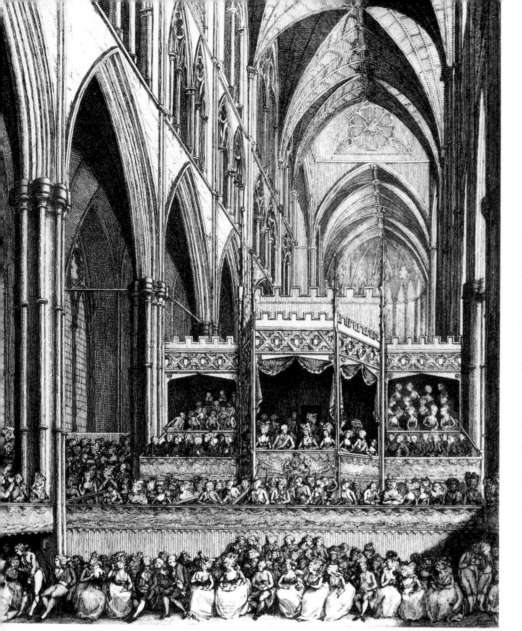

107, 108, 110 Among the social events which particularly impressed Haydn was the annual Handel Festival held in Westminster Abbey. In the early summer of 1791 Haydn attended this event; the engraving *(above)* shows the interior of the Abbey with the Royal box at the 1784 festival.

The statue of Handel (1738) by Louis-François Roubiliac *(above, right)*, was observed by Haydn in Vauxhall Gardens and recorded by him in his notebook entry for 4 June 1792, when the king's birthday celebrations took place. Vauxhall was then a fashionable place of entertainment, as can be seen from the spectators in Rowlandson's well-known watercolour *(opposite, above)*.

109, 111 The Pantheon *(left)* in Oxford Road was opened in 1772 as a venue for lavish balls and masquerades; the interior is seen here in a mezzotint by R. Earlom after C. Brandoin. Haydn's Cantata *Arianna a Naxos* was performed here on 24 February 1791 at a concert given by the New Musical Fund. The building, designed by James Wyatt in imitation of the Pantheon in Rome, was later converted for use as a theatre and opera house, but was destroyed by fire early in 1792 and subsequently rebuilt.

The rival King's Theatre in the Haymarket was the other principal opera house in London. In a satirical engraving by Cruikshank *(right)* published in 1791, the Prince of Wales is depicted as the 'Modern Atlas', carrying the theatre (the colonnaded façade of Carlton House – cf. ill. 119 – is shown in the background), reflecting his backing of Sir John Gallini's opera house.

The MODERN ATLAS

112, 113 Prince Anton Esterházy and his wife, Maria Anna Theresia (*née* Hohenfeld); details from an anonymous painting and a portrait by Angelika Kauffmann, respectively. Prince Anton was head of the family from 1790 to 1794, during which period Haydn returned to Vienna (1792–3); the prince was not in favour of Haydn's second visit to England, but was eventually persuaded to allow his *Kapellmeister*, who had no formal duties, to leave.

114–116 While in England, Haydn made a number of journeys by coach to visit various parts of the country: in August 1794 he travelled to Bath and Bristol, and while in Bath he stayed at Perrymead, the house of the famous Italian-born castrato Venanzio Rauzzini *(far right)*, from the garden of which a panoramic view of the city *(above)* could be admired. Rauzzini, like the composer Dr Henry Harington *(right)*, was one of the leading figures in the musical life of the city.

117, 118 In July 1794, Haydn visited the naval base at
Portsmouth, seen here in an engraving by R. Dodd, 1796.
This journey to the coast was broken at the Palace of
Hampton Court *(top)*; the east front, with the formal
garden, is shown in an engraving by J. Toomey.

119, 120 Haydn's principal royal benefactor in England was the Prince of Wales, portrayed *(above)* by Sir Thomas Lawrence (detail); Haydn was frequently a guest at Carlton House, the Prince's London residence, where concerts – including works by Haydn – were regularly given; the lavish interior of the Crimson Drawing Room is shown *(left)* in an engraving by W. H. Pyne.

121 At Oatlands, near Weybridge in Surrey, Haydn was entertained in November 1791 by the Duke and Duchess of York. The scene which Haydn describes in his Notebooks is shown in this engraving, after a drawing by E. Dayes, published in 1795.

122–124 London, as the musical capital of the world, attracted many of the leading composers and performers of the day: the composer Muzio Clementi *(left)*, who had settled in England as a young man, found his reputation overshadowed by that of the newly arrived Haydn; Vincente Martín y Soler (Martini; *centre*) came to England in 1794 during Haydn's second visit, while the child prodigy George Polgreen Bridgetower *(right)*, made a great impression as a violinist from 1789 on.

125, 126 Among works by Haydn published in London with formal dedications were two groups of Piano Trios issued by Longman & Broderip as Op. 70 and Op. 73; the first group *(left)* was dedicated to Princess Maria Anna Theresia Esterházy, who had become a widow by the time the works appeared in November 1794, while the second, which includes the Trio with the famous Rondo 'in the Gypsies' style', was issued in 1795 with a dedication to Haydn's intimate friend Mrs Rebecca Schroeter.

127–129 Other notable personalities with whom Haydn was associated in London included: the soprano Anna Morichelli *(left)*, who appeared, *inter alia*, in Haydn's benefit concert on 4 May 1795; Mrs Elizabeth Billington *(centre)*, to whom Haydn presented (via his friend William Shield) his *Terzetto* 'Pietà di me'; and Giovan Battista Viotti, the violinist and composer with whom Haydn collaborated in 1794 and at the Opera Concerts in 1795.

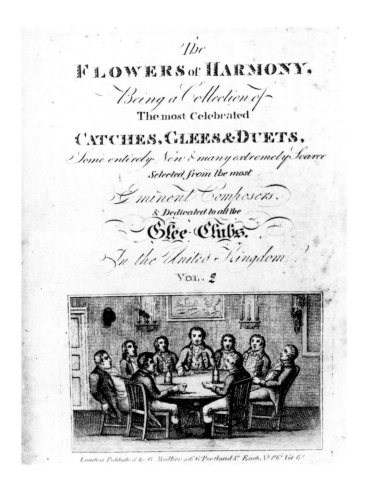

130, 131 Two title pages of contemporary London publications: an edition of 'catches, glees and duets' *(left)* – many of them composed by friends and acquaintances – includes an engraving showing how multi-voiced glees were frequently performed – Haydn's 'Ten Commandments', composed for the Saxonian Minister in London, were often sung in this manner around a table, with a bottle of port circulating; the Longman & Broderip edition of six Trios by Ignaz Joseph Pleyel *(above)* includes a portrait of the composer – a former pupil of Haydn's – and a formal dedication to Queen Charlotte.

132 A grand pianoforte 'with the additional keys' (i.e. with extended compass), similar to the instrument which Longman & Broderip presented to Haydn in 1794 and which the composer took back to Vienna in 1795, where it was admired by Beethoven. The music open on the piano is Haydn's Divertimento 'Il maestro e lo scolare' (originally for harpsichord/four hands) in a version for two harpsichords and strings. The portrait hanging on the wall is of the Emperor Joseph II; it was painted shortly before his death in 1790.

On arriving in England, Haydn's first goal, geographically, was London. Its very size amazed him, but more than that, it was his first experience of a great and worldly metropolis (for Vienna, at that time, was a beautiful but still smallish city with walls dating from the time of the last Turkish siege). Later, on the library table in one of the great English country houses to which he was invited, Haydn might have found the following note in *The Sporting Magazine* (January 1794, p. 220):

Perhaps in no age or country has a metropolis been better characterized than the metropolis of England, in the words of Johnson. 'If you wish to have a just notion of the magnitude of this City, you must not be satisfied with feeling its great streets and squares, but must survey the innumerable little alleys and courts. It is not in the shewy evolutions of buildings, but in the multiplicity of human habitations which are crowded together, that the immensity of London consists. I have often amused myself with thinking how different a place London is to different people. They whose narrow minds are contracted to the consideration of some one particular object, view it only through that medium. A politician thinks of it merely as a seat of government in its different departments; a grazier, as a vast market for cattle; a mercantile man, as a place where a prodigious deal of business is done upon 'Change; a dramatic enthusiast, as the grand scene of theatrical entertainments; a man of pleasure, as an assemblage of taverns, and the great emporium for ladies of easy virtue; but the intellectual man is struck with it, as comprehending the *whole of human life in all its variety*, the contemplation of which is inexhaustible.'

Haydn's curiosity extended to everything he saw in England: the people, the customs, the climate, the music-making, the women (all his biographers stress that he was very fond of women – 'in younger years he is said to have been most susceptible to love'); and he kept a series of notebooks, of which three have survived complete and a fourth in extracts, that give us a humorous, sarcastic, naïve, clever and sometimes shocked account of his life in England. Many different kinds of people became Haydn's friends in England (as much as their different stations would allow): from the Duchess of York to 'Mister March ... a dentist, coach-maker and dealer in wines ... a man 84 years old (with) a very young mistress'; from Dr Charles Burney to the Earl of Abingdon (Haydn must have been utterly fascinated to see the latter put in prison, like any commoner, for a vicious libel); from the violent revolutionary poet and playwright Thomas Holcroft (again Haydn must have watched his treason trial and acquittal with astonishment) to the gentle Mistress Schroeter, the 'amiable widow' whom Haydn might have married had he been single; from the banker Nathaniel Brassey to the naval captain who had the delighted Haydn to lunch on his East India merchantman 'with six cannon' and told the composer how to preserve cream or milk 'for a long time'. Haydn blossomed; but neither the flattery, the adulation of the public,

105
102

nor the constant mentions in the London daily newspapers went to his head. The English loved him, and thought his music, after Handel's, the greatest they knew.

Within a week of his arrival, Haydn had resumed his correspondence with Maria Anna von Genzinger:

London, 8th January 1791.

Nobly born,

Gracious Lady!

I hope that you will have received my last letter from Calais. I should have written you immediately after my arrival in London, but I wanted to wait a few days so as to be able to write about several things at once. So I can tell you that on the 1st inst., New Year's Day, after attending early mass, I boarded the ship at 7:30 a.m. and at 5 in the afternoon I arrived, thank God! safe and sound in Dower [*sic*]. At the beginning, for the first 4 whole hours, we had almost no wind, and the ship went so slowly that in these 4 hours we didn't go further than one single English mile, and there are 24 between Calais and Dower. Our ship's captain, in an evil temper, said that if the wind did not change, we should have to spend the whole night at sea. Fortunately, however, towards 11:30 o'clock a wind arose and blew so favourably that by 4 o'clock we covered 22 miles. Since the tide, which had just begun to ebb, prevented our large vessel from reaching the pier, 2 small ships came out to meet us as we were still fairly far out at sea, and into these we and our luggage were transferred, and thus at last, though exposed to a medium gale, we landed safely. The large vessel stood out to sea five hours longer, till the tide turned and it could finally dock. Some of the passengers were afraid to board the little boats and stayed on board, but I followed the example of the greater number. I remained on deck during the whole passage, so as to gaze my fill at that mighty monster, the ocean. So long as it was calm, I wasn't afraid at all, but towards the end, when the wind grew stronger, and I saw the monstrous high waves rushing at us. I became a little frightened, and a little indisposed, too. But I overcame it all and arrived safely, without (excuse me) vomiting, on shore. Most of the passengers were ill, and looked like ghosts, but since I went on to London, I didn't feel the effects of the journey right away; but then I needed 2 days to recover. Now, however, I am fresh and well again, and occupied in looking at this endlessly huge city of London, whose various beauties and marvels quite astonished me. I immediately paid the necessary calls, such as to the Neapolitan Ambassador and to our own; both called on me in return 2 days later, and 4 days ago I lunched with the former – N.B. at 6 o'clock in the evening, as is the custom here.

My arrival caused a great sensation throughout the whole city, and I went the round of all the newspapers for 3 successive days. Everyone wants to know me. I had to dine out 6 times up to now, and if I wanted, I could dine out every day; but first I must consider my health, and 2nd my work. Except for the nobility, I admit no callers till 2 o'clock in the afternoon, and at 4 o'clock I dine at home with *Mon.* Salomon. I have nice and comfortable, but expensive, lodgings. My landlord is Italian, and also a cook, and serves me 4 very respectable meals; we each pay 1 fl. 30 kr. a day excluding wine and beer, but everything is terribly expensive here. Yesterday I was invited to a grand amateur concert, but I arrived a bit late, and when I showed my ticket they wouldn't let me in but led me to an antechamber, where I had to wait till the piece which was then being played in the hall was over. Then they opened the door, and I was conducted, on the arm of the *entrepreneur*, up the centre of the hall to the front of the orchestra, amid universal applause, and there I was stared at and greeted by a great number of English compliments. I was assured that such honours had not been conferred on anyone for 50 years. After the concert I was taken to a handsome adjoining room, where a table for 200 persons, with many places set, was prepared for all the amateurs; I was supposed to be seated at the head of the table, but since I had dined out on that day and had eaten more than usual, I declined this honour, with the excuse that I was not feeling very well, but despite this I had to drink the harmonious health, in Burgundy, of all the gentlemen present; they all returned the toast, and then allowed me to be taken home. All this, my gracious lady, was very flattering to me, and yet I wished I could fly for a time to Vienna, to have more quiet in which to work, for the noise that the common people make as they sell their wares in the street is intolerable. At present I am working on symphonies, because the libretto of the opera is not yet decided on, but in order to have more quiet I shall have to rent a room far from the centre of town. I would gladly write you in more detail, but I am afraid of missing the mail-coach. Meanwhile I am, . . .

Your Grace's
most sincere and obedient servant,
Joseph Haydn.

Haydn was now established in quarters at 18 Great Pulteney Street, where Salomon also lived; in addition Haydn had a room at the famous music shop of Broadwood's, which was opposite, and there he could compose. But he found it difficult to concentrate amidst the noise of the city and later in the season he took rooms in a quiet suburb (see below).

Johann Peter Salomon, the remarkable impresario, violinist and composer who brought Haydn to England, was born at Bonn (christening: 20 February 1745); later, in 1770, Beethoven was also born in the very same house. After a successful career in Germany, Salomon emigrated to England where he made his début as a violinist at Covent Garden Theatre on 23 March 1781. He was at first associated with the Professional Concert but later formed his own concert series, at which one of his specialities was the performance of string quartets. 82

In 1791 London was the musical capital of the world, and there was opera or a subscription concert every night of the week. Salomon's series was held at the Hanover Square Rooms, and among the other concert halls regularly in use were Freemasons' Hall, The Rooms in Tottenham Street, the Crown and Anchor in the Strand, and Willis's Rooms in King Street, St James's. The Opera was held at the King's Theatre, which later contained a magnificent concert hall (usually called the 'New Room') where Haydn's last three symphonies were first performed. Sir John Gallini's rival opera company, supported by the Prince of Wales, was at the Pantheon, and it was there that Haydn's new Opera, *L'anima del filosofo*, was to have been staged; as it happened, Haydn's most popular vocal work, the *Maccone* for Sir John Gallini, was given there many times during the 1791 season (Haydn called it *Maccone*; it was a seven-part Catch and is, alas, lost). The two principal concert series were the Professional Concert (Hanover Square, Mondays) and the Haydn-Salomon series (Hanover Square, Fridays). Haydn was, of course, expected to provide numerous new works for the Friday concerts, but he could also supply as 'new' works several symphonies (Nos. 90 and the soon very popular No. 92, to be nicknamed 'The Oxford'), a set of six quartets (Opus 64, composed in 1790), and some of the Notturni for the King of Naples (1790) as well some vocal works not known in England (such as 'Ah, come il core' from *La fedeltà premiata*, which Haydn offered as a concert aria, and the Cantata *Arianna a Naxos*). Apart from a new Aria for the singer Davidde, 'Cara deh torna in pace' (lost), and the *Maccone* for Gallini, Haydn composed two new symphonies, Nos. 96 ('Miracle') and 95, both specifically signed and dated London 1791, for Salomon's first season. The new Opera *L'anima del filosofo*, which was based on the Orpheus legend (and was later 83, 92

111

109

86

published in fragments as *Orfeo ed Euridice*), had a libretto by Carlo Francesco Badini, a clever Italian journalist and rival of Mozart's librettist, Lorenzo da Ponte; Badini had settled in London and contributed regularly to various newspapers; like Da Ponte he was something of a scandalous figure.

Haydn was soon swept into the musical and social life of the capital. He made friends with men and women of widely diverse social backgrounds and nationalities; be became a popular figure and his comings and goings were soon noted by the daily Press. Among his influential friends was Dr Charles Burney, composer, writer, and father of the famous novelist, Fanny Burney (who later married a French émigré named D'Arblay); Burney welcomed the Austrian composer with a long poem, published as 'Verses on the Arrival of Haydn. Price one shilling.' An announcement in the *Public Advertiser* of 7 January 1791 whetted its readers' appetites thus:

MUSICAL ARRANGEMENTS FOR EVERY DAY IN THE

WEEK, THROUGH THE WINTER SEASON.

Never could this country boast of such a constellation of musical excellence as now illuminates our fashionable hemisphere. No one Metropolis can exhibit such a union of Masters as London now possesses: and therefore as Music will be the chief pleasure of the season, we shall endeavour to give a faithful representation of the Performances.

The Meeting, which through the condescension of the Prince of Wales, was to be held yesterday at Carlton House, may finally arrange the great affair of the rival Operas; but there is no doubt from the auspices, but that it will be settled to give the Opera a national establishment.

In the meantime our Readers may be pleased to see what will be the arrangements of musical pleasures for the week; even if the coalition of the two Operas should not take place.

We shall announce whatever change may be made; at present they stand as follow:

SUNDAY. – The Noblemen's Subscription, is held every Sunday at a different House.

MONDAY. – The Professional Concert – at the Hanover-Square Rooms – with Mrs. Billington.

TUESDAY.– The Opera.

WEDNESDAY.– The ancient music at the rooms in Tottenham Street, under the Patronage of their Majesties.

— – The Anacreontic Society also, occasionally, on Wednesday.

THURSDAY. – The Pantheon. – A Pasticcio of Music and Dancing, in case that the Opera Coalition shall take place; if not, a concert with Madame Mara and Sig. Pacchierotti.

— – Academy of Ancient Music, every other Thursday, at Freemason's Hall.

FRIDAY. – A Concert under the auspices of Haydn at the Rooms, Hanover Square, with Sig. David.

SATURDAY. – The Opera.

This is the arrangement for each week throughout the season; and so full is the town of eminent professors in every department of the science, that there may be a double orchestra found of admirable performers, so as to open two places of musical entertainment every evening.

> If Music be the food of Love, play on,
> Give me excess of it; that surfeiting,
> The appetite may sicken, and so die.' –

SHAKESPEARE.

On 15 January, we read the important announcement (in the *Public Advertiser*, the *Gazetteer*, etc.) of the Haydn–Salomon concerts:

HANOVER SQUARE. MR. SALAMON [*sic*] respectfully acquaints the Nobility and Gentry, that he intends having TWELVE SUBSCRIPTION CONCERTS in the Course of the present Season. The first of which be on Friday the Eleventh of February next, and so continue on the succeeding Fridays. Mr. HAYDN will compose for every Night a New Piece of Music, and direct the execution of it at the Harpsichord.

The Vocal as well as Instrumental Performers will be of the first Rate, and a List of them will appear in a few Days.

Subscriptions, at Five Guineas, for the Twelve Nights, to be held at Messrs. Lockhard's, No. 36, Pall-Mall.

Tickets transferable Ladies to Ladies, and Gentlemen to Gentlemen.

There was a Court ball at St James's on 18 January, Queen Charlotte's Birthday. Haydn was present, and from that evening his future in London's aristocratic society was assured. The *St James's Chronicle* reported the occasion, and a similar report in the *Daily Advertiser* (20 January 1791) informs us that 'A remarkable Circumstance happened on Thursday Evening'. 94, 97

In the Ball-Room at St. James's: Haydn, the celebrated Composer, though he has not yet been introduced at our Court, was recognized by all the Royal Family, and paid them his silent Respects. Mr. Haydn came into the Room with Sir John Gallini, Mr. Wills and Mr. Salomon. The Prince of Wales first observed him, and upon bowing to him, the Eyes of all the Company were upon Mr. Haydn, every one paying him Respect.

Haydn came to know a great many members of the aristocracy. King George III, who was a much more astute and sensitive man than is often realized, asked him to stay in England; and in 1795 the Queen offered Haydn a suite in Windsor Castle. Haydn was entertained many times by the Prince of Wales, his brother, the Duke of York and especially the handsome Duchess of York. The composer soon became immensely popular; he spent weekends in beautiful houses all over England, and his hosts obviously found him a delightful guest. Haydn's special friend and patron was Lord Abingdon, who took the composer around with him. 93 · 119 · 102

Haydn was no snob, however. He said, with great pride, 'I have been in the company of emperors, kings and many great gentlemen, and I received many a compliment from them: but I do not wish to live on terms of intimacy with such persons and prefer to be with people of my class' (Griesinger, 55). In England, Haydn found a middle class much older-established, much richer, and with much more influence than in his native Austria. The aristocracy may have been the ones to send Haydn fifty guineas for a ticket to his benefit concert but it was the solid (in those days not stolid) middle class who flocked to Haydn's and Salomon's concerts, cheered their lungs out after hearing the 'Military' Symphony and avidly bought up Haydn's piano trios and English canzonettas. It was from this same large segment of British society that Haydn drew his many English friends, the Mister Marches and Mistress Schroeters and all the other names that adorn his London notebooks.

Even before the Salomon concerts began, Haydn was having a frantically busy life. In demand at one concert after another, composing the new opera and the two new symphonies, the strain began to tell; and, sometime in that spring he took quarters in Lisson Grove, then a quiet suburb with cows grazing in the nearby fields. Apart from his 'guest appearances' at concerts,

Haydn also gave lessons 'to various people on the fortepiano, and every lesson was paid for by a guinea' (Griesinger, 35). Said Haydn; 'Da machte ich große Augen' (ibid.; a colloquial translation would be, 'My eyes popped out of my head').

After several delays the Haydn–Salomon concerts finally got under way on 11 March 1791. The following announcement appeared several times in the *Public Advertiser*:

HANOVER-SQUARE. MR. SALOMON respectfully acquaints the Nobility and Gentry, that his CONCERTS will open without further delay on Friday next, the 11th of March, and continue every succeeding Friday.

PART I.

Overture – Rosetti.

Song – Sig[nor] Tajana.

Concerto Oboe – Mr. Harrington.

Song – Signora Storace.

Concerto Violin – Madame Gautherot [Composed by Viotti].

Recitativo and Aria – Signor David [Composed by Rusi].

PART II.

New Grand Overture [i.e. Symphony, probably No. 92] – Haydn.

Recitative and Aria – Signora Storace.

Concertante, Pedal Harp and Pianoforte – Madame

Krumpholtz and Mr. Dusseck,

Composed by Mr. Dusseck.

Rondo – Signor David [Composed by Andreozzi].

Full Piece – Kozeluck [*sic*].

Mr. HAYDN will be at the Harpsichord.

Leader of the Band, Mr. SALOMON.

Tickets transferable, as usual, Ladies to Ladies and

Gentlemen to Gentlemen only.

The Ladies' tickets are Green, the Gentlemen's Black.

85

The Subscribers are intreated to give particular orders to their Coachmen to set down and take up at the Side Door in the Street, with the Horses' Heads towards the Square.

The Door in the Square is for Chairs only.

People were curious, of course. Some thought that Haydn must by now have written himself out. Even such a great admirer as the Rev. Thomas Twining (a friend of Burney's and a fine amateur musician) had written to Burney on 15 February 1791:

If the resources of any human composer could be inexhaustible, I should suppose Haydn's would; but as, after all, he is but a mortal, I am afraid he must soon get to the bottom of his genius-box.   [Lonsdale, 355]

Twining need have had no fear: the genius-box was still bottomless. There are at least three contemporary criticisms of the concerts in London newspapers, one in the *Morning Chronicle* on 12 March:

SALOMON'S CONCERT.

The First Concert under the auspices of HAYDN was last night, and never, perhaps, was there a richer musical treat.

It is not wonderful that to souls capable of being touched by music, HAYDN should be an object of homage, and even of idolatry; for like our own SHAKSPEARE [*sic*], he moves and governs the passions at his will.

His *new Grand Overture* was pronounced by every scientific ear to be a most wonderful composition; but the first movement in particular rises in grandeur of subject, and in the rich variety of *air* and passion, beyond any even of his own productions. The *Overture* has four movements – An Allegro – Andante – Minuet – and Rondo – They are all beautiful, but the first is pre-eminent in every charm, and the Band performed it with admirable correctness.

Signor DAVID exhibited all the wonders of his voice, and never surely was there heard a tenor of such riches and beauty. His first song was a *Recitativo* and *Aria*, by RUSI; and his second *a Rondo*, by ANDREOZZI.

There was an exquisite *concertante* between M. DUSSECK and Madame KRUMPHOLLZ [*sic*]; Signora STORACE sung two songs in a very fine style.

We were happy to see the Concert so well attended the first Night; for we cannot suppress our very anxious hopes, that the first musical genius of the age may be induced, by our liberal welcome, to take up his residence in England.

Happily, we have another contemporary report, less reliable, perhaps, than the newspapers but interesting all the same: it is the diary of Charlotte Papendiek, whose husband, a flautist, had played in Vienna in 1779 (Haydn may have met him there) and now taught music to the royal family.   103

... The wished-for night at length arrived, and as I was anxious to be near the performers I went early. Mr. Papendiek followed from Queen's House, and I got an excellent seat on a sofa at the right-hand side. The orchestra was arranged on a new plan. The pianoforte was in the centre, at each extreme end the double basses, then on each side two violoncellos, then two tenors or violas and two violins, and in the hollow of the piano a desk on a high platform for Salomon with his ripieno. At the back, verging down to a point at each end, all these instruments were doubled, giving the requisite number for a full orchestra. Still further back, raised high up, were drums, and other side the trumpets, trombones, bassoons, oboes, clarinets, flutes, &c., in numbers according to the requirements of the symphonies and other music to be played on the different evenings.

The concert opened with a symphony of Haydn's that he brought with him, but which was not known in England. It consisted of four movements, pleasing lively, and good. ...

The second act invarably opened with a new symphony composed for the night. Haydn of course conducted his own music, and generally that of other composers, in fact all through the evening.

The Hanover Square Rooms are calculated to hold 800 persons exclusive of the performers. By the beginning of the second act we concluded that all had arrived who intended to come, and though we knew that Salomon's subscription list was not full, we had hoped for additions during the evening. But no; and I regret to make this observation of my countrymen, that until they know what value they are likely to receive for their money they are slow in coming forward with it. An undertaking of this magnitude, bringing such a superior man from his own country as Haydn to compose for an orchestra filled with the highest professional skill and talent, would have met with every encouragement, first to show respect to the stranger and then to Salomon, who ... had done so much for the musical world, in this case having taken such infinite trouble and incurred so much risk.

From the evidence at our disposal, it would seem that the 'new symphony' (or, as the *Morning Chronicle* called it, 'new Grand Overture') played at this first Salomon concert was No. 92 in G, which in fact had been composed in

1789. Something of the thrill of Haydn's early concerts with his friend Salomon may be caught in the following entry from Dr Burney's memoirs:

1791. – This year was auspiciously begun, in the musical world, by the arrival in London of the illustrious Joseph Haydn. 'Tis to Salomon that the lovers of music are indebted for what the lovers of music will call this blessing. Salomon went over himself to Vienna . . . purposely to tempt that celebrated musical genius hither; and on February 25 [*sic*], the first of Haydn's incomparable symphonies which was composed for the concerts of Salomon was performed. Haydn himself presided at the piano-forte; and the sight of that renowned composer so electrified the audience, as to excite an attention and a pleasure superior to any that had ever, to my knowledge, been caused by instrumental music in England. All the slow middle movements were encored; which never before happened, I believe, in any country.

[Scholes II, 110]

The report is useful for one further point regarding the instrument from which Haydn conducted. In most of the 1791 newspapers, it is referred to as a harpsichord; but although the British continued to make powerful and mechanically the best harpsichords the world had ever seen down to the last decade of the century, Burney, a professional musician, says specifically 'piano-forte'; and it may be doubted if Haydn would have chosen the harpsichord when the new English pianos were obviously much more powerful.

The Haydn–Salomon series of 1791 turned out to be a spectacular success for everyone concerned. Haydn presented the London public with a judicious selection of vocal and instrumental pieces, most of which were immediately published by British houses (Quartets Op. 64, *Arianna a Naxos*, Symphonies Nos. 90 and 92). It was not hard to persuade Haydn to stay on for another year, and Salomon was soon able to announce a new season 'with the assistance of Mr Haydn'. The last part of May was given over to a gigantic Handel Festival, 'by command and under the patronage of their Majesties', in Westminster Abbey. There were over a thousand performers, including the cream of all the orchestras and singers; the famous 'large double basses', 'double bass Kettle drums' (tuned an octave below the normal pitches) and double bassoons. Haydn could hear magnificent performances of *Israel in Egypt*, the Coronation Anthem 'Zadok the Priest', *Messiah* and extracts from numerous other oratorios. Haydn was astonished and deeply moved.

Many years later in Vienna, Haydn gave his biographer Dies one of the London notebooks. Dies (133f.) writes:

I opened it up and found a couple of dozen letters in the English language. Haydn smiled and said: 'Letters from an English widow in London, who loved me; but she was, though already sixty years old, still a beautiful and charming woman and I would have married her very easily if I had been free at the time.'

This woman [continued Dies] is the widow, still living, of the famous pianist Schröter [*sic*], whose melodious song Haydn emphatically praised. . . . If he was not invited elsewhere, he usually dined with her.

Johann Samuel Schroeter (1750–88) had in 1782 succeeded J. C. Bach as Master of the King's Musick. Rees's *Cyclopaedia* (1819–20) says, 'He married a young lady of considerable fortune, who was his scholar, and was in easy circumstances.' Schroeter published many works for the keyboard and

HANOVER-SQUARE.

MR. HAYDN's NIGHT.

MAY the 16th, 1791.

PART THE FIRST.

New Grand Overture———HAYDN.

Aria———Signora STORACE.

Concertante for Two Corni Baffetti,
Meffrs. SPRINGER and DWORSACK.

New Aria, with Oboe and Baffoon obligati,
Signor DAVID.———*Haydn.*

Concerto, Violin———Mr. GIORNOVICHI.

PART THE SECOND.

By particular Defire, the New Grand Overture, *Haydn,*
as performed at Mr. Salomon's firft Concert.

Cantata—Signor PACCHIEROTTI.——*Haydn.*

Concertante for Piano Forte and Pedal Harp,
Mr. DUSSECK, and Madame KRUMPHOLTZ.

Duetto—Sig. DAVID and Sig. PACCHIEROTTI.

Finale———HAYDN.

RONDO. Signora STORACE.

Cimarofa.

INFELICE ch'io fono !
A tè diedi il mio core
Di tè mi fido, e tù m'inganni !
Oh Dio ! qual pena amara
Qual affanno è il mio
Mifera in tale ftato che mai far deggio
Porgerti la deftra farai viltà
Gl' affetti a un traditore
Pria di giurar, m'incenerifca amore.

    Il mio cor, gl' affetti miei
    A chi mai più donerò
    Se crudel con me tù fei
    Di chi fidarmi oh Dio non sò
    Cari amici ... il cor vi lafcio ...
    Tù rammenta ... ah fi crudele ...
    Di queft' alma a tè fedele
    Sentirai mà invan pietà
    Son oppreffa dal deftino
    Mi divora in fen l'affanno
    Fiera forte amor tiranno
    Perchè tanta crudeltà.

ARIA. Signor DAVID.

Haydn.

CARA deh torna in pace
Non ti fdegnar ben mio
Troppo m'affanno oh Dio
La pena del tuo cor.
Barbaro io vado a morte
Ah che l'affanno mio
Mi porta a delirar.

CANTATA. Signor PACCHIEROTTI.

RECIT.   *Haydn.*

AH come il core mi palpita nel feno
Per Fillide infedel mori Fileno.
Omnipotenti Numi, che leffi !
Ah mia tiranna inumana pieta
Tu per falvarlo fofti l'empia cagion della fua morte,
Crudeliffima legge ingrata forte !
Ohime ! di fofco velo fi fcopre il giorno
Io gelo, il piè vacilla oh Dio !
Ombra dell' Idol mio, fra mirti degli Elifi
Il noftro amor fi eternerà frà poco
Teco farò ... Che fento ? ... Ah ! tu fdegnofa
Dal margine di lete mi rifpondi
Tra fofpiri funefti. Fuggi infida da me,
Tu mi uccidefti.

ARIA.

    Ombra del caro bene
    Ah non chiamarmi infida
    Fidati a me, e fida
    Verro frà la ombre ancor.
    Tiranna a me ti refe
    Una pieta fedele
    Mi refe a te crudele
    Un infelice amor.

DUETTO.
Signor DAVID and Signor PACCHIEROTTI.

RECIT.   *Bianchi.*

PADRE fon teco ;
    Io della morte la via t' infeguerò

A. 2.   Ho non la temo.
    Così ci ferba o Ciel nel punto eftremo.

DUETTO.

Gual.   Caro Padre a te vicino
    Infelice io non fon più

Ermes.   Figlio amato del deftino
    Ta trionfa la virtù

A. 2.   Già ritorna alfin queft' alma
    A goder la dolce calma
    Già ritorna à refpirar.

J.8 - 340

Printed by H. REYNELL, (No, 21,) Piccadilly, near the Hay-Market.

A copy of the handbill for Haydn's benefit concert at the Hanover Square Rooms, 16 May 1791; in addition to the programme for the evening, it also includes the texts of the vocal items performed, among them a lost Aria written for Giacomo Davidde (cf. ill. 86), 'Cara deh torna in pace'.

Haydn owned several, which Rebecca probably gave him. It has been doubted if she was really sixty; but in any case she grew to love Haydn and certainly introduced him to a delightful group of people in London. Her first letter reads as follows:

> Mrs. Schroeter presents her compliments to Mr. Haydn, and informs him, she is just returned to town, and will be very happy to see him whenever it is convenient for him to give her a lesson. James str. Buckingham Gate. Wednesday, June 29th 1791.

Both Dies and Griesinger relate how even in his old age Haydn loved women. Dies (134) writes:

> He freely admitted that he loved pretty women, but he couldn't understand how it happened that in his life he had been loved by many a pretty woman. 'They can't have been led to it by my beauty.' . . .

104 In July 1791, Haydn received the honorary degree of Doctor of Music from Oxford University. Happily, we have many documents which tell us, in considerable detail, of the three concerts that took place and of the ceremony itself. The concerts took place in the handsome Sheldonian Theatre, one of Sir Christopher Wren's masterpieces, based on Marcellus's Theatre in Rome and erected in 1664–69; Griesinger (34) relates:

105 Dr. Burney suggested to Haydn that he should be given a doctor's degree at Oxford. The ceremony during which the degree was given took place in a cathedral [*sic*] with great solemnity; the doctors enter in procession and put questions to the candidates, if they wish to be admitted and so forth. Haydn answered what his friend Salomon told him to say. The election is put to the assembly from a raised platform; the speaker enlarged upon Haydn's merits, listed his works, and to the question, would Haydn be admitted, there arose a general cry of assent. The doctors dress in a small gown with frills at the collar and they have to wear it for three days. 'I would have dearly liked my Viennese acquaintances to see me in this dress!' The Storaces and some other musical friends waved to him from the orchestra. The day after the election Haydn conducted the music. 'I thank you,' he answered [in English], raising the ends of his gown. That caused much jubilation . . . It happened several times to Haydn that Englishmen went up to him, looked at him from top to toe, and left him saying, 'You are a great man.'

Dies (135f.) relates much the same story but supplies some new details:

Dr. Burney was the moving spirit: he talked Haydn into it and went with him to Oxford. At the ceremony in the University Hall, the assembled company was encouraged to present the doctor's hat to a man who had risen so high in the service of music. The whole company was loud in Haydn's praises. Thereupon Haydn was presented with a white silk gown, the sleeves in red silk, and a little black hat, and thus arrayed, he had to seat himself in a doctor's chair. . . . Haydn was asked to present something of his own composition. He climbed up to the organ loft, turned to the company, took his doctorial robes in both hands, opened them at his breast, closed them again and said as loudly and clear as possible [in English], 'I thank you.' The company well understood this unexpected gesture; they appreciated Haydn's thanks and said, 'You speak very good English.' 'I felt very silly in my gown, and the worst of it was, I had to drag it round the streets for three whole days. But I have much to thank this doctor's degree in England; indeed, I might say everything; as a result of it, I gained the acquaintance of the first men in the land and had entrance to the greatest houses.'

Haydn said this with that openness which is so characteristic of him, so that I simply could not understand how it is possible for such a genius to be so completely unaware of his own strength and to ascribe everything to the doctor's hat and nothing to his art. Self-adulation could not be seen in his words, much less any hidden pride. . . .

The *Morning Herald* of 11 July tells us not only of the ceremony but also of the concert that evening:

On Friday morning the annual Commemoration took place at OXFORD, when the celebrated HAYDN was admitted to a DOCTOR'S DEGREE in a manner highly flattering to him and creditable to the University, being the free gift and unanimous desire of that learned body.

Between the parts of the Latin and English oration, upon this occasion the band performed pieces adapted to the situation. On the return of the procession from the theatre, and on HAYDN's retiring, the applause which arose, was perhaps equal to any that ever attended a similar occasion.

At five in the evening the concluding Concert took place; and several performers were all well received on their entrance, particularly CRAMER, who was honored with warm tokens of general respect.

The opening piece was the Overture from ESTHER, performed with great spirit. KELLY followed with 'why does the Go[d], etc.' from Samson, with good expression. MATTHEWS and BELLAMY, then sung 'The Lord is a Man of War' tolerably. The next in order was, a beautiful Cantata by HAYDN, who appeared in his gown and conducted it; – this charming air used to be finely sung by MARCHES[I]; therefore STORACE was injudicious in attempting it on this occasion, and indeed, obtained less applause than HAYDN's *Doctorial Robe*. The first act terminated with the Recitative 'Search round the, etc.' and Chorus 'May no rash, etc.' from Handel's Solomon by KELLY. This was repeated.

A new Overture by PLEYEL led on the second act. The composition was much admired and the Band played it with very great correct[n]ess and spirit, though they never saw it till that evening. STORACE then sung. 'The Prince unable to conceal, etc.' from Alexander's Feast, with such *expressive gesture* that the young gentlemen in the *Black Gowns* were highly gratified and unanimously *encored* it. The next was a Concerto on the Violin by CRAMER, executed in his best style, and with such brilliancy that the applause was very great from all quarters. DAVID was followed with 'Comfort ye my People', but not with such success as he gave at the Abbey. This act concluded with the Chorus, 'And the Glory, etc.'.

KELLY before the third act sung an Italian Air, the music of which was not very striking; and he made as much of it as it deserved.

The last act commenced with an Overture of HAYDN, very fine, but well known. HAYDN was not present at this performance. STORACE followed with the Air 'with lowly suite' in which she was very deservedly *encored*. DAVID next sung 'Pensa che in [campo] etc.' an Air of PAESIELLO, but in too flourishing a style of execution with a want of neatness in his divisions.
. . .

106

Haydn, methodical as always in money matters, recorded the cost of the trip to Oxford in one of his notebooks (in German, of course).

I had to pay 1½ guineas for having the bells rung at Oxforth [*sic*] in connection with my doctor's degree, and ½ a guinea for the robe. The trip cost 6 guineas.

Luigia Polzelli had written to Haydn saying that her husband, Antonio Polzelli had at last died; he had been an invalid for years. Haydn's answer (in Italian) reads:

London, 4th August 1791.

Dear Polzelli!

I hope that you will have received my last letter through Count Fries and also the hundred florins [Gulden] which I transferred to you. I would like to do more, but at present I cannot. As far as your husband is concerned, I tell you that Providence has done well to liberate you from this heavy yoke, and for him, too, it is better to be in another world than to remain useless in this one. The poor man has suffered enough. Dear Polzelli, perhaps, perhaps the time will come, which we both so often dreamt of, when four eyes shall be closed. Two are closed, but the other two – enough of all this, it shall be as God wills. Meanwhile, pay attention to your health. I beg of you, and write me very soon, because for quite some time now I have had days of depression without really knowing why, and your letters cheer me, even when they are sad. Good bye, dear Polzelli, the mail won't wait any longer. I kiss your family and remain always

Your most sincere
Haydn.

On 17 September, Haydn writes again to Frau von Genzinger in Vienna:

... Now, may dear good gracious lady, how is your fortepiano? Is a Haydnish thought brought to mind, now and then, by your fair hand? Does my dear *Fräulein* Pepi sometimes sing poor *Ariadne*? Oh yes! I can hear it even here, especially during the last two months, when I have been living in the country, amid the loveliest scenery, with a banker's family where the atmosphere is like that of the Gennzinger family, and where I live as if I were in a monastery. I am all right, thank the good Lord! except for my usual rheumatism; I work hard, and when in the early mornings I walk in the woods, alone, with my English grammar, I think of my Creator, my family, and all the friends I have left behind – and of these you are the ones I most value. Of course I had hoped to have the pleasure of seeing you sooner, but my circumstances – in short, fate – will have it that I remain in London another 8 or 10 months. Oh, my dear gracious lady! how sweet this bit of freedom really is! I had a kind Prince, but sometimes I was forced to be dependent on base souls. I often sighed for release, and now I have it in some measure. I appreciate the good sides of all this, too, though my mind is burdened with far more work. The realization that I am no bond-servant makes ample amends for all my toils. But, dear though this liberty is to me, I should like to enter Prince Esterházy's service again when I return, if only for the sake of my family. I doubt whether this will be possible, however, for in his letter my Prince strongly objects to my staying away for so long, and absolutely demands my speedy return; but I can't comply with this, owing to a new contract which I have just made here. And now, unfortunately, I expect my dismissal, whereby I hope that God will give me the strength to make up for this loss, at least partly, by my industry. Meanwhile I console myself by the hope of hearing something soon from Your Grace. You shall receive my promised new Symphony in two months, but in order to inspire me with good ideas, I beg Your Grace to write, and to write a long letter, too, to one who is ever

Your Grace's
most sincere friend and obedient
servant,

Jos: Haydn.

Esterházy's demand for Haydn's return was to compose an *opera seria* to be performed on the occasion of the Prince's installation as Governor of the County of Oedenburg; the event took place at Eszterháza Castle on 3 August 1791 and was the last great *festa* to take place there. The festivities were

37

commemorated in a handsome engraving with some gypsy musicians in the right foreground – no doubt to compensate for *Kapellmeister* Haydn's absence. In the event, Prince Anton made it up with Haydn, and when they met in Frankfurt in 1792 (see p. 135), the Prince simply said, 'Haydn, you could have saved me 40,000 Gulden', reputedly the staggering price paid to stage Joseph Weigl's *Venere e Adonis* with an imported Viennese cast.

Meanwhile, in the summer of 1791, Haydn was invited to stay at Roxford, the home of a banker named Nathaniel Brassey, near Hertingford-bury in Hertfordshire (north of London). During the quiet summer weeks at Roxford, Haydn will have composed Symphony No. 93 and probably some of No. 94 and No. 98, which he now had to complete for the new Salomon season of 1793. By the end of September, if not before, Haydn was back in London: on 26 September 1791, he signed the guest book at Broadwood's piano shop across the street from his lodgings on Great Pulteney Street.

To a certain extent, Haydn was no longer master of his own fame. His reputation began to exist as a thing almost separate from the man. While on the one hand, like all other composers of the period, he had no control of the publication and dissemination of his music once it left his hands; on the other, he was, like all famous men, subjected to intense scrutiny. It could not be thought, of course, that everyone approved of his music; it had been in years past far too controversial for that; but as far as his music was available, it was now being played all over Europe. Even his operas, those stepchildren of his muse which Haydn loved particularly, were beginning to circulate on the Continent: too late, for they were already 'old' compared to Haydn's own style *de anno* 1791 and, even more, to Mozart's brilliant works.

Early in November Haydn was invited to an official lunch given by the Lord Mayor of London. The description of it in the First London Notebook is a brilliant piece of reportage which shows that like all aspects of England in which noise dominated, Haydn was slightly repelled:

On 5th Nov. I was guest at a lunch given in honour of the Lord Mayor. The new Lord Mayor and his wife ate at the first table No. 1, then the Lord Chanceler and both the Scherifs, Duc de Lids [Leeds], Minister Pitt and the other judges of the first rank. At No. 2 I ate with Mr Silvester, the greatest lawyer and first Alderman of London. In this room (which is called the geld Hall [Guildhall]), there were 16 tables besides others in adjoining rooms; in all nearly 1200 persons dined, all with the greatest pomp. The food was very nice and well-cooked; many kinds of wine in abundance. The company sat down at 6 o'clock and arose at 8. The Lord Mayor was escorted according to rank before and also after dinner, and there were many ceremonies, a sword was carried in front of him, and a kind of golden crown, to the sound of trumpets, accompanied by a wind band. After dinner the distinguished company of [table] No. 1 retired to a separate room which had been chosen beforehand, to drink coffee and tea; we other guests, however, were taken to another adjoining room. At 9 o'clock No. 1 rose and went to a small room, at which point the ball began: in this room there is, *a parte*, an elevated place for the high *Nobless* where the Lord Mayor is seated on a throne together with his wife. Then the dancing begins according to rank, but only 1 couple, just as at Court on the King's Birthday, 6th January [*recte*: 4th June]. In this small room there are 4 tiers of raised benches on each side, where the fair sex mostly has the upper hand. Nothing but minuets are danced in this room; I couldn't stand it longer than a quarter of an hour; first, because the heat caused by so many people in such a small room was so great; and secondly, because of the wretched dance band, the entire orchestra consisting only of two violins and a violoncello. The minuets were more Polish than in our or the Italian manner. From there I went to another room, which was more like a subterranean cavern, and where the dance was English; the music was a little better, because there was a drum in the band which drowned the misery of the violins. I went on to the great hall, where we had eaten, and there the band was larger and more bearable. The dance was English, but only on the raised platform where the Lord Mayor and the first 4 numbers had dined; the other tables, however, were all occupied again by men who, as usual, drank enormously the whole night. The most curious thing, though, is that a part of the company went on dancing without hearing a single note of the music, for first at one table, then at another, some were yelling songs and some swilling it down and drinking toasts amid terrific roars of 'Hurrey, H[urrey], H[urrey]' and waving of glasses. The hall and all the other rooms are illuminated with lamps which give out an unpleasant odour. It is remarkable that the Lord Mayor requires no knife at table, for a carver . . . cuts up everything for him in advance. . . .

91 On 23 November, the second son of King George III, Frederick, Duke of York, married Princess Friederike Charlotte Ulricke, eldest daughter of the Prussian King Friedrich Wilhelm II. The royal pair had already been married in Berlin, but British law required that they marry again on English soil. The ceremony took place at seven o'clock in the evening, at Buckingham House (now Palace). The Duke of York was described by Mirabeau as 'puissant chasseur, puissant buveur, et puissant homme en cordialité pour les femmes mariées, et libre Comme un Seigneur Anglais'. Haydn adored the Duchess at first sight, and she was to become his faithful benefactress and patron. Everybody tried to make the girl feel at home. The handsome Prince of Wales went to greet the couple when they arrived at York House. The *European Magazine*, November 1791 (pp. 323ff.) reports:

On their arrival at York House they were received by his Royal Highness the Prince of Wales, who came thither about twenty minutes before. The Prince received the Duchess in the Great Hall, with that elegance so peculiar to him; his Highness taking her by the hand, saluted his royal sister, and congratulated her on her arrival in the German language, which the Prince speaks with great perfection.

121 The very next day, Haydn was whisked away to Oatlands, near Weybridge in Surrey, with the new royal couple:

On 24th Nov., I was invited by the Prince of Wales to visit his brother, the Duc du York, at eatland [Oatlands]. I stayed there 2 days and enjoyed many marks of graciousness and honour, not only from the Prince of Wales but also from the Duchess, daughter of the King of Prussia. The little castle, 18 miles from London, lies on a slope and commands the most glorious view. Among its many beauties is a most remarkable grotto which cost £25,000 Sterling, and which was 11 years in the building. It is very large and contains many diversions, *inter alia* actual water which flows in from various sides, a beautiful English garden, various entrances and exits, besides a most charming bath. The Duke bought this country estate for some £47,000 Sterling. On the 3rd day, the Duke had me taken 12 miles towards London with his horse and carriage.

The Prince of Wales wants my portrait. For 2 days we played music for 4 hours in the evening, that is, from 10 o'clock till 2 o'clock in the morning, then we had supper and went to bed at 3 o'clock.

98 The portrait mentioned was to be executed by John Hoppner and is one of the best known likenesses of Haydn; it is in the Royal Collection. He refers to

it again when writing a long report to Frau von Genzinger in Vienna, dated 20 December:

... I must take this opportunity of informing Your Grace that 3 weeks ago I was invited by the Prince of Wales to visit his brother, the Duke of York, at the latter's country seat. The Prince presented me to the Duchess, the daughter of the King of Prussia, who received me very graciously and said many flattering things. She is the most delightful lady in the world, is very intelligent, plays the pianoforte and sings very nicely. I had to stay there 2 days, because a slight indisposition prevented her attending the concert on the first day. On the 2nd day, however, she remained continually at my side from 10 o'clock in the evening, when the music began, to 2 o'clock in the morning. Nothing but Haydn was played. I conducted the symphonies from the pianoforte, and the sweet little thing sat beside me on my left and hummed all the pieces from memory, for she had heard them so often in Berlin. The Prince of Wales sat on my right side and played with us on his violoncello, quite tolerably. I had to sing, too. The Prince of Wales is having my portrait painted just now, and the picture is to hang in his room. The Prince of Wales is the most handsome man on God's earth; he has an extraordinary love of music and a lot of feeling, but not much money. *Nota bene*, this is between ourselves. I am more pleased by his kindness than by any financial gain. On the third day the Duke of York sent me two stages with his own span, since I couldn't catch the mail-coach.

Now, gracious lady, I would like to take you to task a little, for believing that I prefer the city of London to Vienna, and that I find the sojourn here more agreeable than that in my fatherland. I don't hate London, but I would not be capable of spending the rest of my life there, even if I could amass millions. I shall tell Your Grace the reason when I see you. I look forward tremendously to going home and to embracing all my good friends. I only regret that the great Mozart will not be among them, if it is really true, which I trust it is not, that he has died. Posterity will not see such a talent again in 100 years! I am delighted that Your Grace and your family are well. I have enjoyed excellent health up to now, thank God! but a week ago I got an attack of English rheumatism which was so severe that sometimes I had to cry aloud. I hope soon to get rid of it, however, inasmuch as I have adopted the usual custom here of wrapping myself in flannel from head to foot. I must ask you to excuse the fact that my handwriting is so poor today. ...

Unknown to Haydn, Mozart had died in Vienna on 5 December. When 78 the full details reached London, he was stunned; he never got over Mozart's loss and in later years tears would spring to his eyes whenever he saw one of the composer's sons. Haydn knew that Mozart's brother-Mason, Johann Michael Puchberg, the banker, had a special relationship to the young composer. Early in the New Year – the letter has survived only in fragments – Haydn wrote to Puchberg in Vienna:

[*German*]   London, January 1792.
... For some time I was beside myself about his [Mozart's] death, and I could not believe that Providence would so soon claim the life of such an indispensable man. I only regret that before his death he could not convince the English, who walk in darkness in this respect, of his greatness – a subject about which I have been sermonizing to them every single day. ... You will be good enough, my kind friend, to send me a catalogue of those pieces which are not yet known here, and I shall make every possible effort to promote such works for the widow's benefit; I wrote the poor woman three weeks ago, and told her that when her favourite son reaches the necessary age, I shall give him composition lessons to the very best of my ability, and at no cost, so that he can, to some extent, fill his father's position ...

Haydn must have remembered, with a stab of pain, how he and Mozart and Puchberg ('I am inviting only Haydn and yourself') had listened first to piano rehearsals and then to the orchestral rehearsals of *Così fan tutte* in January 1790. Haydn will probably not have known the extent of Mozart's debts to Puchberg (1,000 Gulden, equal to Haydn's annual salary in 1790). On 14 January 1792, Haydn wrote a long letter to his ex-mistress Luigia Polzelli, who had now found a position in the opera house at Piacenza.

[*Italian*]

My dearest Polzelli! This very moment I received your letter, and hasten to answer it. I am relieved that you are in good health, and that you have found a position in a little theatre; not so much because of the payment but to have the experience. I wish you every possible success, in particular a good rôle and a good teacher, who takes the same pains with you as did your Haydn. You write that you would like to send your dear Pietro to me; do so, for I shall embrace him with all my heart; he is always welcome, and I shall treat him as if he were my own son. I shall take him with me to Vienna. I shall remain in London until the middle of June, not longer, because my Prince and many other circumstances make it imperative that I return home. Nevertheless I shall try, if possible, to go to Italy, in order to see my dear Polzelli, but meanwhile you can send your Pietro to me here in London; he will always be either with me or with your sister, who is now alone and who has been separated quite some time now from her husband, that beast. She is unhappy, as you were, and I am very sorry for her. I see her but rarely, for I have a lot to do, especially now, when the Professional Concert has had my pupil Pleyel brought over, to face me as a rival; but I'm not afraid, because last year I made a great impression on the English and hope therefore to win their approval this year, too. My opera was not given, because *Sig.* Gallini didn't receive the licence from the King, and never will; to tell you the truth, the Italian opera has no success at all now, and by a stroke of bad luck, the Pantheon Theatre burned down just this very day, two hours after midnight. Your sister had been engaged in the last piece; I am sorry for all of them.

I am quite well, but am almost always in an 'English humour', that is, depressed, and perhaps I shall never again regain the good humour that I used to have when I was with you. Oh! my dear Polzelli: you are always in my heart, and I shall never, never forget you. I shall do my very best to see you, if not this year, then certainly the next, along with your son. I hope that you won't forget me, and that you will write me if you get married again, for I would like to know the name of him who is fortunate enough to have you. Actually I ought to be a little annoyed with you, because many people wrote me from Vienna that you had said the worst possible things about me, but God bless you, I forgive you everything, for I know you said it in love. Do preserve your good name, I beg you, and think from time to time about your Haydn, who esteems you and loves you tenderly, and will always be faithful to you. Write me, too, if you have seen and spoken with anyone who was formerly in Prince Esterházy's service. Good bye, my dear, that's all for this evening: it's late.

Today I went to see your dear sister, to ask her if she would be able to put up Pietro in her house. He will be received with the greatest pleasure; he can sleep there and have his meals there, too, since I always eat out and am invited out every day; but Pietro can come every day to me for his lessons – I live only a little way from your sister's. I give your sister a bit of money, because I am very sorry for her; she is not exactly poor, but she has to be very economical. I shall clothe your son well, and do everything for him. I don't want you to have any expense on his account; he shall have everything he needs. I shall certainly leave for Vienna in the middle of June, but I shall take the route *via* Holland, Leipzig and Berlin (in order to see the King of Prussia); my Petruccio will always be with me. I hope, however, that up to now he has been an obedient son to his dear mother, but if he hasn't been, I don't want him, and you must write me the truth. I don't want to have an ungrateful boy, for then I would be capable of sending him away at a moment's notice. Your sister embraces you and kisses you thousands and thousands of times. Write me often, dear Polzelli, and remember that I shall be always your faithful

Haydn.

Haydn and Salomon had been so successful in their 1791 season that it was to be expected that rival organizations would be jealous. The directors of the Professional Concert series, having tried without success to lure Haydn away from Salomon, now persuaded Haydn's star pupil, Ignaz Pleyel, to come to London as the principal composer for their organization's 1792 season. It is hard for us today to appreciate how popular Ignaz Pleyel's music 131 – which is all but forgotten today – was in 1792. Indeed, Pleyel was more popular in many parts of Europe than his master, and publishers vied with each other for Pleyel's latest compositions, which were clever but superficial imitations of the Haydn manner – a watered down version of the original, but easier on the minds, ears and fingers of many young ladies in London, Paris, Berlin and Vienna. Mozart thought very highly of Pleyel and imagined that one day the pupil might supplant the master; so we must realize that Pleyel was a formidable, potentially even dangerous, rival to Salomon and his series. Haydn alludes to the pressures on him in a letter to Frau von Genzinger dated 2 March 1792:

... there isn't a day, not a single day, in which I am free from work, and I shall thank the dear Lord when I can leave London – the sooner the better. My labours have been augmented by the arrival of my pupil Pleyel, whom the Professional Concert have brought here. He arrived here with a lot of new compositions, but they had been composed long ago; he therefore promised to present a new work every evening. As soon as I saw this, I realized at once that a lot of people were dead set against me, and so I announced publicly that I would likewise produce 12 different new pieces. In order to keep my word, and to support poor Salomon, I must be the victim and work the whole time. But I really do feel it. My eyes suffer the most, and I have many sleepless nights, though with God's help I shall overcome it all. The people of the Professional Concert wanted to put a spoke in my wheel, because I would not go over to them; but the public is just. I enjoyed a great deal of success last year, but still more this year. Pleyel's presumption is sharply criticized, but I love him just the same. I always go to his concerts, and am the first to applaud him. I am delighted that Your Grace and the family are well. Please give my kind respects to all of them. The time is drawing near when I must put my trunks in order. Oh! how happy I shall be to see Your Grace again, to show you how much I missed you and to show the esteem in which, gracious lady, you will ever be held by

Your most obedient servant,
Jos: Haydn.

At the Sixth Concert, on 23 March 1792, Haydn's Symphony No. 94 in G, soon to become known as the 'Surprise' Symphony, had its first performance. 201 According to the *Oracle* of 24 March:

The Second Movement was equal to the happiest of this great Master's conceptions. The surprise might not be unaptly likened to the situation of a beautiful Shepherdess who, lulled to slumber by the murmer of a distant Waterfall, starts alarmed by the unexpected firing of a fowling-piece. The flute obligato was delicious.

Griesinger elaborates on this slow movement in his biography of the composer (p. 32):

I asked [Haydn] once in jest if it were true that he wrote the Andante with the kettledrum beat in order to awaken the English public that had gone to sleep at his concert. 'No', he answered me. 'Rather it was my wish to surprise the public with something new, and to make a début in a brilliant manner so as not to be outdone by my pupil Pleyel, who at that time was engaged by an orchestra in London (in the year 1792) which had begun its concert series eight days before mine. The first *Allegro* of my symphony was received with countless bravos, but the enthusiasm reached its highest point in the *Andante with the kettledrum beat. Ancora, Ancora!* sounded from every throat, and even Pleyel complimented me on my idea.'

Haydn was clearly seeing a good deal of Rebecca Schroeter in his free moments. On 6th March they were together in the evening. Her letter the next day shows that their relationship had crossed a certain line and become a real love-affair. From her letters she sounds like a dear and attractive person:

March 7th 92.
My D: I was extremely sorry to part with you so suddenly last Night, our conversation was particularly interesting and I had [a] thousand affectionate things to say to you, my heart was and is full of TENDERNESS for you, but no language can express HALF the LOVE and AFFECTION I feel for you, you are DEARER to me EVERY DAY of my life. I am very sorry I was so dull and stupid yesterday, indeed my DEAREST it was nothing but my being indisposed with a cold occasion'd my Stupidity. I thank you a thousand times for your concern for me, I am truly sensible of your goodness, and I assure you my D. if any thing had happened to trouble me, I wou'd have open'd my heart, & told you with the most perfect confidence. Oh, how earnes[t]ly [I] wish to see you, I hope you will come to me to morrow. I shall be happy to see you both in the Morning and the Evening. God Bless you my love, my thoughts and best wishes ever accompany you, and I always am with the most sincere and invariable Regard my D:

My Dearest I cannot be happy
till I see you if you know,
do, tell me, when you will come

Mrs Schroeter liked to write notes the last thing before retiring so that her servant could deliver them the following morning. On 1 June she wrote:

My D^r I beg to know HOW YOU DO? hope to hear you[r] Head-ach is ENTIRELY GONE, and that you have SLEPT WELL. I shall be very happy to see you on Sunday any time convenient to you after one o'clock – I hope to see you my D^r L on tuesday as usual to Dinner, [crossed out: "and all (?night ? p.m.) with me"] – and I shall be much obliged to you if you will inform me what Day will be agreeable to you to meet M^r M^tris and MISS STONE at my house to Dinner, I shou'd be glad if it was either Thursday or Friday, whichever Day YOU PLEASE to fix, I will send to Mr Stone to let them know. I long to see you my D^t H, let me have that pleasure as soon as you can, till when and Ever I remain with the FIRMEST attachment My D^r L:
most faithfully and affectionately
yours [etc.]
Friday June ye 1st 792.

However, she soon disappears as a letter writer from Haydn's life: there are no known letters from the 1794–5 period. If they existed, were they, perhaps, copied into the Fourth London Notebook, which has come down to us incomplete? Or did the fact that Haydn lived in Bury Street, St James, in

1794–5, very near Mistress Schroeter, remove the necessity of their corresponding? She appears twice more in Haydn's 'official' biography: to her are dedicated three of Haydn's greatest piano Trios, Opus 73, in 1795; and she is known to have been a subscriber to *The Creation*. She also helped Haydn with an important contract in 1796 in which she appears as a witness.

Earlier that year, on April 10, Haydn had written to Prince Anton Esterházy in Austria, offering his services to the family once again.

112

Most Serene Prince of the Holy Roman Empire,
Gracious Lord and Sire!

Since I must leave England in a short time, I hasten to place my entire faithful services in all matters – as far as I shall be able to fulfil them – at Your SERENE HIGHNESS' disposal. Our concerts will be finished at the end of June, after which I shall begin the journey home without delay, in order to serve my most gracious Prince and Lord again. I am, in humble submission,

Your SERENE HIGHNESS'
Most humble Joseph Haydn, m.p.,
Capellmeister.

Haydn travelled back to Vienna via Bonn (July 1792), where he met a talented young man who was viola player in the Electoral Orchestra and who had composed in 1790 two spectacular Cantatas ('On the Death of Joseph II'; 'On the Elevation of Leopold II to Emperor'); one of these (or possibly both) was submitted to Haydn. The older composer was impressed and it was agreed that Beethoven, then aged 22, would accompany Haydn to England in the following year. In November 1792, Beethoven came to Vienna to begin his studies (in counterpoint and harmony) with Haydn but, as we know, the 1793 visit to England never materialized.

From Bonn, Haydn journeyed to meet his Prince at Frankfurt-am-Main, where on 14 July Leopold II was crowned Holy Roman Emperor. A few days later Haydn went to discuss publishing affairs with Bernhard Schott in the town of Biebrich on the Rhine; but Schott was never to become one of Haydn's personal publishers. On 24 July, Haydn arrived back in Vienna and took up his old quarters on the Wasserkunstbastei No. 992, at Herr Hamberger's (this historic house, now destroyed, was to be Beethoven's residence some years later). No Viennese newspaper recorded Haydn's arrival. If Viennese newspapers were reticent about Haydn's presence in the Imperial and Royal capital city, there was a general awareness of the triumphs achieved by Austria's leading composer while in England. Perhaps the most touching honour of all was a pyramid-shaped monument erected in 1793 by Count Harrach, the Lord of Rohrau, where Haydn had been born sixty-one years earlier. Count Harrach, upon being asked by Dies to explain how the monument came into being, wrote the following in a letter, which Dies quotes (140f.):

5

... The reason why I had a monument to Haydn placed in my garden was none other than the fact that, having come of age, I wanted to reorganize the flower-, vegetable-, fruit- and pheasant-gardens round my castle – a total of some forty *Joch* [= 16·83 hectares, or about $41\frac{1}{2}$ acres] – into, I won't dare say an English park, but at least a proper promenade, in the planning of which economic restrictions had of necessity to play a certain part.

I thought it right and proper, and also honourable for my park, to erect a monument for the so famous J. Haydn in the castle grounds which encompassed his birthplace. Haydn was

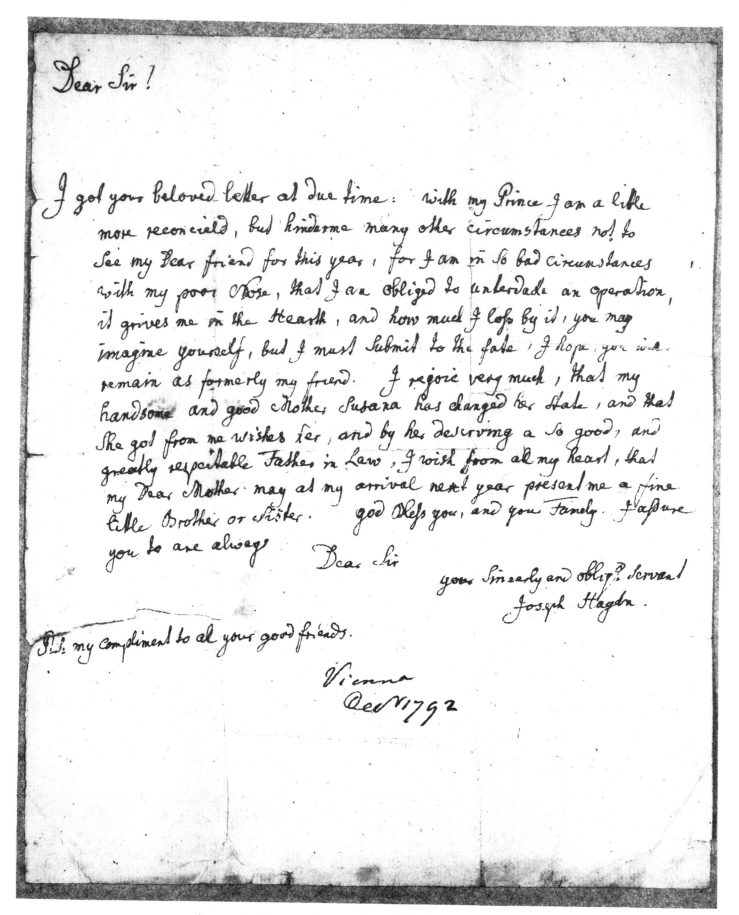

Dear Sir !

I got your beloved letter at due time : with my Prince I am a like more reconcield, but hinderme many other circumstances not to see my Dear friend for this year, for I am in so bad circumstances with my poor Nose, that I am obliged to unterdate an operation, it grieves me in the Hearth, and how much I loss by it, you may imagine yourself, but I must submit to the fate, I hope, you will remain as formerly my friend. I rejoic very much, that my handsome and good Mother Susana has changed her State, and that she got from me wishes for, and by her deserving a so good, and greatly respcitable Father in Law, I wish from al my heart, that my Dear Mother may at my arrival next year present me a fine little Brother or Sister. god bless you, and your Family. I assure you to are always

Dear Sir

your sincearly and oblig? servant
Joseph Haydn.

P.S. my compliment to al your good friends.

Vienna
Dec: 1792

A recently discovered letter written in English which Haydn sent from Vienna after he had returned there at the end of his first visit to England (the date was added in an unknown, but contemporary, hand). The friend to whom the letter was addressed and the members of his family referred to in it cannot be identified from the scanty evidence contained in Haydn's message.

then in England [so the plan must have been made in 1791 or 1792] and was but little known to me and had no idea of my undertaking; and it was not until two or three years later that he happened to hear that this monument in Rohrau existed and without my knowing it went to see it. . . .

Haydn offered, in 1804, to make provision in his Will to ensure that after his death the monument would continue to be cared for, and Count Harrach, not to be outdone, offered to subscribe a trust fund of 500 or 600 Gulden to see that the monument was protected. In any event, it is now in Haydn's birthplace, so beautifully restored by the Lower Austrian Government.

On 13 November Haydn wrote what would prove to be his last letter to Frau von Genzinger; she died a little over two months later – not yet forty-three years of age – on 20 January 1793.

Gracious Lady!

Apart from wishing you a Good Morning, this is to ask you to give the bearer of this letter the final big Aria in F minor from my opera, because I must have it copied for my Princess. I will bring it back to you myself in 2 days at the latest. Today I take the liberty of inviting myself to lunch, when I shall have the opportunity of kissing Your Grace's hands in return. Meanwhile I am, as always,

> Y[our] G[race's]
> Most obedient servant,
> Joseph Haydn.

Haydn had loved Frau von Genzinger perhaps more than he dared show in his letters. She had occupied a special place in his heart that neither *la* Polzelli nor even Rebecca Schroeter could replace.

The Napoleonic Wars soon made it problematical for Haydn to return to England across Europe in time for the new season of 1793, and on 21 January 1793, when Louis XVI was guillotined in Paris, it seemed that history had entered a new phase. The next month, George III, flanked by the Prince of Wales and the Duke of York, reviewed the first British expeditionary force to be sent to the Continent.

Prince Anton Esterházy was all against Haydn undertaking a new visit to England (Haydn had 'acquired enough fame for himself'), and for the moment, the old composer acquiesced. He busied himself with many activities: in November 1792 he wrote Twelve German Dances and Twelve Minuets (IX:11 and 12) which were performed with a huge orchestra (the original parts have survived) including double woodwind (4 flutes, 4 oboes, etc.) and sixteen (or for the Minuets ten) first violins. These were the greatest sets of Dances he had hitherto composed, and are rivalled in strength, sophistication and beauty only by the Twenty-Four Minuets for orchestra (1795–8?; IX:16). Haydn spent the summer months of 1793 at Eisenstadt, taking his pupil Beethoven with him, and in the autumn he wrote to inform Maximilian Franz, Elector of Cologne and Beethoven's patron, that the young man 'will in time fill the position of one of Europe's greatest composers, and I shall be proud to be able to speak of myself as his teacher.' That summer of 1793, Haydn purchased a pretty little house in the Viennese suburb of Gumpendorf, where he intended to retire; it is now the Haydn Museum of Vienna. 185

In June, from Eisenstadt, Haydn had to write to the tiresome Polzelli about money (as usual) and other devious manipulations of his ex-mistress:

Dear Polzelli!

I hope that you will have received the two hundred florins [Gulden] which I sent *via* Sig. Buchberg [Puchberg] – and perhaps also the other hundred, a total of 300 florins; I wish I were able to send more, but my income is not large enough to permit it. I beg you to be patient with a man who up to now has done more than he really could. Remember what I have given and sent to you; why, it's scarcely a year ago that I gave you six hundred florins! Remember how much your son costs me, and how much he will cost me until such a day as he is able to earn his own daily bread. Remember that I cannot work so hard as I have been able to do in the years past, for I am getting old and my memory is gradually getting less reliable. Remember, finally, that for this and many other reasons I cannot earn any more than I do, and that I don't have any other salary except the pension of my Prince Nicolaus Esterházy (God rest his soul), and that this pension is barely sufficient to keep body and soul together, particularly in these critical times. . . . At present I am alone with your son in Eisenstadt, and I shall stay here for a little while to get some fresh air and have a little rest. You will receive a letter from your son along with mine; he is in good health, and kisses your hand for the watch. I shall stay in Vienna until the end of September, and then I intend to take a trip with your son, and perhaps – perhaps – to go to England again for a year; but that depends mainly on whether the battleground changes; if it doesn't, I shall go somewhere else, and perhaps – perhaps – I shall see you in Naples. My wife is still sick most of the time, and is always in a foul humour, but I don't really care any more – after all, this woe will pass away one day. Apart from this, I am much relieved that you, for your part, are a little more relieved about your dear sister. God bless you and keep you in good health! I shall see to it that you receive what

A page from Haydn's *Andante con variazioni* in F minor for piano (1793), from a copy made by Johann Elssler; the passage reproduced shows the dramatic and stormy coda, the turbulent style of which looks forward to Beethoven's middle period (as it happens, the date of composition of this work – generally regarded as Haydn's greatest 'small' piano piece – coincides with Beethoven's studies as a pupil of Haydn) and even to Chopin.

little I can offer you, but now you really must be patient for a while, because I have other onerous debts; I can tell you that I have almost nothing for all my pains, and live more for others than for myself. I hope to have an answer before you leave for Naples. . . .

While in Vienna during 1793, Haydn gave two public performances of his new London works. The first was at the Small Redoutensaal on 15 March and it included three of the London Symphonies; it was a great success ('Il etoit charmant', writes Count Zinzendorf in his Diary). At the end of the year, the Tonkünstler-Societät invited Haydn to conduct their annual Christmas concert for the benefit of the widows and orphans of poor musicians. Although Haydn had long not been 'on speaking terms' with the Society – the rupture had occurred over his successful oratorio *Il ritorno di Tobia*, performed in 1775, and repeated in revised form in 1784, and performance rights that the Society wanted Haydn to give them at their discretion – he agreed and gave his *Madrigal* 'The Storm' (XXIVa:18), originally composed with English words for the Salomon series of 1792 and now offered in a new German translation, possibly by Baron Gottfried van Swieten, who would, in due course, provide the libretto for each of the late oratorios; he also conducted a chorus from *Il ritorno di Tobia* and three of the London Symphonies (No. 94 certainly, No. 95 probably, and a third, unidentified, work). The daughter of Haydn's old friend, *Hofrat* Franz von Greiner, Caroline (later married Pichler, a court official) wrote some appalling dedicatory verses to commemorate the performance of Haydn's 'six new Symphonies written in England'.) The *Wiener Zeitung* wrote:

Haydn himself conducted the orchestra, which consisted of over 180 persons, and the excellent performance moved the public, which appeared in large numbers, to show its complete satisfaction by often repeated and vigorous demonstrations of its undivided approval.

Eventually, Haydn persuaded his benign Prince Anton Esterházy to allow a new English trip; Baron van Swieten lent his travelling coach, and this time, taking his valet and excellent music copyist, Johann Elssler, Haydn set off for London on 19 January 1794. He installed himself at No. 1 Bury Street (St James's), near Rebecca Schroeter, whose house at No. 6 James Street, Buckingham Gate, lay an easy ten minutes' walk via St James's Palace and The Mall, along St James's Park. On his return, Haydn brought with him, complete, a new symphony (usually referred to as 'Overture') to be performed at the first Salomon concert; this was No. 99 in E Flat, the first symphony in which he used clarinets. The 1794 concert series was to have opened on 3 February, but in the event was postponed for a week partly owing to Haydn's arrival having been delayed until 5 February. The following announcement was placed by Salomon in several London newspapers (*Oracle*, *Public Advertiser*, *Morning Chronicle* etc.) during January:

MR. SALOMON'S CONCERT, HANOVER-SQUARE.
MR. SALOMON most respectfully acquaints the Nobility and Gentry, that his CONCERTS will open on Monday the 3rd of February next, and continue on every succeeding Monday (Passion and Easter Week excepted).

Dr. HAYDN will supply the Concerts with New Compositions, and direct the Execution of them at the Piano Forte.

Principal Vocal Performers are, MADAME MARA, and Mr. FISCHER, One of the King of Prussia's principal opera Singers, who never appeared in this Country before.

Principal Instrumental Performers, who will play Concertos and Concertantes on their respective Instruments, are – Violins, Signor Viotti and Mr. Salomon – Piano Forte, Mr. Dussek – Oboe, Mr. Harrington – German Flute, Mr. Ash[e]. – Pedal Harp, Madame KRUMPHOLTZ.

Besides other distinguished Performers, who will appear occasionally.

Subscriptions at Five Guineas for the Twelve Concerts received, and Tickets delivered, at Messrs Lockarts, Maxtone, Wallis, and Clark, Pall Mall.

The Ladies' Tickets are blue, and transferable to Ladies; and the Gentlemen's are red, and transferable to Gentlemen only.

No less than four daily newspapers reviewed the first concert of Salomon's series; the whole of London's non-operatic musical attention was now centred on this series, the Professional Concert having ceased to exist after the abortive 1793 season. On 11 February the *Morning Chronicle* reported:

SALOMON'S CONCERT.

This superb Concert was last night opened for the season, and with such an assemblage of talents as make it a rich treat to the amateur. The incomparable HAYDN, produced an Overture of which it is impossible to speak in common terms. It is one of the grandest efforts of art that we ever witnessed. It abounds with ideas, as new in music as they are grand and impressive; it rouses and affects every emotion of the soul. – It was received with rapturous applause.

VIOTTI produced a new Concerto, in which his own execution was most delicate and touching; nothing could be more exquisite than his tones in the second movement. We have no doubt but both these pieces will be called for again; for they are to be ranked among the finest productions of which music has to boast.

DUSSEK had also a new Concerto on the *piano forte*, in his best manner; and Madame MARA sung divinely.

Symphony No. 99 was repeated at the Second Concert (17 February), and the critic of the *Morning Chronicle* singled out the beautiful woodwind playing in the famous solo wind section of the second movement: but '... indeed the pleasure the whole gave was continual; and the genius of Haydn, astonishing, inexhaustible, and sublime, was the general theme.'

Apart from the new symphonies, Haydn brought to Salomon the new Quartets (Opp. 71 and 74), which this great leader performed during the course of the season and which were subsequently published in London. In the Fourth Concert (3 March), Haydn conducted the première of his newest symphonic masterpiece, No. 101 ('The Clock'), which was received with jubilation. Both the first and second movements had to be repeated – 'It was HAYDN: what can we, what need we say more', concluded the *Morning Chronicle*; while the *Oracle* noted of 'The Clock' that 'the connoisseurs admit [it] to be his best work.'

In the Eighth Concert (31 March), Haydn conducted the first performance of the third of his new symphonies, No. 100 in G ('The Military') which, as the criticisms were soon to show, would be the greatest success of his whole career, surpassing even the popularity of 'The Surprise': he had somehow caught the spirit of the day in a miraculous way. The *Morning Chronicle* of 9 April reported:

... Another new Symphony, by Haydn, was performed for the second time; and the middle movement was again received with absolute shouts of applause. Encore! encore! encore! resounded from every seat: the Ladies themselves could not forbear. It is the advancing to battle; and the march of men, the sounding of the charge, the thundering of the onset, the clash of arms, the groans of the wounded, and what may well be called the hellish roar of war increase to a climax of horrid sublimity! which, if others can conceive, he alone can execute; at least he alone hitherto has effected these wonders.

The review obviously refers to bars 152ff. of the Allegretto; 'the climax of horrid sublimity' describes the ominous kettledrum roll (bars 159f.) and the ensuing tutti (bar 161).

Salomon's last concert of the season took place on 12 May, and it is clear from the criticisms, that men in London realized more than ever before that these concerts were continually creating musical history and it must have occurred to more than one astute mind that these great Haydn symphonies were in fact entering the permanent repertoire on the first night of their respective débuts. Haydn had been persuaded to remain another season, and this fact was apparently announced to the, no doubt delighted, audience on 12 May.

One reason why Haydn may have shown himself willing to stay on in England had been the death of Prince Anton Esterházy ('from a sudden bursting of a pus sac in his rib-cage'). In such circumstances there seemed to be no reason why Haydn should not settle permanently in England – his professional future was, after all, assured – and there is every evidence to suggest that he was seriously considering the prospect during the season of 1794. However, at this critical juncture in his career Haydn received an all-important letter containing the intentions of Prince Anton's successor, Nicolaus II, who was visiting Italy; the letter, which has not survived, was sent from Naples, as Dies (155f.) records:

About half a year after Haydn's arrival in London, a letter was sent him in the name of the [then] reigning Prince Nicolaus [II] Esterházy (who was at that time travelling through Italy) from Naples, which contained the news: 'The Prince has named Haydn his *Kapellmeister*, and wishes to restore the whole band again.' Haydn received this news with the greatest pleasure. He had entertained for a long time the warmest sympathy for the Princes Esterházy; they had offered him his daily bread and (what was more important) given him the opportunity of developing his musical talents. Haydn saw, of course, that his income in England was large, and that it by far exceeded that in his fatherland. Moreover, it would have been easy for him to secure any kind of well-paid position there [in England]. Since the death of Prince Anton, he was a completely free man; nothing bound him to the princely house except love and gratitude. It was those things, however, that silenced every opposition and persuaded him to accept the offer of Prince Nicolaus with joy and, as soon as his commitments in London were fulfilled, to return to his native country.

There were probably three important reasons which motivated Haydn's decision to return: (1) The pace at which he lived in England was simply too quick for a man of over sixty to be able to keep up for any length of time; he had especially felt this towards the end of the 1792 season. (2) The Terror in France was approaching its ghastly climax, and with the war going badly for the Allies: on 10 July the French occupied Brussels, in August Trier (Trèves) which they successfully defended against Allied counter-attacks, and in

October they attacked Holland and drove out the English troops. In view of all this, Haydn thought it was best to be in his own country and where his own native language was spoken (he never achieved fluency in English). (3) Haydn knew that in his old age, he would be taken care of by Prince Esterházy, that he would never starve or lack for bodily comforts; and who, in England, would do that for him? Perhaps with some deep-rooted instinct, Haydn sensed that he would live to be (for the times) a very old man and would stop composing. In the event, he did have a comfortable old age, honoured by the Esterházy family (especially Nicolaus II's wife, the Princess

139 Marie Hermenegild), by the Emperor, and especially by the Empress Marie Therese. His decision was a wise one, even if he had grown very fond of England and his English friends.

For the moment, however, Haydn stayed on. He had always enjoyed travelling in England, and in the summer of 1794, his journeyings outside the

117 capital were widespread. In July he visited Hampton Court and from
118 there went on to Portsmouth: Haydn loved ships and was friends with several British captains, one of whom had given him a memorable lunch on board an East India merchantman in August 1791. From Portsmouth, the composer crossed the Solent to the Isle of Wight. In August he went with two friends to

114 Bath, where he stayed at Perrymead, the house of the famous Italian-born
116 castrato, Venanzio Rauzzini, for whom Mozart had composed 'Exsultate, jubilate' (K.165) in Milan in January 1773. In his notebook, Haydn recorded his impressions in some detail:

On 2nd August 1794, I left at 5 o'clock in the morning for Bath, with Mr Ashe and Mr Cimador, and arrived there at 8 o'clock in the evening. It's 107 miles from London. The Mail Coach does this distance in 12 hours. I lived at the house of Herr Rauzzini, a *Musicus* who is very famous, and who in his time was one of the greatest singers. He has lived there 19 years, supports himself by the Subscription Concerts which are given in the Winter, and by giving lessons. He is a very nice and hospitable man. His summer house, where I stayed, is situated on a rise in the middle of a most beautiful neighbourhood, from which you can see the whole city. Bath is one of the most beautiful cities in Europe. All the houses are built of stone; this stone comes from quarries in the surrounding mountains; it is very soft, so soft, in fact, that it's no trouble to cut it up into any desired shape; it is very white, and the older it is, once it has been taken from the quarry, the harder it gets. The whole city lies on a slope, and that is why there are very few carriages; instead of them, there are a lot of sedan-chairs, who will take you quite a ways for 6 pence. But too bad that there are so few straight roads; there are a lot of beautiful squares, on which stand the most magnificent houses, but which cannot be reached by any vehicle: they are now building a brand new and broad street.

N.B. Today, on the 3rd, I looked at the city, and found, half-way up the hill, a building shaped like a half-moon, and more magnificent than any I had seen in London. The curve extends for 100 fathoms, and there is a Corinthian column at each fathom. The building has 3 floors. Round about it, the pavement in front of the houses is 10 feet broad for the pedestrians, and the street as wide *a proportione*; it is surrounded by an iron fence, and a terrace slopes down 50 fathoms in successive stages, through a beautiful expanse of green; on both sides there are little paths, by which one can descend very comfortably.

Every Monday and Friday evening all the bells are rung, but apart from this, you don't hear many bells being rung. The city is not thickly populated, and in Summer one sees very few people; for the people taking the baths don't come till the beginning of October, and stay through half of February. But then a great many people come, so that in the year 1791, 25,000 persons were there. All the inhabitants live off this influx, without which the city would be very poor: there are very few merchants and almost no trade, and everything is very dear. The baths are by nature very warm; one bathes in the water, and one also drinks it – generally the latter. And one pays very little: to bathe it costs 3 shillings at all times. I made the acquaintance there of Miss Brown, a charming person of the best *conduit*; a good pianoforte player, her mother a most beautiful woman. The city is now building a most splendid room for guests taking the cure.

A touching story concerning Rauzzini is recounted by Dies (127f.):

Rauzzini had in his garden a monument to his best friend, who had been snatched from him by death. In the inscription, he lamented the loss of such a true friend, &c., and concluded his lament with the words: 'He was not a man – he was a dog.'

Haydn secretly copied this inscription and composed a four-part canon to the words. Rauzzini was surprised: he liked the canon so much that he had it incised on the monument, to the honour of Haydn's and the dog's.

Another personal touch is revealed in the compliment paid to Haydn by Dr Henry Harington, a composer then living in Bath, who wrote a poem of praise' What art expresses'; on receiving this tribute, Haydn promptly set it to music. This episode inspired Muzio Clementi to observe: 115
122

The first doctor [Harington] having bestowed much praise on the second doctor [Haydn], the said second doctor – out of doctorial gratitude – returns the first doctor thanks for all favour received, and praises in his turn the said first doctor most handsomely.

From Bath Haydn went on to visit Bristol, and three weeks later the indefatigable composer went to visit Sir Charles Rich at Waverley Abbey, near Farnham in Surrey – 'I must confess that whenever I looked at this beautiful wilderness, my heart was oppressed at the thought that all this once belonged to my religion' (Haydn's Diary).

Haydn now came more and more to the attention of the Royal Family. In the Fourth Notebook, is his description:

On 1st February 1795, I was invited by the Prince of Wales to attend a musical soirée at the Duke of York's, which the King, the Queen, her whole family, the Duke of Orange &c. attended. Nothing else except my own compositions was played; I sat at the pianoforte; finally I had to sing, too. The King, who hitherto could or would only hear Handel's music, was attentive; he chatted with me, and introduced me to the Queen, who said many complimentary things to me. I sang my German song, 'Ich bin der verliebteste'. On 3rd Feb., I was invited to the Prince of Wales'; on 15th, 17th and 19th Apr. 1795, I was there again, and   119
on the 21st at the Queen's in Buckingham House.   91

There are many descriptions of this event, which must have been one of the highpoints of Haydn's whole life. By far the most interesting description is in William Parke's *Memoirs* (I,196f.) published in 1830:

... At the end of the first part of the concert Haydn had the distinguished honour of being formally introduced to His Majesty George III., by His Royal Highness the Prince of Wales. My station at the time was so near to the King, that I could not avoid hearing the whole of their conversation. Amongst other observations, His Majesty said (in English) 'Doctor Haydn, you have written a great deal.' To which Haydn modestly replied, 'Yes, Sire, a great deal more than is good.' To which the King neatly rejoined, 'Oh no, the world contradicts that.'

After his introduction, Haydn, by desire of the Queen, sat down to the pianoforte, and, surrounded by Her Majesty and her royal and accomplished daughters, sung, and accompanied himself admirably in several of his *Canzonets*. The gracious reception Haydn experienced from the King was not only gratifying to *his* feelings, but flattering to the science he professed; and while it displayed the condescension and liberality of a great and good monarch, it could not fail proving a powerful stimulus to rising *genius*.

The 'German Song' referred to by Haydn in his Notebook is in fact a translation of 'Transport of Pleasure' from the Second Set of Canzonettas.

Meanwhile, Salomon had come to a momentous decision: he was going to relinquish his concerts and merge forces with the Opera. In a very long open letter to the Press, he gives his reasons for so doing, the principal one being the difficulty of finding singers willing to cross the English Channel. The great Salomon concerts were at an end, then – but not in fact, for very long, for in 1796 Salomon found that he could start them up again. Haydn was not particularly worried, since the new organization had obviously approached him at once and secured his services. The Opera Concert series of 1795 was led by the great violinist and composer Giovan Battista Viotti, who fled from France to England in 1793; he was at the head of a very large orchestra of sixty players, and it was for this splendid group that Haydn composed his last three symphonies, Nos. 102–4. The first of these was the *pièce de résistance* of the First Concert (2 February), while the 'Drum Roll' Symphony (No. 103) was first played at the Fourth Concert (2 March) and 'excited the deepest attention'. Coincidentally, that very night, in Vienna, Beethoven made his début at a concert given by Prince Lobkowitz and 'made everyone sit up and listen' (Zinzendorf, Diary).

The big event of the London season was Haydn's benefit concert on 4 May, perhaps the greatest concert of his life. At this spectacular event, two new pieces by Haydn were played for the first time: Symphony No 104, 'The 12th which I have composed in England', wrote Haydn on the autograph, perhaps with a certain sense of destiny; and the beautiful *Scena di Berenice* for Brigida Giorgi Banti, one of the great cantatas of the century and the model for Beethoven's *Scena* 'Ah, perfido!' composed a year later in Prague. Some of the greatest singers in the world participated, not only *la* Banti but also *la* Morichelli, her great rival, and Morelli.

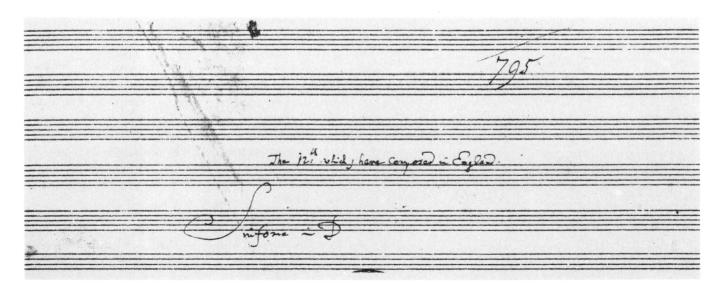

Haydn's inscription on the title page of Symphony No. 104 (1795); cf. text above.

NEW MUSICAL FUND,

Under the PATRONAGE of Their ROYAL HIGHNESSES

The PRINCE of WALES and DUKE of YORK.

At the KING's *THEATRE, in the* HAY-MARKET,

On MONDAY the 20th of APRIL, 1795,

WILL BE PERFORMED

A Grand Miscellaneous Concert

OF

VOCAL AND INSTRUMENTAL MUSIC,

FOR THE BENEFIT OF

The New Musical Fund,

ESTABLISHED FOR

The Relief of Decayed Musicians, their Widows and Orphans,

RESIDING IN ENGLAND.

Leader of the Band, Mr. CRAMER.

Conductors, Dr. HAYES and Dr. MILLER,

Dr. HAYDN will preside at the Forte Piano.

Mr. GREATOREX at the Organ, built for the Occasion, by Mr. ELLIOTT, with the Long Movement.

N. B. The Band will consist of Four Hundred Performers, for which an Orchestra will be erected on the Stage.

ACT I.		ACT II.	
GRAND CHORUS in the Dettengen Te Deum	HANDEL.	GRAND SYMPHONY, M. S.	HAYDN.
SONG, Mrs. SECOND		and performed under his immediate Direction	
CONCERTO GRAND FORTE PIANO, Mr. SMART, Jun.	CRAMER.	SONG, Mr. HARRISON	
SONG, Mr. BARTLEMAN		PLEYEL'S CELEBRATED CONCERTANTE (*by desire*) Messrs. CRAMER, F. CRAMER, H. SMART, SMITH, &c.	
CONCERTO VIOLONCELLO, Mr. LINDLEY		A Favorite GLEE	
SONG, Madam BANTI, with Violin Obligato, Mr. CRAMER		SONG, Mrs. HARRISON	
CONCERTO GERMAN FLUTE, Mr. ASHE		CONCERTO VIOLIN, Madam GILLBERG, being her Second Public Performance in England	
AIR and GRAND CHORUS, " Glory to God"	HANDEL.	GRAND CHORUS, " How excellent Thy Name" (Saul)	HANDEL.

PIT and BOXES, 10s. 6d.   GALLERY, 5s.

☞ The Doors to be opened at SEVEN o'Clock, and the Performance begin at EIGHT precisely.

Subscriptions are received, and Tickets delivered, at Messrs. Ransom, Moreland, Hammersley, and Co.'s, Bankers, Pall Mall; Messrs. Longman and Co.'s Music Warehouses, Cheapside and Haymarket; Messrs. Thompson's, St. Paul's Church-yard; Mr. Fentum's, No. 78, Strand; Mr. Forster's, No. 348, ditto; Mr. Preston's, ditto; Mr. Buckinger's, ditto; Messrs. Lewis, Houston, and Hide's, Holborn; Mr. Birchall's, New Bond Street; Mr. Miller's, Stationer, Old Bond Street; Messrs. Bett's, Royal Exchange; at the Secretary's, Mr. H. King, No. 358, near the Pantheon, Oxford Street; and of the Society's Treasurer, Mr. Smart, at his Music Warehouse, Corner of Argyll Street, Oxford Street.

N. B. A Subscriber, paying ONE GUINEA, will have TWO TICKETS, each of which will admit One Person to any Part of the House.

Such LADIES and GENTLEMEN as may be desirous of encouraging the Society, by subscribing to the Annual Performance, are respectfully informed, that Tickets (emblematical of the Institution, and which may be retained by Subscribers) are ready for Delivery at the above-mentioned Places.

The Subscribers to the OPERA, who may wish to retain their Boxes for the above Benefit, are respectfully intreated to signify their Intentions to Mr. SHELMANDINE, at the Theatre, on or before Tuesday, April 14th, otherwise they will be disposed of.

SAMPSON LOW, Printer, No. 7, Berwick Street, Soho, opposite the Chapel.

A copy of the handbill for the charity concert at the King's Theatre, Haymarket, 20 April 1795; on this occasion Haydn, as well as presiding 'at the Forte Piano', conducted one of his own Symphonies – as was customary in his London concert appearances – immediately after the interval.

After this spectacular benefit concert, which brought the composer 4,000 Gulden in cash, Haydn continued to appear, not only at the Opera Concert (which extended its season by two concerts), but at the benefit concerts for his friends, such as Miss Corri (now Mrs Dussek), the oboist Hindmarsh or the flautist Andrew Ashe ('The house was quite full', wrote Haydn in his diary); these concerts took place in late May and early June.

On 16 May, Haydn was a witness at the marriage between Therese Jansen and Gaetano Bartolozzi at St James's Church, Piccadilly. The other witnesses were Charlotte Jansen, Gaetano's father Francis (Francesco) Bartolozzi, the famous engraver, and Maria Adelaide de la Heras. Haydn composed his last three Piano Sonatas (Nos. 60–62; XVI:50–52) in 1794 for Miss Jansen and would later write three Piano Trios for her.

For the next two months Haydn lived quietly in London, supervising publications of his latest works (e.g. Three Piano Trios Nos. 35–37, XV:21–3, dedicated to Princess Marie Hermenegild Esterházy; they appeared in London on 13 June), and completing various new pieces, such as the final six English Canzonettas, and three Piano Trios (including the celebrated 'Gypsy Rondo') dedicated to Mrs Schroeter. He made a catalogue of his works composed in England which he put into one of his Notebooks: it comprises what Haydn called '768 sheets', a sheet meaning four pages, i.e. a total of over 3,000 pages – and almost every work a masterpiece. It was a staggering achievement for a man in his sixties.

126

On 15 August, Haydn left England, never to return. Griesinger (23) tells us that the composer

made through his three-year sojourn in England some 24,000 Gulden, of which about 9,000 were used for the trips, for his stay, and for other costs. . . . Haydn often repeated that he first became famous in Germany through England . . . [p. 35]. [He] considered the days spent in England the happiest of his life. He was everywhere appreciated there, it opened a new world to him, and he could, through his rich earnings, at last escape the restricted circumstances in which he had grown grey: for in the year 1790 he had owned barely 2,000 Gulden capital.'

The entry for 16 May 1795 in the marriage register of St James's, Piccadilly, where Haydn acted as a witness at the wedding of Gaetano Bartolozzi and Therese Jansen; cf. text above.

IV
THE LATE YEARS
IN VIENNA
1796~1809

'... I was also never so devout as during that time
when I was working on *The Creation*; every day
I fell on my knees and asked God to give me strength to
enable me to pursue the work to its successful conclusion ...'

GRIESINGER, 54

133 Wax portrait bust of Haydn by Franz Christian
Thaller, *c.* 1799. Of the three busts known to have been
made by Thaller, this is the only surviving example;
extremely life-like, it is reputed to be clothed in garments
worn by the composer and to show his wig made from his
own hair. The bust is preserved in the Kunsthistorisches
Museum, Vienna.

The Emperor Franz II and the new Austrian anthem, 1797

134–138 In the midst of the upheaval in Europe caused by Napoleon's territorial ambitions, Haydn composed his *Volcks Lied* 'Gott erhalte' (in the general manner of the British anthem 'God Save the King' and as a counter to France's *Marseillaise*) for the birthday of the Emperor, seen *(right)* in a portrait by Carl Kaspar (1747–1809); the courtyard of the Imperial Palace in Vienna – the Hofburg – is seen (below) in an engraving after a drawing by C. Schütz, 1785.

The commissioning of a new anthem designed to boost patriotic morale was largely due to the initiative of Franz Joseph, Count Saurau, portrayed *(opposite, below)* by F. H. Füger, 1797. Haydn's 'Gott erhalte' won immediate and lasting approval; his final draft of the vocal part is shown opposite, with *(below)* a Vienna porcelain plate decorated with the four verses of the anthem by Painter No. 77 (Johann Georg Gment) in 1809.

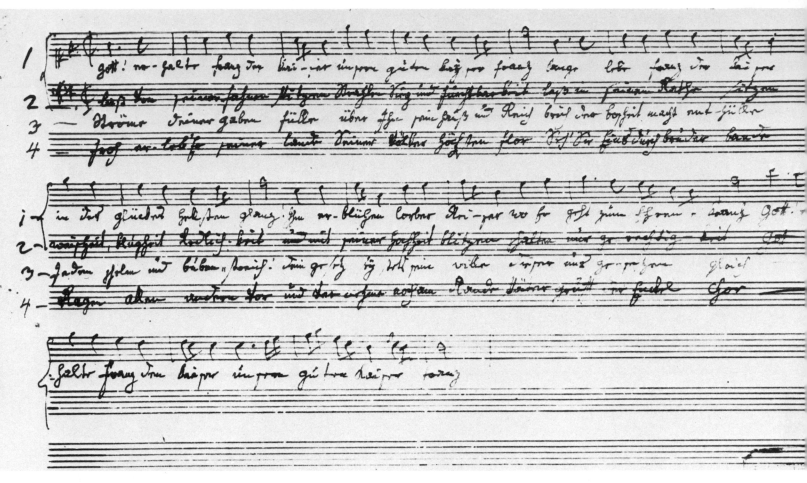

139 Princess Marie Hermenegild Esterházy (*née* Princess Liechtenstein), portrayed by Elisabeth Vigée-Lebrun, 1798. The Princess, with whom Haydn was on excellent terms, helped him in many ways in his late years, interceding when necessary with her husband, Prince Nicolaus II (cf. p. 173); the six great Masses of the period 1796–1802 were composed by Haydn for performance on her name-day.

140 Haydn at the age of 67, as depicted by J. C. Roesler. This portrait in oils, painted in Vienna, is dated 1799; it now hangs in the Music Faculty of Oxford University.

141 The young Beethoven *(below)*, the rising star of the Viennese musical scene, about the turn of the century; this somewhat idealized portrait by J. W. Mähler, *c.* 1804/5, is one of four portraits of the composer painted by this artist.

142 Therese Saal, the leading soprano who was the toast of Vienna in the early years of the new century; in this painting by F. H. Füger the singer is shown holding music from Haydn's *Creation*, in which work she sang the part of Eve at its first public performance in 1799.

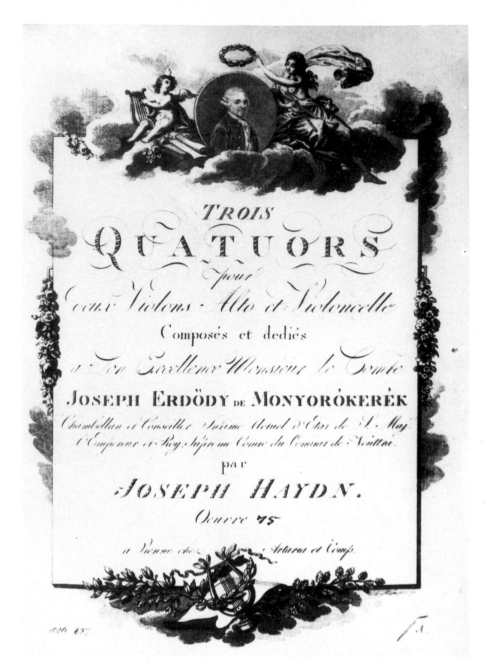

143, 144 The title page *(left)* of the Artaria edition (1799) of Haydn's String Quartets, Nos. 1–3 of Op. 76 – here listed as 'Op. 75'; this group of Quartets, completed in 1797, was commissioned by and dedicated to Joseph, Count Erdödy *(below)*, with whose family Haydn was on friendly terms for many years.

145 Franz Joseph Maximilian, Prince Lobkowitz, another of Haydn's patrons and subsequently one of Beethoven's principal Viennese patrons; the two Quartets of Haydn's Op. 77, composed in 1799, were dedicated to the Prince (cf. ill. 205).

146–148 Much of our authentic information about Haydn's late years and Viennese society of the period derives from the first-hand accounts of G. A. Griesinger *(left)*, Frederik Samuel Silverstolpe *(centre)* and Carl, Count von Zinzendorf. Griesinger, an official at the Saxonian Embassy, was for many years Haydn's go-between in his dealings with the Leipzig publishers Breitkopf & Härtel, while Silverstolpe – who was attached to the Swedish Embassy in Vienna – left invaluable notes about the composer; for his part, Zinzendorf kept detailed MS. diaries recording events in the Austrian capital.

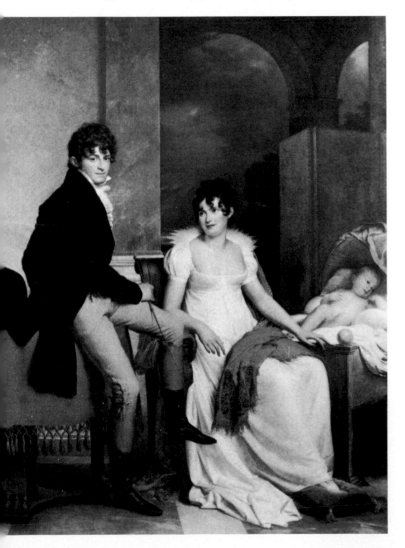

149, 150 Among Haydn's patrons were Moritz, Count Fries (a prominent Viennese banker), and his wife; the Fries family is depicted *(left)* in an informal group portrait by François Gérard, and a musical soirée at the palace of Count Fries – the type of social event in which Haydn frequently participated – is shown *(above)* in a drawing by J. Fischer, 1800. Haydn's last (unfinished) String Quartet, 'Op. 103' of 1803, was dedicated to the Count.

151, 152 The first performance of Haydn's great Oratorio was given in Vienna at the Palace of Johann Joseph Nepomuk, Prince Schwarzenberg, in April 1798; a coloured engraving by Carl Schütz *(above)* shows the Neuer Markt (Mehlmarkt), as it was in that year, with the Schwarzenberg Palace, since destroyed, in the centre background. The regular semiprivate concerts for the nobility given by the Prince, seen *(left)* in a portrait by Oelenhainz, were witnessed by, among others, Silverstolpe and Zinzendorf (cf. ills. 147, 148).

153-155 Three aspects of the realization of what was to become the *chef d'œuvre* of Haydn's late years: the opening of the autograph libretto by Baron Gottfried van Swieten (with, in the left margin, suggestions to the composer) shows the German text as adapted by Swieten from the English originally intended for Handel (Haydn's oratorio was published with parallel texts); Haydn's sketch for the orchestral Introduction 'Chaos' is compared *(below)* with the opening of the first violin part from the original performance material copied out by Johann Elesler (with some dynamic markings added by the composer).

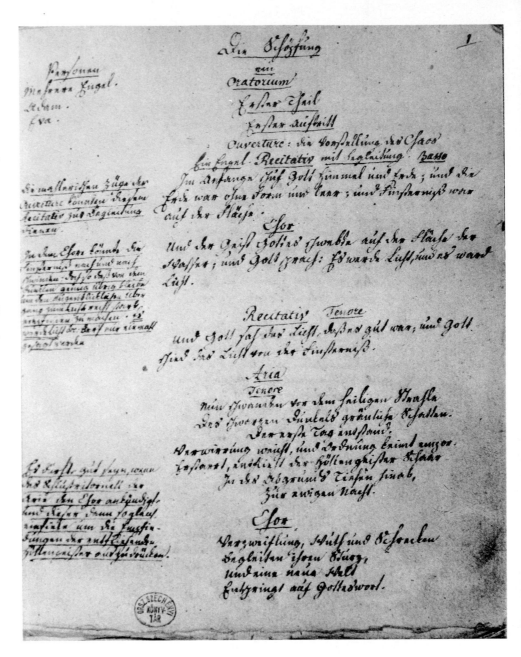

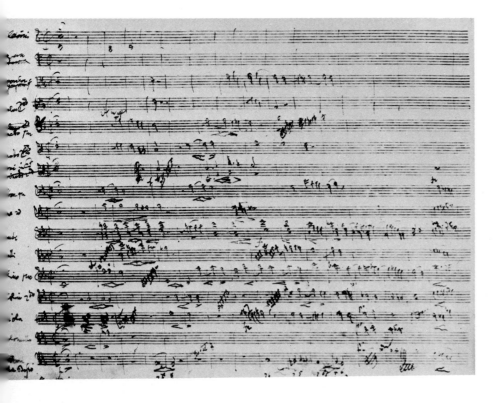

156, 157 The first edition (1800) of *The Creation* in full score and with German and English text, was published – with an impressive list of subscribers from all over Europe – by Haydn himself; the title page of his edition is shown below, with *(right)* an engraved portrait of Haydn's librettist, Baron Gottfried van Swieten (cf. ill. 153), who held the office of Imperial and Royal Librarian.

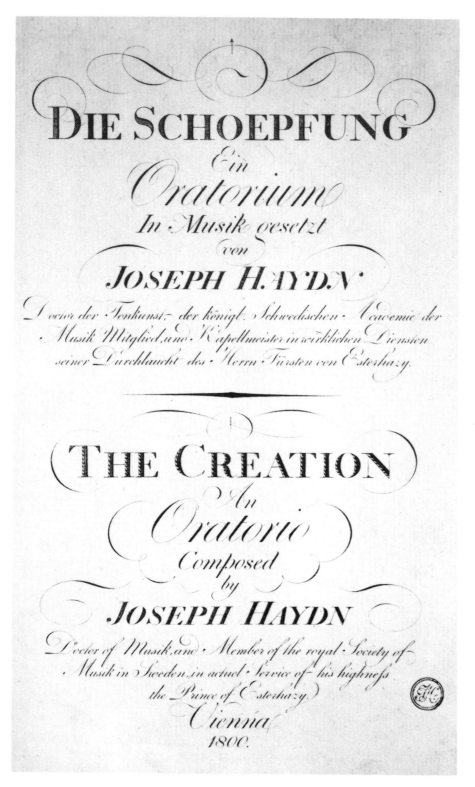

158, 159 The leader of the orchestra at the respective first performances of *The Creation* (1798) and *The Seasons* (1801) was Paul Wranizky *(above)*, while another leading figure in the Viennese musical scene was the Italian composer Antonio Salieri *(below)* who in 1808 conducted a performance of *The Creation* given in honour of Haydn's seventy-sixth birthday (cf. ill. 181).

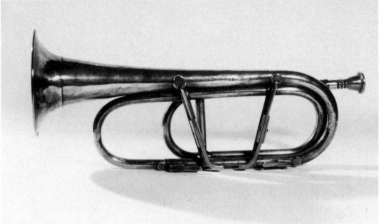

160, 161 Haydn's Trumpet Concerto of 1796 has become in modern times the most popular of all the composer's orchestral works; the closing *tutti* of the Finale is shown in the last page of the autograph *(above)*, with a keyed trumpet *(clarino; right)* of the type invented by the Court Trumpeter Anton Weidinger, for whom the Concerto was written and who gave the first public performance at the Burgtheater on 28 March 1800.

The late Masses

162–164 The six great settings by Haydn of the years 1796–1802 are scored for soloists, chorus and orchestra; the theatrical atmosphere of a full-scale church performance is conjured up in an engraving by J. E. Mansfeld *(left)*, published in a work criticizing practices in the Roman Catholic Church tending to distract the congregation from their proper devotions. Of these Masses, one – the *Missa in tempore belli* – was probably first performed on 26 December 1796 in the church of the Piarists (in the Josephstadt suburb of Vienna; *below*) seen here in a coloured engraving by Carl Schütz, 1780; four of the other works were first performed in the Bergkirche in Eisenstadt *(opposite)* to celebrate the name-day of Princess Marie Hermenegild Esterházy (at this stage of his career Haydn's only formal duty as *Kapellmeister* was the annual composition of a Mass for this occasion).

Frater Felix Niering Ord. S. Francisci
Architectus Inven. et fecit

Ioan Vinca Bibergar sculp. Calcogra Vaicego Fa.

165 One of the most popular of Haydn's late Masses has always been the *Missa in angustiis* – the so-called 'Nelson' Mass; the composition of this work, written in 1798 in the space of fifty-three days, coincided with the period when the British Admiral, Horatio, Lord Nelson *(right)* was seeking out and eventually destroying the French fleet in the Battle of the Nile. Nelson's success on 1 August 1798 – a morale-boosting breakthrough in the long drawn-out struggle against Napoleon – led to him being greeted as a hero by the Austrians when he arrived in Vienna (en route from Naples to London) in August 1800; on this occasion Nelson and Emma, Lady Hamilton, who accompanied him, also visited Prince Nicolaus II Esterházy at Eisenstadt and heard the Mass performed there.

166–168 Haydn's domestic and family life included a close relationship with Antonio Polzelli *(left)* – the youngest son of the composer's former mistress – and with his own younger brother Michael *(right)*; the Haydn brothers met only occasionally (Michael lived in Salzburg), but maintained a regular correspondence. Joseph's principal residence during his later years was in the Viennese suburb of Gumpendorf *(below*; cf. ill. 185), seen here in a drawing dated 1798.

169 A fan presented by Haydn to the wife of the porter at the Esterházy Palace in the Wallnerstraße, *c.* 1800; this gift – sent to Frau Pointner with an accompanying letter – was a personal gesture to thank the porter's wife for looking after him during an illness.

170–172 (opposite) Among the buildings in Vienna which had special links with Haydn were the old Burgtheater (since replaced), of which both the interior *(above)* and exterior *(below, right)* are shown in contemporary engravings; the first public performances of the Trumpet Concerto and *The Creation* were given in this theatre, which stood in the Michaelerplatz. Haydn's principal Viennese publisher, Artaria & Co., had its offices in the Kohlmarkt *(below, left)*.

DIE JAHRESZEITEN

nach Thomson,

in Musik gesezt von

JOSEPH HAYDN.

PARTITUR.

Originalausgabe.

Bey Breitkopf & Härtel in Leipzig.

14.

173–175 Haydn's last great oratorio, *The Seasons*, with libretto (based on the poem by James Thomson) by Baron Gottfried van Swieten, received its first public performance in 1801. Haydn entrusted the publication of the Oratorio to Breitkopf & Härtel of Leipzig; the title page of this first edition (1802) is shown opposite. The large Redoutensaal *(above)*, which was used for many important social events, was sadly empty when Haydn's Oratorio was given there in May 1801; one of the witnesses to this and other events whose diaries have survived was Joseph Carl Rosenbaum *(right)*, who noted that only 'a little over 700 people' were present.

176 A page from the so-called 'Haydn-Verzeichnis' ('Haydn index') of 1805, copied out by Johann Elssler. This MS. catalogue included all the works that Haydn could remember having composed between *c.* 1749 and 1803; the list of Symphonies shown here begins with the first compositions in this *genre* written for Prince Paul Anton Esterházy in 1761 – Nos. 6–8, known respectively as 'Le Matin', 'Le Midi' and 'Le Soir' – and ends with No. 28, composed in 1765.

177–180 A selection of portraits dating from Haydn's later years: *(top, left)* lithograph by A. Kunike, published after the composer's death and showing him without his habitual wig; *(above, left)* a life-size lead bust – now attributed to F.C. Thaller (cf. ill. 133) – *c.* 1800, formerly in Haydn's possession and bequeathed by him to Count Harrach, whose descendants still own the piece; *(top, right)* engraving by Edmé Quenedey, published in Paris; and a lost miniature by Christian Horneman, *c.* 1803, depicting the composer in a somewhat idealized manner.

181, 182 On 27 March 1808 a special performance of *The Creation* conducted by Antonio Salieri was given in Vienna, in the hall of Old University, to mark the composer's impending seventy-sixth birthday; the by now frail Haydn was brought from Gumpendorf in a carriage provided by Prince Nicolaus and – after being greeted by his wife, Princess Marie Hermenegild, and other notable figures, Beethoven among them – was borne into the hall (see the reconstruction opposite, in which a similar chair and the placard announcing the event are shown); the scene within the hall *(above)*, with the composer in the centre surrounded by friends and admirers, was recorded on a box-cover by the miniaturist Balthasar Wigand. Although the original box is missing – stolen from the Museum der Stadt Wien in 1945 – a copy of the cover (seen here) made in 1909 records the scene of Haydn's last public appearance.

183–185 Haydn's last weeks, spent at his home in the
Kleine Steingasse, Gumpendorf *(opposite, above)*, were
disturbed by the French bombardment of the city of
Vienna; a lithograph *(above)*, after a drawing by J. N.
Höchle, recreates the atmosphere of a night attack by
cannon fire. In this terrifying situation the old composer
calmed his servants' anxiety with the words 'Fear not,
children, where Haydn is no harm can come to you.' Three
days before the composer's death, a French cavalry officer
visited him and the two men talked about *The Creation*;
before leaving, the young officer sang an aria from the
Oratorio – a gesture that gave Haydn much pleasure. After
taking the city of Vienna, one of Napoleon's first official acts
was to despatch a guard of honour to Haydn's house in the
suburbs.

During these last dark days Haydn was cared for by his
faithful servant and copyist Johann Elssler *(right)* who, after
his master's death on 31 May 1808, wrote a long letter to
G. A. Griesinger reporting the sad news.

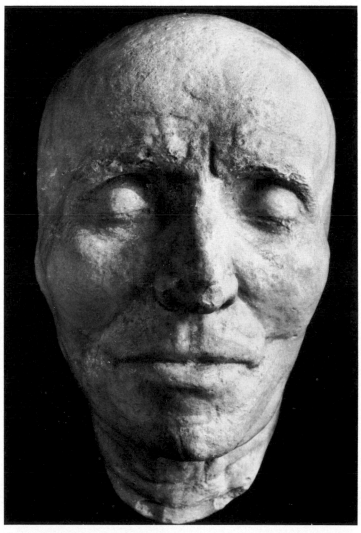

186, 187 The death-mask in plaster of the composer was taken by Johann Elssler; today it is preserved as a treasured relic in Haydn's former home, now the Haydn Museum. Although the funeral and interment took place on the outskirts of Vienna, Haydn's remains were later removed on the instructions of Prince Nicolaus II Esterházy to the Bergkirche in Eisenstadt (cf. ill. 188); the tomb (with its Latin inscription), designed by Haydn's pupil Sigismund von Neukomm, is surmounted overall by a quotation from Psalm 117 (118), v. 17: 'I shall not die, but live, and declare the works of the Lord.' – a sentiment reflecting the composer's lifelong devotion to the Church.

188 The Bergkirche, Eisenstadt, scene of the first performances of four of Haydn's six late Masses and his final resting place.

On 8 September 1795 the following announcement appeared in the *Preßburger Zeitung*:

> According to letters from Hamburg, the princely Esterházy *Kapellmeister*, Herr Joseph Haydn, that universally esteemed and indeed very great composer whose excellent compositions are everywhere received with the greatest approbation, arrived there from London on the 20th of last month [August], continuing his journey to Vienna the next day.

After Haydn's return from his second triumphal visit to England, the city of Vienna was to be his principal place of residence until his death in 1809. Haydn's new patron, Prince Nicolaus II Esterházy, found Vienna attractive – unlike Nicolaus I, who had disliked the Austrian capital and preferred the isolation of Eszterháza Castle in Hungary. Eszterháza was now completely abandoned, and the best furniture and pictures were removed to Vienna or to the family castle in Eisenstadt, where Nicolaus II spent the summers and from which the huge Esterházy estates were managed.

Haydn followed the Esterházy court to Eisenstadt in summer, and while there he had quarters near the castle; but otherwise he lived in Vienna and became the doyen of musical life there. During the period 1796–1802 Haydn's only formal duty as *Kapellmeister* was to compose a new setting of the Mass each year for performance in Eisenstadt to celebrate the name-day of Nicolaus II's wife, Princess Marie Hermenegild; the result was the series (with the exception of the year 1800) of six great Masses (see below). In 1796, Haydn's *Capelle* included the princely *Feldharmonie* (a wind band consisting of pairs of oboes, clarinets, bassoons and horns), a small group of voices, strings and another bassoon player who usually played kettledrums.

It would be pleasing to record that Haydn's late years were spent in the employ of a prince whose instinct for music was of the kind displayed by Nicolaus I; but, alas, not only was Nicolaus II basically unmusical, but personal relations between the prince and his *Kapellmeister* were, in the beginning, somewhat strained. Evidence of this is to be found in a number of episodes. Most revealing is a story concerning an orchestral rehearsal, probably *c.* 1795–6, at which Haydn was conducting; the prince entered and made a criticism, whereupon Haydn replied – in the presence of all the musicians – 'Your Highness, that is my business.' Nicolaus, white with fury, strode from the room. Another aspect of the prince's attitude towards the venerable composer recalls Haydn's position in the early years of his service with the Esterházys, when (cf. p. 41) he was addressed in the third person (e.g., 'He will conduct a symphony tomorrow.'). This mode of address, appropriate to a lackey, had long since been dropped under Nicolaus I, and Haydn justifiably objected to its use; it now required the good offices of Princess Marie Hermenegild – with whom Haydn had always been on the

Prince Nicolaus II Esterházy; pencil drawing by the Rev. William Bradford, Chaplain to the British Embassy in Vienna.

139

best of terms and to whom he had dedicated three piano trios while absent in England – to restore a dignified form more suited to a Doctor of Music of Oxford University and one who had not long before chatted *tête-à-tête* with the King and Queen of England. As time went on, relations between the prince and his *Kapellmeister* improved, but Nicolaus was at best a difficult and unsympathetic man.

18   Now that Eisenstadt was again the centre of the Esterházy administration, elaborate plans were drawn up for rebuilding the rather ugly Castle and the architect's plans are impressive; but Charles de Moreau was able to realize only a very small part of his plans (e.g. the handsome stables in front of the building). Here is how an Englishwoman, Martha Wilmot, described Eisenstadt in 1828:

> 26th [September, 1828].
> ... Eisenstadt, Prince Esterházy's celebrated Chateau, surrounded by lands, woods, and every possible luxury, save that of good taste was our next station. The town is a very poor one, ill-paved and dirty. Even the Chateau stands in a square the pavement of which is enough to break the springs of a carriage, altogether it was very desolate looking, and grass grew (amidst the stones and large flags) before the door ... There are soldiers guarding the entrance, and a great deal of military parade and pride but a desolate appearance about the place, however, when his Chateau is thrown open during the hunting season, which sometimes happens, he can receive and accommodate with their attendants, 80 visitors. The bedrooms too, are in general, excellent, and some very handsome. The reception rooms are nothing remarkable considering the great scale of everything, except the grand banqueting room, and this is 180 feet long ... here 300 guests dine sometimes, sometimes plays are acted by performers from Vienna, and in short it is a noble piece ...

27   Apart from the Castle, where Haydn gave concerts (on a large scale in the Great Hall, now known as the 'Haydnsaal'; on a smaller scale in some of the attractive rooms on the first [American, second] floor), our musical interest in 164 Eisenstadt must concentrate on the Bergkirche (Mountain Church); it was there that Haydn – with one major exception – conducted the first 165 performances of his last six Masses. The first performance of the 'Nelson' Mass (*Missa in angustiis* [XXII:11]) took place in 1798 in the parish church 32   (now Cathedral) of St Martin on Sunday, 23 September. Haydn himself probably played the many organ solo parts on the great organ – now beautifully restored and one of the greatest instruments in the south German territory – it was built in 1778 by J. G. Malleck, who also, many years later (1797), built the present organ in the Bergkirche. The great flowering of Haydn's choral style is reflected as much in these Masses as it is in his late Oratorios. The Masses are scored for a large orchestra and the usual four-part complement of soloists and choir with supreme skill and audacity, but basically they remain lasting tributes to Haydn's belief in the order of the universe and the omnipresent and beneficent influence of God's goodness. On this aspect of Haydn's character Griesinger (53ff.) tells us:

> Haydn was very religiously inclined, and a devoted follower of the religion in which he grew up. In his heart he was most firmly convinced that all human destiny lies under God's guiding hand; that God is the rewarder of good and evil; that all talents came from above. All his larger scores begin with the words 'In nomine Domini' and close with 'Laus Deo' or 'Soli Deo gloria'. 'If, when I am composing, things don't go quite right,' I heard him say, 'I

walk up and down the room with my rosary in my hand, say several Aves, and then the ideas come again.' In religion, he also found the strongest consolation for his physical debility; in the final years of his life, he was quite reconciled to the idea of death, and prepared himself for it daily. Without speculating on the principles of faith, he accepted the 'what' and 'how' that his Catholic Church taught . . .

. . . Haydn left every man to his own conviction, and he recognized them all as his brothers. Altogether his devotion was not of a sort which is gloomy and forever in penance but rather cheerful, reconciled, trusting – and in this mould his church music, too, is composed . . .

A natural consequence of Haydn's religiosity was his modesty; for his talent was not of his own doing but a gracious gift of Heaven, to whom he considered he must show himself grateful.

Haydn's pupil, Sigismund von Neukomm, commenting on a passage in Dies's biography concerning the so-called 'Creation' Mass of 1801, states:

The newer Masses by Haydn, against which the critics have been ruthlessly opposed because of their more elegant and less ecclesiastical style, were composed in Haydn's last and glorious period and each year for the birth- or rather the name-day of his deeply respected patroness the Princess Esterházy, for whom a Mass in an attractive, elegant style would have more value than a learned or more serious work. [*Bemerkungen*, 30]

In Vienna the amount of musical activity was, if anything, even greater than in the era of Haydn's youth; but now the nobility could ill afford the full orchestras they had employed in Haydn's youth; instead they had wind bands which were used for *Tafelmusik*. One popular kind of repertoire for this *Feldharmonie* was the transcription of operas, and many such arrangements, even of Mozart's operas, have survived (also in the Esterházy Archives at Eisenstadt). There were two opera orchestras in the city, one for the German and one for the Italian repertoire; most of the singers were primarily engaged for the one or for the other, seldom for both. Haydn, and later Beethoven, 141 drew upon this pool for their benefit concerts. Of the private orchestras, apart from the Esterházy *Capelle*, perhaps the most famous was that of Prince Lobkowitz, at whose concerts Haydn and, later, Beethoven appeared 145 regularly. The leading public concerts were still the Easter and Christmas double evenings by the Tonkünstler-Societät, which now – after the long estrangement referred to above – asked Haydn to become an honorary officer. These concerts were usually in the form of an oratorio, with concertos or other music between the sections. Haydn later came to be their principal benefactor, performing *The Seven Words* (choral version), *The Creation* and *The Seasons* for their semi-annual concerts of the Society and bringing in huge sums of money for musicians' widows and orphans. In fact Haydn's principal public appearances – apart from the first performances of his Oratorios – were now devoted to charity, in the Handelian tradition of the Foundling Hospital in London.

When Haydn returned from London, he and Beethoven frequently gave concerts together, Beethoven as piano soloist and Haydn conducting his London Symphonies. Beethoven was, of course, no longer Haydn's pupil, and the young man's relationship to his former teacher was highly ambivalent. On the one hand he dedicated to Haydn his newest piano sonatas (Opus 2, 1796), on the other he is said to have told Haydn, 'I never learned anything from you' – hardly an objective statement. To clarify the whole question of Beethoven and Haydn at this relatively early period in their relationship we would quote from an interesting document which for some reason has for the most part escaped the biographers of both composers. It is a rather journalistically conceived but none the less characteristic report from the French flautist, Louis François Drouet (1792–1873) who knew Beethoven in Vienna; Drouet made an extended European tour in 1816, which took him as far as Naples, and it was probably on this tour that he stopped in Vienna, made Beethoven's acquaintance and became an enthusiastic admirer of his music. Drouet describes his relationship to Beethoven in a series of conversations with 'a highly educated, musical lady, the wife of an Englishman', which were published for the first time in 1858 in a Hamburg paper entitled *Zeitung für Gesangvereine und Liedertafeln*.

'Haydn,' said Drouet, 'was certainly a great *Musikus*, one of the greatest who ever lived, and yet he made a mistake about Beethoven, whom you love so much. When he saw his first trios, about which his opinion had been sought, he said: "Nothing will ever come of that young man".'

'Not true at all,' answered the lady. 'These words are attributed to Haydn, but he never said them and you know it, too, because you said so yourself in front of the Duchess of Belgiojoso ... When Beethoven, still very young [continued the lady], showed his first compositions to Haydn and asked him for his opinion, Haydn said to him: "You have a great talent, and you will have still more, enormously more, talent. Your powers of imagination are an inexhaustible source of ideas, but ... do you really want my frank opinion?" "Certainly," said Beethoven, "I came here to have your opinion." – "Well, then," said Haydn, "you will accomplish more than has ever been accomplished hitherto; you will have thoughts that no one has yet had; you will never (and you're quite right about this) sacrifice a beautiful thought to a tyrannical rule; but the rules will be sacrificed to your moods, for you make the impression on me of a man with several heads, several hearts and several souls, and ... but I fear I annoy you". "You will annoy me," said Beethoven, "if you don't continue." – "Well," continued Haydn, "because you want me to do so, I will tell you that in my opinion there will always be something – if not eccentric, then at any rate unusual in your works: one will find beautiful things in them, even admirable passages, but here and there something peculiar, dark, because you yourself are a little sinister and peculiar, and the style of the musician is always that of the person himself. Look at my compositions. You will often find something jovial about them, because that's the way I am; next to a serious thought you will find a cheerful one, as in Shakespeare's tragedies." ... By the way, at the time when Haydn saw the first works of Beethoven, the latter was very young, the tree was too heavily covered with foliage and needed pruning; in the first compositions by Beethoven, everything was in superabundance...'

The Lady: 'You find the first compositions by Beethoven very good, because you know them as they are printed, but not in the form in which he showed them to Haydn.'

Drouet: 'This remark is quite correct, I didn't think of that, but now I remember very well that Beethoven told me, when he was speaking about his first efforts, "They are not printed as I first wrote them; when, after some years, I examined my first manuscripts once again, I asked myself if I had not been insane to cram into one single piece that which was sufficient for twenty. I burned these manuscripts, so that no one could see them, and I would have committed many foolish mistakes in my first appearance as a composer if it had not been for the good advice of Papa Haydn and Albrechtsberger."'

157   The first official collaboration between Haydn and Gottfried van Swieten

– the Baron had probably 'unofficially' furnished the German text of 'The Storm' in 1793 – was a new version of *The Seven Words* which Haydn had composed for Cádiz in 1786 as a purely orchestral work. Now, a decade later, Haydn added new instruments to the orchestra (e.g., clarinets and trombones), made other revisions, and added a new instrumental interlude for solo wind band, an extraordinary and chilling Largo in which the double bassoon appears for the first time in Haydn's scores – clearly a reminder of that instrument's presence in the great Handelian festivals of London. A discussion of the differences between the instrumental and the choral versions, apropos a performance in Bückeburg in 1802, clearly mirrors most contemporary thought on the subject:

> Saturday, 12 June, 1802. Haydn's *Seven Words* in Bückeburg.
>
> I shall tell you, my Dear Countess, that Haydn's *Seven Words* was given here on Good Friday, and with the new inserted choral parts, I shall tell you so as to make your musical heart doubly heavy not to have been present. If you knew what an effect this beautiful music produced when it was only instrumental music, you must believe me if I tell you that through the words which have been suitably added to it, the music gained much by a certain reinforcement of expression. Of course it remains a work that is not really suited to the general public: to appreciate six [*recte*: seven] adagios one after another [is at best difficult], and the satisfaction of our audience derived perhaps from the special emotion that fills all of us on Good Friday, thus linking the idea of a worthy composition with the feeling of boredom. The dynamic gradations with which the choruses were performed certainly pleased the connoisseurs doubly because they happen so rarely. The opening words, or rather the Seven Words themselves, created the most solemn impression before each chorus through their being only for human voices alone, without accompaniment, and in pure chanting. It was rather difficult to find the right pitch, with a long pause after the chorus, and with no instruments to give the pitch. Our concert was given only out of love for music; none of the usual reasons were necessary for the performance; it was not even for the benefit of the poor; sacred music ought to be free for every man who wishes to listen quietly.

Readers of the *Wiener Zeitung* were informed on 14 January 1797 that

> His I.R. Majesty has graciously condescended to receive with every mark of approbation the very considerable financial contributions to the war effort made since the year 1793 by Prince Niklas [*sic*] Esterházy von Galantha, Councillor, Major-General, and the First Lieutenant of the Noble Hungarian Bodyguard... and has now seen fit to confer on [Prince Esterházy] the Grand Cross of the Order of St Stephen ...

Haydn, of course, was hardly in a position to make large financial gifts to help in the war effort against Napoleon; but he was able to make a contribution more lasting than any gift of money. For this is the period in which Haydn composed his gravely beautiful 'Volcks Lied' (People's Song), later known as the Austrian (and still later the German) national anthem.

One version of the *Volkslied's* origin comes from Anton Schmid, Custodian of the Austrian National Library in Vienna, who wrote in 1847:

> As far as the reasons for which the wonderful Haydn Song was composed, we may present to our readers the following plausible circumstances, which several of the finest composers in Vienna, some of whom are dead and some still alive, remembered from those times and communicated to us.

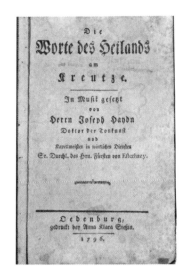

The Seven Words (choral version): the title page of the German text book printed at Oedenburg for the performance of Haydn's Oratorio which took place in the Great Hall of Eisenstadt Castle on 27 October 1797. The printer had previously enjoyed a long and close relationship with the operatic troupe at Eszterháza, furnishing most of the printed libretti for operas performed in the theatre there under Haydn's direction.

134

136, 138

In England, Haydn came to know the favourite British national anthem, 'God save the King', and he envied the British nation for a song through which it could, at festive occasions, show in full measure its respect, love and devotion to its ruler.

When the Father of Harmony returned to his beloved *Kaiserstadt*, he related these impressions to that real friend, connoisseur, supporter and encourager of many a great and good one of Art and Science, Freiherr van Swieten, Prefect of the I.R. Court Library, who at the time was at the head of the Concert Spirituel (supported by the high aristocracy) and likewise Haydn's particular patron. Haydn wished that Austria, too, could have a similar national anthem, wherein it could display a similar respect and love for its Father [*Landesvater*]. Also, such a song could be used in the fight then taking place with those forcing the Rhine; it could be used in a noble way to inflame the hearts of the Austrians to new heights of devotion to the princes and fatherland, and to incite to combat, and to increase, the mob of volunteer soldiers who had been collected by a general proclamation.

137

Freiherr van Swieten hastily took counsel with His Excellency, the then President of Lower Austria, Franz Count von Saurau ...; and so there came into being a song which, apart from being one of Haydn's greatest creations, has won the crown of immortality.

It is also true that this high-principled Count used the most opportune moment to introduce a *Volksgesang*, and thus he called to life those beautiful thoughts which will delight connoisseurs and amateurs here and abroad.

He ordered forthwith the poet Lorenz Haschka to draft the poetry and then requested our Haydn to set it to music.

In January 1797, this double task was resolved, and the first performance of the Song was ordered for the birthday of the Monarch.

On 30 January 1797, Saurau wrote to the authorities in Prague as follows:

Nobly born Count!

Your Excellency will be aware of the effect on the populace caused by the well-known English song [*Volkslied*]: God save the King; and how for a long time it has admonished that people to a common defence against foreign foes.

The Song which is herewith enclosed, written by Haschka and set to music by the famous Haydn, will be sung by the people in all the theatres of Vienna on 12 February, and I take the liberty of sending it in confidence to Your Excellency, in order that the Song, if you judge it to be a good idea, may be sung that same day also in Prague; and may the wishes of the whole populace for the continued welfare of His Majesty resound on that day!

> I remain with every respect,
>> Your Excelllency's
>> obedient servant
>> Saurau.

The *Magazin der Kunst und Literatur* carried a report:

Gott erhalte den Kaiser

The twelfth of February, the birthday of our exalted and much beloved Emperor, was celebrated this year in a fashion that was up to now unknown in Austria. A warm admirer of this monarch found a way – and in this he could not have approached closer to the general desire – for the loyal subjects in all places of the Austrian monarchy to display the sensitivity of their hearts for the well-being of their beloved Prince of the Land, and to show it openly and in consort. A *Volkslied* in the manner of that in which the loyal Englishmen sing for the preservation of their king, seemed to be the most efficacious means. Haschka wrote the song and Haydn set it to music; a choice that reflects credit on the highly placed men who made it.

It was sung this year on 12 February in all the theatres. The enthusiasm of the public which was displayed on this occasion as on several others allows us to hope that we will have frequent occasion to hear the voices of the people joined together for the preservation of the Emperor ...

Although Haydn never composed any more symphonies after he left England, there are two types of purely instrumental works that flowered in the present period: the Trumpet Concerto (VIIe:1) of 1796, for a keyed trumpet invented by Anton Weidinger, Court Trumpeter in Vienna; and the series of string quartets. Both represent commissions, the one for a talented player, the others for aristocratic patrons. It was becoming the custom for someone to commission a series of (say) quartets from a composer; these quartets remained the exclusive property of the commissioner for a certain period of time (usually a couple of years), after which the composer was free to have them published or to reap whatever other reward he could from the music. Prince Lobkowitz was to 'purchase' Beethoven's 'Eroica' Symphony on such terms, and it was for him that Haydn composed his last completed string quartets, Opus 77 (1799). Before then, Count Apponyi had made a similar arrangement with the composer for the six quartets of Opus 71 & 74 (1793) and Count Erdödy for the famous series of Opus 76 (1797?).

On 14 June 1797 the Swedish diplomat Frederik Samuel Silverstolpe writes to Stockholm:

160
161

205

143, 144
148

... A few days ago I went to see Haydn again, who now lives right next to me, since he gave up his customary winter and spring lodgings in one of the suburbs [Gumpendorf] and moved a whole quarter-of-a-mile away. On this occasion he played to me, on the piano, violin quartets which a certain Count Erdödi has ordered from him and which may be printed only after a certain number of years. These are more than masterly and full of new thoughts. While he played, he let me sit beside him and see how he divided the various parts in the score ...

The new quartets from Op. 76 were performed in September at Eisenstadt on the occasion of a visit by the Viceroy of Hungary, Palatine Archduke Joseph. The diary of Joseph Carl Rosenbaum describes the festivities:

175

Wednesday, 27th: The Viceroy arrived in Eisenstadt at about 12 noon. His approach was announced by the thunder of cannon, which lasted until he arrived and was received in the castle. He was received on the steps by a cordon of princely officials, in the anteroom by the liveried servants, and in the small hall by the house officials. On the square were the princely grenadiers, then the free citizens of the town with their clergy and town council, then the princely subjects from Oberberg and the Jewish community. It was a most ceremonious reception, a brilliant demonstration of the greatness of Prince Esterházy. At mid-day there was a banquet in the grand hall; places were laid for 800 persons, on two tables. As toasts were drunk, trumpets and drums sounded from the balcony of the hall, and cannon fired in the garden of the castle ...
Thursday, 28th: At about 10 a.m. the Viceroy, in the company of the Prince and several cavaliers ... went hunting ... At midday a banquet was held in the small hall. In the afternoon the citizens of the town, then the princely citizens and the Jewish community, all with their superiors, and the musicians, gathered on the square and welcomed the Viceroy with a display of flags and with music ... The town parson, the magistrate and the town council then went into the small hall where they were received by the Viceroy who thanked

them for the particular attentions which had been paid him. New quartets by Haydn were played, [one of them] based on the song *Gott erhalte Franz den Kaiser*, and a seven-year-old boy by the name of Böhm played the violin, earning unanimous applause. At the Viceroy's departure, cannon were fired and trumpets and drums resounded from the balcony of the castle.

168, 185 During this final period, although Haydn had his own house in the Viennese suburb of Gumpendorf (Kleine Steingasse No. 73), during the winters he took a *pied-à-terre* in the inner city so that he would not have to make the lengthy journey back to the suburbs late at night. Later, after he had given up this *pied-à-terre*, he lived entirely in Gumpendorf; in an undated MS. (now in the Mozarteum, Salzburg) written after the composer's death, 184 Haydn's faithful servant Johann Elssler set down a record of the living habits of his aging master:

Daily Schedule of the late Herr v. Haÿdn

In the summertime he rose at half-past six. The first thing he did was to shave, which he did for himself up to his 73rd year. After shaving, he got dressed completely. If a pupil were present, he had to play the lesson he had been assigned on the piano [*Clavier*] to Hr. v. Haydn as he was dressing. The mistakes were at one corrected, the pupil instructed about the reasons therof, and then a new task was assigned. For this one and a half hours were required. On the dot of 8 o'clock breakfast had to be on the table, and right after breakfast Haÿdn sat down at the piano and improvised, whereby at the same time he worked out the sketch of the composition; for this, a daily period from 8 to 11:30 in the morning was required. At 11:30 visits were paid or received; or he took a walk until 1:30. From 2 to 3 o'clock was the hour for lunch. After lunch Haÿdn always concerned himself with some small domestic task, or he went into his small library and read a book. At 4 o'clock Haÿdn returned to musical affairs. He took the sketch which had been prepared that morning and put it into score, for which task he took three to four hours. At 8 p.m. Haÿdn usually went out, but came home again at 9 and either sat down to write scores or took a book and read until 10 o'clock. The hour of 10 o'clock was supper time, which consisted of bread and wine. Haÿdn made it a rule not to have anything else except bread and wine in the evening, and he broke the rule now and then only when he was invited out for dinner. At table Haÿdn liked light conversation and altogether a merry entertainment. At half past eleven Haÿdn went to bed – in old age even later. – The wintertime made no appreciable difference in the daily schedule except that Haÿdn got up in the morning a half hour later, otherwise everything was as in the summer. In old age, mainly during the last 5 to 6 years of his life, physical weakness and illness disturbed the above schedule. The active man could, at last, find no occupation. In this latter period Haÿdn used to lie down for half an hour in the afternoon.

Silverstolpe reported on a visit to Haydn in 1797:

During the conversation which followed, I discovered in Haydn as it were two physiognomies. The one was penetrating and serious, when he talked about anything exalted, and only the expression 'exalted' was enough to show him visibly moved. In the next moment this atmosphere of exaltation was chased away, quick as lightning, from his every-day expression, and he became jovial with a force that showed on his features and which then passed into waggishness. This was his usual physiognomy; the other one had to be induced. – As I left him, he said, 'Do you know that his house has something remarkable about it: here, and just in these very rooms, we lost Mozart; what a gap that has left for us!' – I felt that I stood on hallowed ground.

Just before Haydn left England, his friend and 'manager' J. P. Salomon had pressed into the master's hand a handwritten libretto entitled 'The Creation'. It had been intended for Handel, but he had not composed it. Haydn had been profoundly moved by his Handelian experiences in England, and he had the idea that the old Baroque oratorio form could be given new life, particularly as regards the new school of orchestration, of which he was one of the founders and leaders. When Haydn returned to Vienna, he and Gottfried van Swieten first collaborated on 'The Storm', then on the revised *Seven Words*; now van Swieten examined the libretto of 'The Creation' and thought it would make an inspiring book for Haydn. The Baron adapted the text and translated it into German, but in such a way that Haydn could also use the original English text as well (hence the bilingual edition of the score that Haydn himself published by subscription in 1800). The original author is now thought to be Thomas Linley senior (1733–95), Richard Brinsley Sheridan's father-in-law and, during Haydn's visits to England, co-director with Samuel Arnold of the Drury Lane oratorio concerts.

In a letter from Johann Georg Albrechtsberger to his and Haydn's erstwhile pupil, Ludwig van Beethoven, we have the first written reference to Haydn's new oratorio:

Vienna, 15 December 1796.

My dear Beethoven!

For your name-day [*recte*: birthday] tomorrow, I wish you all the best. God give you health and happiness and grant you much luck. If you, my dear Beethoven, should have a free hour, your old teacher invites you to spend it with him. It would give me great pleasure if you would bring the Trio with you, we could rehearse it straight away, and since I now have more time I will start directly making the scores.

Yesterday Haydn came to me, he is carrying round in his head the idea of a big oratorio which he intends to call 'The Creation' and hopes to finish it soon. He improvised some of it for me and I think it will be very good.

Don't forget to look in tomorrow and meanwhile hearty greetings from

Your Johann Georg Albrechtsberger.

Silverstolpe reported on a visit he made to the composer in 1797 as follows:

When Summer began Haydn moved back to his own home in the suburb of Gumpendorf, ... When I entered the room I heard a parrot calling 'Papa Haydn!' In one of the rooms to the right one often saw the great man with his undistinguished features getting up from his work, but also sometimes remaining seated at it until the Aria from *The Creation* ['Rollend in schäumenden Wellen'/'Rolling in foaming billows'] which describes the sea moving and the waves breaking on the shores. 'You see,' he said in a joking tone, 'you see how the notes run up and down like the waves: see there, too, the mountains that come from the depths of the sea? One has to have some amusement after one has been serious for so long.' – But when we arrived at the pure stream, which creeps down the valley in a small trickle, ah! I was quite enthusiastic to see how even the quiet surface flowed. I could not forbear putting an affectionate hand on the old and venerable shoulder and giving it a gentle squeeze, as he sat at the piano and sang with a simplicity that went straight to the heart.

It must have been about June 1797 that Haydn reached the halfway mark in composing *The Creation*. We learn from Griesinger (54f.) that

His patriarchal, devout spirit found particular expression in *The Creation*, and therefore this composition must have been more successful than if it had been written by a hundred other masters. 'It was not till I completed half of my composition that I noticed that it had turned out well; I was also never so devout as during that time when I was working on *The Creation*; every day I fell on my knees and asked God to give me strength to enable me to pursue the work to its successful conclusion ...

151, 152   Later, when the time came for rehearsals of *The Creation* preceding its first performance at the Palace of Prince Schwarzenberg in the Mehlmarkt, we are informed by Silverstolpe:

This work was first given on 30 April 1798. I was among the audience, and a few days beforehand I had attended the first rehearsal. At the latter Haydn was surprised afterwards by a present. Prince Schwarzenberg, in whose rooms the work was prepared and later also performed, was so utterly enchanted by the many beauties of the work that he presented the composer with a roll containing one hundred ducats, over and above the 500 that were part of the agreement. – No one, not even Baron van Swieten, had seen the page of the score wherein the birth of light is described. That was the only passage of the work which Haydn had kept hidden. I think I see his face even now, as this part sounded in the orchestra. Haydn had the expression of someone who is thinking of biting his lips, either to hide his embarrassment or to conceal a secret. And in that moment when light broke out for the first time, one would have said that rays darted from the composer's burning eyes. The enchantment of the electrified Viennese was so general that the orchestra could not proceed for some minutes.

We have seen Haydn almost at the summit of his career with the first, semi-private performance of *The Creation*; we say 'almost' because the actual summit may be reckoned the first public performance in 1799. In its issue of 20 February 1799 the *Allgemeine Musikalische Zeitung* carried the following from a Viennese correspondent:

170, 171   ... We shall get this masterpiece [*The Creation*] performed here in public and at a ceremonious occasion. On 19 March it will be given in our Court Theatre. The orchestra will consist of 180 persons. The aristocracy pays for the costs of the performance, so that the whole income goes to the composer. And that this will be respectable you can see from the fact that now, at present writing, not a box more is to be had. We are just now beginning to know and appreciate our Father Haydn; ...

Johan Frederik Berwald, the Swedish child prodigy (born 1787) who was touring Europe at this period, reported on the occasion in his memoirs:

158   ... As early as 4 o'clock in the afternoon, our temporary servant came and said we should hasten to the theatre, because it was besieged by a large number of people, even though the concert was not to start until 7 o'clock. When we entered, we saw that the stage proper was set up in the form of an amphitheatre. Down below at the fortepiano sat *Kapellmeister* Weigl, surrounded by the vocal soloists, the chorus, a violoncello and a double bass [as *continuo*]. At one level higher stood Haydn himself with his conductor's baton. Still a level higher on one side were the first violins, led by Paul Wranitzky and on the other the second violins, led by his brother Anton Wranitzky. In the centre: violas and double basses. In the wings, more double basses; on higher levels the wind instruments, and at the very top: trumpets, kettledrums and trombones. That was the disposition of the orchestra which, together with

the chorus, consisted of some 400 persons. The whole went off wonderfully. Between the sections of the work, tumultuous applause; during each section however, it was still as the grave. When it was over, there were calls, 'Father Haydn to the front! Father Haydn to the front!' Finally the old man came forward and was greeted with a tumultuous *Applaudissement* and with cries, 'Long live Father Haydn! Long live music!' Their imperial majesties were all present and joined in the 'bravo' calls. . . .

Haydn had entered the hearts of his countrymen in a way that no composer had ever done to that extent previously. It is really almost as if *The Creation* was man's hope for a peaceful future (uncertain, at best, in 1799) and man's consolation for a clouded present. That it brought real comfort, consolation and joy to thousands of Viennese and, very soon, other Europeans, is clear from every document that survives. Never in the history of music, not even Handel with his *Messiah* (hardly known, for example, in France, Spain, Italy, or Russia), had a composer judged the temper of his time with such smashing success.

Before Haydn went to England in 1790, his principal publisher had been Artaria of Vienna; and Artaria – though 'sleepy' (Haydn) – was still entrusted with such essential publications as the Quartets, Opus 76. But a new publisher now entered Haydn's horizon and gradually became all-important: Breitkopf & Härtel of Leipzig. Haydn came into intimate contact with this firm *via* a middle-man, the composer's later biographer, Georg August Griesinger, who was sent to Vienna in 1799 as a tutor to the Saxon Ambassador's son and who subsequently became Secretary of Legation at the Embassy. Much of our knowledge about Haydn's activities comes from this three-way relationship. In a letter from Haydn to the Leipzig firm (then directed by Christoph Gottlob Breitkopf, and later, after 7 April 1800 – when Breitkopf died – by Gottfried Christoph Härtel), we read:

171

146

Vienna, 12th June 1799.

Dearest Friend!

I am really very much ashamed to have offended a man who has written so often and honoured me with so many marks of esteem (which I do not deserve), by answering him at this late date; it is not negligence on my part but the vast amount of BUSINESS which is responsible, and the older I get, the more business I have to transact daily. I only regret that on account of growing age and (unfortunately) the decrease of my mental powers, I am able to dispatch but the smallest part of it. Every day the world pays me compliments on the fire of my recent works, but no one will believe the strain and effort it costs me to produce them: there are some days in which my enfeebled memory and the unstrung state of my nerves crush me to the earth to such an extent that I fall prey to the worst sort of depression, and thus am quite incapable of finding even a single idea for many days thereafter; until at last Providence revives me, and I can again sit down at the pianoforte and begin to scratch away again. Enough of this!

Yesterday Herr Griesinger brought me the 2nd, 3rd and 4th volumes of our immortal Mozart, together with the musical periodical. Please let me know how much I owe you for them, and to whom I should give the money here in Vienna.

The publication of both these things does you great credit. I WOULD ONLY WISH, AND HOPE, THAT THE CRITICS DO NOT DEAL TOO SEVERELY WITH MY CREATION. . . .

Meanwhile, my dear friend, I remain, with every esteem,

Your obliging and obedient servant,
Joseph Haydn

The announcement of the benefit concert given at the Burgtheater, Vienna, on 28 March 1800 for Anton Weidinger, Court trumpeter and inventor of the keyed trumpet. The programme opened with a Symphony by Haydn, followed by the first public performance of his Trumpet Concerto with Weidinger – for whom the work had been written in 1796 – as soloist.

Throughout the period of Haydn's married life, his wife, Maria Anna, remains a rather shadowy figure. In fact one of the few concrete documents about her is her last Will and Testament, which she drew up in Vienna on 9 September 1799, when her husband was still at Eisenstadt. The document is not without interest, particularly since she made Haydn her residuary legatee. Far be it from us to attempt an analysis of the ills of the Haydns' marriage, but Maria Anna may have been something less of an ogre than she has been made to appear in the Haydn literature. That she was uneducated may be seen from the incredible spelling and grammar of her last Will, alas untranslatable in this respect, yet it is in fact a rather sympathetic document. She died of arthritis at Baden in March 1800. She had been boarding with Anton Stoll, Chapel Master of the Parish Church at Baden, for whom Mozart had composed the *Ave verum Corpus* (K.618) and with whom Haydn was on intimate terms.

Hardly had Haydn's wife been laid to rest, when his past once again rose to meet him in the person of his former mistress, Luigia Polzelli (Catherine Csech, his lady friend at Pressburg, was still alive, but we know nothing about her except that the composer was about to leave her the huge sum of 1,000 gulden in his own Will).

Polzelli had at one time extracted a promise from Haydn to marry her as soon as he and she were free. Now that Frau Haydn had died, Luigia actually managed to extract the following promise in writing from the good-natured Haydn:

[Statement to Luigia Polzelli. Italian]

    I, the undersigned, promise to Signora Loisa Polzelli (in case I should consider marrying again) to take no wife other than said Loisa Polzelli, and should I remain a widower, I promise said Polzelli to leave her, after my death, a pension for life of three hundred gulden (in figures, 300 fl.) in Viennese currency. Valid before any judge, I herewith set my hand and seal,

Joseph Haydn
Maestro di Capella di S. Alt. il Principe
Esterhazy.
[Haydn's seal]

Vienna, 23rd May 1800.

Haydn was no longer in the least interested in marrying the olive-skinned Italian soubrette whom he had loved in the decade 1780–90 at Eszterháza. He was quite content to remain single and, with a few more letters to *la* Polzelli sending her money, she fades quietly out of his life: for, having extracted this promise from Haydn, she was still free to marry whomsoever she pleased, which she proceeded to do, leaving for Italy with her new husband, Luigi Franchi, a singer. Haydn (who always expected Luigia to remarry – he had written from London to ask her to tell him the name of the one 'who is fortunate enough to have you') was probably not sorry to see the last of her. He did not forget her in his Will, however, but reduced the amount of money previously promised.

The final Oratorio on which Haydn and Gottfried van Swieten collaborated was *The Seasons*, based on James Thomson's popular and influential poem. If relations between Haydn and Swieten had been – as far as their different social statuses allowed – cordial, the new work soon drove

173

them apart. Haydn considered much of the new libretto trivial and frivolous (such as 'Praise of Industry'), but nevertheless he poured a lifetime of experience into the work's composition; nor did the Swieten adaptation lack for words to inspire the old composer to his greatest efforts, but a certain pessimism now began to enter Haydn's life-enhancing philosophy. For example, he thought of 'Winter' as a portrayal of his own declining years, and perhaps we may regard that incredible orchestral introduction (now available in its original, uncut version) as being Haydn's farewell to music. A report published in Leipzig in the *Allgemeine Musikalische Zeitung*, dated 24 March 1799, reads:

Now Haydn is engaged on a new great work, which the worthy *Herr Geheimrath Freyherr* van Swieten has arranged metrically from Thomson's 'Seasons', and of which he [Haydn] has already completed the first part, 'Spring'. The curiosity of all music lovers is already stretched to breaking-point. . . .

Haydn refers to the new oratorio in a letter to Ernst Ludwig Gerber, the famous German musical lexicographer:

Vienna 23rd September 1799.
. . . Since this subject cannot be as sublime as that of *The Creation*, comparison between the two will show a distinct difference. Despite this, and with the help of Providence, I shall press on, and when this new work is completed I shall retire . . .

In practice, the winter of 1800–01 saw a change of Haydn's living arrangements. On 19 November Griesinger again wrote to Leipzig:

. . . Haydn will not move into town this winter as he usually does, but will remain in his house in one of the most remote suburbs. He lives more quietly there but every visit to him is an expedition in itself. 'Even if I have to spend 1 fl. every day for a *Fiaker*' [carriage], he said to me, 'it costs less than having a *pied-à-terre* in town.' Judge the domestic man from this statement. . . .

In the Spring of 1801 Silverstolpe writes to Stockholm:

Vienna, 28 March 1801.
. . . Haydn's Seasons is finished, however, but a sickness which Haydn suffered postponed everything for so long that I think the performance will be put on next year. Too bad, for who can guarantee that the master will then be able to perform his work. He is too old. His works can only lose if they later fall into strange hands.

In the event, the performance was not postponed. Possibly the most important contemporary criticism was that written by Griesinger for the *Allgemeine Musikalische Zeitung*:

Vienna, 2 May 1801.
The Seasons, after Thomson, arranged by Baron Swieten and set to music by J. Haydn, was performed in the rooms of Prince Schwarzenberg on 24 and 27 April and on 1 May. Silent devotion, astonishment and loud enthusiasm relieved one another with the listeners; for the most powerful penetration of colossal ideas, the immeasurable quantity of happy ideas surprised and overpowered even the most daring of imaginations.

151, 152

The very subject of this poem invites everyone to participate. Who does not long for a return of spring? Who is not crushed by the heat of summer? Who does not rejoice over the fruits of autumn? To whom is the numbing frost of winter not tiresome? The wealth of such a subject makes great demands on the poetry. But even if all are fulfilled, a special talent is required for judging musical effects, choosing the metre and for making a useful order out of the various sections, and this can only be accomplished by a poet who himself has penetrated the secrets of music. Since the reader may acquaint himself with the poem through this musical journal (footnote points out that the poem is printed as appendix No. VII], he will be in a better position to see for himself just what Haydn had to do. That he did all this to perfection, however, is the unanimous opinion of the public here. Every word, under the hands of this musical Prometheus, is full of life and perception. Sometimes the melody of the voice delights, sometimes we are shaken, as a woodland torrent that bursts over its banks, by the mighty entrance of the orchestra; now one delights in a simple, artless expression; or one admires the sumptuous richness of swift and bright harmonies. From the beginning to the end the spirit is involuntarily swept along by emotions that range from the most artful, from the commonplace to the most sublime.

Another interesting report, dated 25 April 1801, with some valuable quotations from Haydn himself, appeared in the *Zeitung für die elegante Welt*:

... It would be more daring to wish to judge such a masterpiece on the basis of a single hearing; thus only a few general remarks here. Even during the composition, Herr Haydn stated the he would rather have composed another subject than the four seasons, for example the last judgement or something similar, because some ideas from *The Creation* involuntarily insinuated themselves into 'Spring'; also one noticed in the new work that some arias and choruses displayed a relationship, albeit a small one, with some numbers of *The Creation*. Who would want to blame the great master for that? *The Four Seasons*, instead, contained many passages which must move the coldest heart to the most gentle emotions, and many which are great, sublime, that sweeps us along like a great river and excite one to the greatest enthusiasm. But the imitation of the cock's crowing at dawn, the gun's explosion during the hunt, seem to me to be a mistaken concept of tone-painting in music, perhaps even a degradation of this divine art.

In Dies's biography (182) we read the following:

It will not displease the reader to learn Haydn's own view in a few words. The Emperor Franz asked him, on the occasion of a performance of *The Seasons*, which product of his art he preferred, *The Creation* or *The Seasons*. '*The Creation*,' replied Haydn. 'And why?' – 'In *The Creation*, angels speak and tell of God, but in *The Seasons* only Simon talks.'

To another friend, Giuseppe Carpani, Haydn said something similar. Carpani (212) writes:

The best of the criticisms was made by Haydn himself. I was present the first time this Oratorio was given in the house of Prince Schwarzenberg. The applause was general, cordial and without end. But I, astonished that two parts of the work containing such variety, quantity and excellence could spring from one brain [una testa sola], hastened at the end of the concert to find my Haydn and convey to him my most lively and sincere congratulations. Haydn, as soon as I opened my mouth, cut me short and spoke the following memorable words: 'It delights me that my music appeals to the public; but I do not accept compliments about it from you. I am sure you yourself realize that it [*The Seasons*] is not another Creation.

I feel it, and you too ought to feel it; but this is the reason why: in the one the characters were angels, in the Four Seasons they are peasants.' One could print tomes about a comparison between the two oratorios, but it could never be said better than in those few words of the composer himself.

172   Haydn decided to give the first public performance of *The Seasons* in the Great Hall of the Redoutensaal on 29 May 1801. After the triumphal first public performance of *The Creation* in 1799, Haydn must have expected a similar reception for this public première of his latest masterpiece. He was mistaken. Rosenbaum's Diary tells the whole story: 'I went ... to the Redouten Saal: *The Seasons* in a benefit performance for Haydn. It was not very well attended, a little over 700 people' – the hall hardly half filled! The fickle Viennese audience were turning away from their darling, and Rosenbaum would also have occasion to record a similar situation when Beethoven's Ninth Symphony was given the second time to a nearly empty hall twenty-three years later.

Haydn was now an old man and infinitely weary after half-a-century of unremitting labour for his Art. He gradually retired from public life, but for a few years he still continued to conduct charity performances of his three late Oratorios. And of course as princely Chapel Master, he continued his duties, administrative and otherwise, which meant that we have two last and glorious flowerings of Haydn's choral music: the *Schöpfungsmesse* of 1801 and the *Harmoniemesse* of 1802, both first given at the Bergkirche in Eisenstadt on 13 September 1801 and 8 September 1802, respectively. On the second of these two celebrations of Princess Marie Hermenegild's name-day Prince Starhemberg was present and noted in his diary:

> Wednesday, 8 September. . . . Splendid Mass, new and excellent music by the renowned Haydn and conducted by him. . . . Nothing more beautiful or better performed; after the Mass returned to the castle. . . . Afterwards, a huge and magnificent dinner ... with music during the meal. The Princess's health proposed by the Prince and echoed by fanfares and cannon, followed by several more [toasts], including one to me and one to Haydn, who was dining with us, proposed by me.
>
> After dinner we dressed for the ball, which was truly superb, like a Court ball. . . .

Here is a picture quite different from that of even a few years earlier. Haydn, we see, is now dining at the same table as the *Herrschaften* while the musicians play *Tafelmusik*; and a distinguished diplomat proposes the toast to Haydn. Within the span of his career in the service of the Esterházys, then, he had seen a complete transformation of his position – from a servant in livery, literally kissing the hem of the Prince's garment, to a distinguished artist invited to dine with the Prince, the Princess and their guests, and the object of affection and adulation. Haydn had accomplished this transformation modestly but no less thoroughly; and it must have been a source of quiet satisfaction to the son of the Rohrau wheelwright and the castle cook.

A local north German music society had sent Haydn a letter of thanks and gratitude after performing *The Creation*. It elicited from the composer a touching response:

[To Jean Phillip Krüger on behalf of the members of the Musikverein in Bergen, on the Island of Rügen, North Germany. German. Only the signature autograph]

Gentlemen,

It was indeed a most pleasant surprise to receive such a flattering letter from a part of the world where I could never have imagined that the products of my poor talents were known. But when I see that not only is my name familiar to you, but my compositions are performed by you with approval and satisfaction, the warmest wishes of my heart are fulfilled: to be considered a not wholly unworthy priest of this sacred art by every nation where my works are known. You reassure me on this point as regards your fatherland, but even more, you happily persuade me – and this cannot fail to be a real source of consolation to me in my declining years – that I am often the enviable means by which you, and so many other families sensible of heartfelt emotion, derive, in their homely circle, their pleasure – their enjoyment. How reassuring this thought is to me! – Often, when struggling against the obstacles of every sort which oppose my labours: often, when the powers of mind and body weakened, and it was difficult for me to continue in the course I had entered on; – a secret voice whispered to me: 'There are so few happy and contented peoples here below; grief and sorrow are always their lot; perhaps your labours will once be a source from which the care-worn, or the man burdened with affairs, can derive a few moments' rest and refreshment.' This was indeed a powerful motive to press onwards, and this is why I now look back with cheerful satisfaction on the labours expended on this art, to which I have devoted so many long years of uninterrupted effort and exertion. And now I thank you in the fulness of my heart for your kindly thoughts of me, and beg you to forgive me for delaying my answer so long: enfeebled health, the inseparable companion of the grey-haired septuagenarian, and pressing business, deprived me till now of this pleasure. Perhaps nature may yet grant me the joy of composing a little memorial to you, from which you may gather the feelings of a gradually dying veteran, who, even after his death, would fain survive in the charming circle of which you draw so wonderful a picture. I have the honour to be, with profound respect.

Your wholly obedient servant,
Joseph Haydn

Vienna, 22nd September 1802.

Haydn's relationship with his brother Johann Michael had always been the happiest, although they were almost always divided from each other geographically. Now, as Joseph intended to retire, Prince Esterházy offered the position of *Kapellmeister* to Michael who, after some vacillation, finally decided to remain in Salzburg. The following two letters in draft are all that survive from what must have been a fascinating correspondence:

[Draft of a letter from Haydn to his brother, Johann Michael, in Salzburg. German, 'Du' form.]

Vienna, 22 January 1803

Thank you heartily for all the kind wishes which you once again showed me in your recent letter. I, too, wish it would be within my power to fulfil your wish about my wretched health, which has plagued me for so long. For the last 5 months I have been subject to a continual nervous weakness which renders me quite incapable of doing anything. You can easily imagine how terribly this sudden change of health has depressed me, but I am not entirely desperate and hope to God that, when the weather changes, my previous health will be restored to at least half of what it once was.

[Draft of a letter from Johann Michael Haydn to Joseph Haydn, Salzburg. German, 'Du' form]

[c. February 1804]

Once again your name-day is approaching, for which I wish you, without further ado, that which is dear and valuable to you; but for my part I, too, wish for myself that you will continue to remember me in brotherly love. – I have long wanted to write to you about our musical organization (which didn't start life until the second part of January [continued in a note at the bottom of the page:] and which you couldn't describe as jammed full) NB. The whole organization was begun with too much enthusiasm; by the time it arrived here, it had already got stuck. The first ones skimmed the cream off, and all that was left for us was a watery soup. Anyway, I didn't write because I was ashamed of myself. I was astonished when I received my contract – they had always kept me in hopes and in promises, and so time went by. I would rather tell you the naked truth myself, before someone else tells you about it with distortions. My entire increase in salary for the whole year consists of not more than 150 gulden. If I could have foreseen this, I would have accepted with both hands the generous offer of your prince. Why didn't I do so at the first opportunity! Well, *tempi passati*! I must comfort myself with the general consolation: it had to happen that way and not otherwise. But just this one thing: I remain with the innermost respect Your o[ld] b[rother] p.p.

Haydn's last appearance as a conductor was at Vienna on 26 December 1803, the Feast of St Stephen. The occasion was a performance of *The Seven Words* (choral version), at 11 o'clock in the morning in the Redoutensaal, the scene of so many triumphs for Haydn, Mozart and Beethoven. The proceeds were for the poor of St Marx, a suburb in Vienna, where Mozart lies in an unmarked grave. Rosenbaum tells us 'It was very crowded. The Emperor gave 1,000 gulden.' It was the last chance for the Viennese to see in action the now frail old man who had changed the history of music.

Haydn had now retired from public life for good, living modestly in his house in Gumpendorf, watched over by the faithful Johann Elssler and other devoted servants, and the object of endless visits by admirers, both young and old. Haydn always liked young people and encouraged them in all sorts of ways. The young Carl Maria von Weber visited Haydn at about this time and wrote the following:

I was at Haydn's several times. Except for the weaknesses of old age, he is still cheerful and in a good humour [*aufgeräumt*], speaks very gladly of his affairs and is especially pleased to talk to pleasant young artists: the real stamp of a great man, and all that is true of Vogler, too; only with the difference that his literary wit is sharper than the natural kind of Haydn's. It is touching to see grown-up men coming to him, and how they call him Papa and kiss his hand.

Now that Haydn had also retired as Prince Esterházy's *Kapellmeister*, a substitute had to be found, and after Michael had declined the offer, the 88 difficult but talented Johann Nepomuk Hummel was engaged; in his turn he contributed several brilliant Masses for Princess Marie, who will have relished the Haydnesque style and orchestration of these new works.

As for Haydn, he now began his final large-scale opus – not a new piece of music but a thematic catalogue of those works which 'he could approximately recall having composed from his 18th to his 73rd year', the so- 176 called 'Elssler Catalogue' or *Haydn-Verzeichnis* (*HV*) of 1805. Elssler drew it up under Haydn's supervision and two copies were made, one for Breitkopf & Härtel and one which remained among Haydn's personal effects and eventually went to the Esterházy Archives (it has been published in facsimile, edited by the great Haydn scholar of our century, Jens Peter Larsen). We have documentary evidence of this project from Griesinger, who on 22 August 1804 reported to Breitkopf & Härtel that

... Haydn has stopped all work because of his health, and a quartet of which he has finished two movements is the child [*Schooßkind*] whom he now cares for and to whom he sometimes devotes a quarter of an hour. Otherwise he is now occupied with the complete catalogue of his works, which he will send you when it is finished.

On 15 April 1805 a visit of considerable importance took place at Haydn's house in Gumpendorf: the painter A. C. Dies paid his first call on the composer, whose biography he would soon undertake. Writing of this visit, Dies tells us that

Grassi [the sculptor] brought me to Haydn. It seemed to me that I did not displease him, for he came towards me, although sick for a long time and with both legs swollen, gave me both his hands, and received me with a cheerfulness that spread over his whole features and with such a penetrating look that I was surprised. This lively expression, the brownish (tinged with reddish) facial colour, the exceptionally neat clothing – Haydn was fully dressed –, his powdered wig and, the swelling notwithstanding, the boots he was wearing, and the gloves; all this made one forget any trace of illness and gave the old man of seventy-three the healthy look of a fifty-year-old, which was supported by his medium height and the fact that he was not at all heavy. 'You seem,' he said to me, 'to be surprised about my being fully dressed, though I'm still sick and weak, can't go out and breathe nothing but indoor air. My parents accustomed me from my earliest youth with discipline concerning cleanliness and order, and these two things have become second nature to me.' He also thanked his parents for encouraging him in fear of God and, because they were poor, they were obliged to be thrifty and hard-working. All things that one encounters very rarely in our young geniuses. [15f.] ... I feared that Haydn's weak state of health might prevent him from further conversation. I told him to look after himself, and my friend [Grassi] and I left him, because it was in any case time for his afternoon nap. They told me that for this nap Haydn undressed completely, put on a night dress and dressing gown and then went to bed. He was strictly punctual and winter or summer he kept to the period from half-past four to five o'clock; thus he slept no more than half-an-hour. After his rest was over he dressed completely, climbed down the stairs with great difficulty and went to the housekeeper's room. There he had some of the neighbour's children come and their cheerful play delighted Haydn; their jokes made him forget his sad condition ... He admits that his spirit is weak. He cannot think, cannot feel, cannot write, cannot hear music ...   [21f.]

Dies's visual description of the old Haydn, as seen through the eyes of an artist, is one of the most accurate we have. The Haydn of 1805 was merely a

A letter (now lost) written by Haydn on 17 August 1805 to his publishers, Artaria & Co. In this letter, which shows how shaky his hand had by then become, the composer states that he hopes to have merited some small reward for the pieces of music he enclosed; the works referred to cannot be identified, but they may well have been autographs (it is known that Artaria later owned many MS. scores which the firm had never published).

shell of his former self; on 5 May, when Dies went to visit Haydn for the third time, Haydn asked to be excused. The housekeeper said, 'He is always depressed when the weather is cold, or windy, or rainy.' Our 'official' biographies of Haydn, whether by Griesinger, Dies or the hopelessly inaccurate Carpani, are vignettes of an old, depressed man; the ruin of a giant intellect whose former wit and penetrating glance could only occasionally be called from its now perpetual slumber.

In 1808, on the Feast of St Joseph, Haydn's name-day, Antonio Polzelli conveyed congratulations to his former *Kapellmeister* on behalf of the members of Prince Esterházy's orchestra; it is not quite clear, from Haydn's answer, whether Polzelli and a few members of the band came to visit Haydn, or whether they wrote.

[To Antonio Polzelli on behalf of the Esterházy band, Eisenstadt. German, 'Du' form. Only the signature autograph]

Vienna, 20th March 1808.

My dear Son!

Your truly heart-warming remarks and those of all the members of the Princely Esterházy band, on the occasion of my name-day, moved me to tears. I thank you and all the others from the bottom of my heart, and ask you to tell all the members in my name that I regard them all as my dear children, and beg them to have patience and forbearance with their old, weak father; tell them that I am attached to them with a truly fatherly love, and that there is nothing I wish more than to have just sufficient strength so that I could enjoy once more the harmony of being at the side of these worthy men, who made the fulfilment of my duties so pleasant. Tell them that my heart will never forget them, and that it is the greatest honour for me, through the grace of my ILLUSTRIOUS PRINCE, to be placed at the head, not only of great artists, but of NOBLE AND THANKFUL HUMAN BEINGS.

Joseph Haydn

Musical Vienna decided to honour Haydn's seventy-sixth birthday with a gala performance of *The Creation*. The Liebhaber-Konzerte (Amateur Concerts), under the sponsorship of Prince Trauttmannsdorf, put on the Oratorio in their regular hall, the Aula (Great Hall) of the (old) University – the hall still exists – with Antonio Salieri as conductor, Conradin Kreutzer at the piano (he would later become a well-known operatic composer) and Therese Fischer, Carl Weinmüller and Julius Radicchi as soloists. The Oratorio was sung in Carpani's Italian translation, and the date of the performance was set for 27 March. Griesinger relates:

181, 182
159

I was surprised that he could make up his mind, considering his failing health, to attend the ...[concert]...on 27 March...He [Haydn] answered: 'Consideration for my health could not stop me. It's not the first time that I have been honoured, and I wanted to show that I'm still capable of receiving it.'

On the day appointed, Haydn was carried into the Great Hall to the sound of trumpet fanfares and tumultous applause, and seated next to Princess Esterházy. The cream of Viennese society was there to pay a last public homage to the Father of the Symphony (as they thought him) and String Quartet. Salieri and Haydn embraced tenderly, surrounded by cheering crowds. Beethoven, the tears streaming down his face, bent and kissed the hand of his former teacher. When the passage, 'And there was Light' was reached, Haydn (as Carpani, who was an eye-witness, relates) 'raised his trembling arms to Heaven, as if in prayer to the Father of Harmony.' At the end of the First Part, it was thought advisable to take Haydn home. Carpani describes the scene:

Two robust athletes picked up the armchair in which he was seated, and amidst the greetings, the applause and the acclamations of the whole room, the harmonious man of triumph approached the stairs; but, having arrived at the doors, he made a sign to stop. The porters obeyed and turned him round to the public; he thanked them with the usual gestures of acceptance, then, looking at heaven, and with tears in his eyes, he blessed his children.

We now come to the last surviving letter sent by Haydn; fittingly, it is addressed to his now much mellowed and indeed almost sympathetic Prince Nicolaus II Esterházy. Only the signature is autograph.

Most Serene Highness,
Gracious Prince and Lord!
    I humbly place myself at Your Serene Highness' feet for the gracious approval of my request, whereby with the utmost kindness you take over my yearly expenditures for the doctor and apothecary. By this new act of generosity Your Serene Highness has freed me from a most pressing anxiety, and thus enabled me to await the end of my earthly existence in peace and serenity. May Heaven grant my zealous wish that Your Serene Highness live in everlasting well-being and Your Gracious Highness' illustrious family in ever increasing prosperity. I remain ever your most devoted and
                                   Your Serene Highness'
                                        humble servant
                                   Joseph Haydn
Vienna, 22nd December 1808.

Haydn died on 31 May 1809; his last days are described by the faithful Johann Elssler in a letter to Griesinger:

                                                            Vienna, 30th June 1809
Most nobly born
    Highly respected Herr v. Griesinger!
It has long been my intention, Sir, to give you news of the death of our beloved benefactor and father. Right after his death I went to [your] H[err] Porter and asked whether I could not send a letter to you, Sir. H[err] Porter said to me, however, that there is no possibility yet because it is not known which roads are open. Now I ask you, Sir, for your pardon and kind patience if I come so late with your request for I know that you, Sir, are always anxious to know how our good and kind Papa Haydn fares. But the confusion at that moment was too great.
    With tears in my eyes I report to you, Sir, our dear Father's death. The day that you, Sir, said good-bye to our good Papa and said, we won't see each other for a long time or perhaps we will see each other soon, just after Your Grace left the room, our good Papa said, we really won't see each other for a long time, he started to weep and said, my dear Johann, I won't be seeing Herr v. Griesinger any more, the war business depresses me right down to the ground. We had a lot of trouble (I and cook Nannerl) to get these thoughts out of our good Papa's mind and to quiet him down, but our good Papa was too weak and altogether couldn't quite pull himself together and was always anxious about how the war was going to continue.

183   When the Imp. French army moved into the Maria Hülfer Lienie [the outer walls of Vienna] on 10th May in the morning at a quarter of seven o'clock, our good Papa was still lying in bed. I and Nannerl were just busy getting Papa out of bed. – For the noise and confusion on the street were too great at this particular moment and we didn't have any people at our side who could comfort our good Papa; anyway as we were still busy getting the Papa out of bed, four canister-shots exploded by the Lienie, one after the other, and indeed, we kept one ball that fell into the courtyard as a souvenir, because of these explosions the door to the bedroom blew wide open and all the windows rattled, our good Papa was shocked and cried in a loud voice, 'Children, don't be afraid, for where Haydn is, nothing can happen' and trembled violently all over his body. But the whole day they were shooting from the fortress [in town], and our good Papa composed himself a bit though it was very hard for him, his nerves were hit too hard, and well! His whole body sank, but he still enjoyed his food and drink but as for walking I couldn't get our good Papa on his feet all by myself and the strongest medicines didn't help any longer. The *Kayser Lied* was still played three times a day, though, but on May 26th at half-past mid-day the Song was played for the last time and that 3 times over, with such expression and taste, well! that our good Papa was astonished about it himself and said he hadn't played the Song like that for a long time and was very pleased about it and felt well altogether till evening at 5 o'clock then our good Papa began to lament that he didn't feel well, but he still stayed up another half-an-hour but at 5:30, Well! Our good Papa asked to be taken right to bed and then he began to shiver a little and had a headache. All sorts of things were given him, and our good Papa felt so much better on that same evening and had quite a good night's sleep and was so well when he got up and the other things were all right too, so that of a dying moment nothing was felt. Saturday the 27th of May our good Papa asked about 8:30 o'clock to get up as usual and get dressed, but his bodily strength wouldn't allow it, and so our good Papa didn't leave his bed any more. The numbing got much worse, but so quietly and willing in everything that we were all astonished, our good Papa didn't complain of any pains, and when we asked him how he felt, we always received the reply, 'Children, be of good cheer, I'm well.'

The 29th of May we asked for a *Consillium* to be held with the permission of H[err] v. Hohenholz. The medicus Doctor Böhm was asked to come, for our good Papa needed it and he [Böhm] is also a very clever man, so the *Consillium* was held on the 30th in the morning, but despite all kinds of medicines administered, it was all of no use, and our good Papa got steadily weaker and quieter, 4 hours before his death our good Papa still spoke but then we didn't hear another sound, our good Papa had reactions and knew us 10 minutes before the end, for our good Papa squeezed Nannerl's hand, and the 31st of May in the early morning five minutes before a quarter to one o'clock our good Papa went quietly and peacefully to sleep, at his death there was no one there but me, the servants and a neighbour who also signed the will as a witness [Anton Meilinger, of 74 Kleine Steingasse]. Our good Papa is buried in God's field [cemetery] in front of the *Hundsturmer Lienie*, in his own grave.

The 31st March 1732 our good Papa was born, and 1809 the 31st of May was for us all the saddest day of death for ever. Our good Papa was 77 years and 61 full days old.

Otherwise everything is in the best order and everything remains until the whole business [of the legacy proceedings] starts, the Nannerl and the niece [*Mum*] of the late Papa and also the maid are still in the house, I'm with my wife and children at home and carry on as best I can in these trying times. May God help us out of our sad position, I eagerly hope to see Your Grace, God keep Your Grace in the best of health and we all kiss your hands

Your thankful
Johann Essler m.p.
Copyist and Servant of the
late Herr v. Haydn.

186   N.B. I have taken my good Papa in plaster.

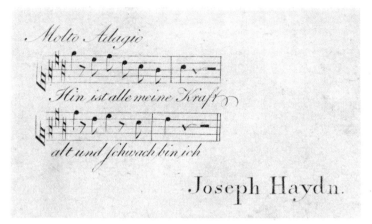

Haydn's visiting card, bearing the opening phrase of his part song 'Hin ist alle meine Kraft, alt und schwach bin ich' ('Gone is all my strength, old and weak am I'), which the aged composer had printed after his last, unfinished, instrumental work – the String Quartet in D minor, 'Op. 103', of 1803 – had been issued by Breitkopf & Härtel; in order to bring home the message that Haydn's creative genius had deserted him, the publishers had included the same phrase at the end of the printed score.

EXAMPLES OF AUTOGRAPH SCORES

189   The first page of Haydn's very early keyboard Sonata
No. 13 in G (Hoboken XVI:6), composed *c.* 1755(?). The
piece, entitled 'Partita per il Clavicembalo Solo', also bears
the composer's familiar dedication 'In Nomine Domini'
and his signature 'Giuseppe Haydn'.

190 The opening of the Divertimento in F (II:15), for two oboes, two bassoons and two horns; the date 1760 (top, right) was originally written 760 and the figure 1 was added later. At the bottom of the page note the word 'daß' in Haydn's hand (possibly trying out a different pen?).

191 (opposite) The first page of Symphony No. 40, dated 1763. At this period Haydn used the spelling 'Synfonia'; later – by 1765 – he adopted the spelling 'Sinfonia'. This work was misplaced in the old chronological list of Breitkopf & Härtel (prepared in 1907 by Eusebius Mandyczewski) because the autograph was not then known to have survived; in Haydn's own *Verzeichnis* (cf. ill. 176) the symphony is listed as No. 15, together with other works composed in 1763 (thus, No. 72 = *Verzeichnis* No. 13, and No. 13 = *Verzeichnis* No. 14).

192 The beginning of an aria sung by Buonafede in Act I
of *Il mondo della luna* (1777), which exists in several different
autograph versions. The sudden substitution of several
singers in Haydn's operatic troupe at Eszterháza shortly
before the Opera received its première forced the composer
to revise many sections of the work.

193 The first insertion aria written by Haydn for his mistress, the soprano Luigia Polzelli: this aria – 'Quando la rosa' (XXIVb:3) – was composed in 1779 for the production at Eszterháza of Anfossi's *La Metilde ritrovata*. Luigia Polzelli had been engaged by Prince Nicolaus, together with her husband Antonio (a violinist), in March 1779; they proved to be less than satisfactory and the Prince dismissed both on Christmas Day 1780; as a result of Haydn's intervention, however, they were reinstated and remained in Esterházy service until Prince Nicolaus's death in 1790.

194 A page from Act I of the Opera *La fedeltà premiata* (1780), showing part of Celia's aria, 'Deh soccorri', in which the original version of the Largo began with a muted horn solo (top line); after the horn player for whom this passage was intended left Eszterháza, Haydn changed the solo from horn to bassoon.

195 The beginning of the Kyrie, from the *Missa Cellensis* in
C ('Mariazellermesse'; XXII:8), 1782. The instrumen-
tation – note that the edge of the page was cropped at the
bindery – reads: 'Clarini' (trumpets); 'Tÿmpano'; '2
oboe'; 'Violino Imo'; [Violino] 2do'; 'Viola'; 'Soprano';
'Alto'; 'Tenore'; 'Basso'; [blank stave]; 'Organo'. The
Mass was intended for the great Benedictine Priory of
Mariazell in Styria, and was commissioned by a friend of
the composer, Anton Lieber von Kreutzner, a retired
military man. In 1766 Haydn had composed a large-scale
work, the *Missa Cellensis in honorem Beatissimae Virginis
Mariae* ('Cellensis' refers to 'Celle' = German, 'Zell'), also
for Mariazell, where – as a penniless student – he had been a
guest of the monks.

196 The beginning of the second movement of Symphony No. 91 in E flat (1788), with the scoring: '2 Corni in b fa'; 'Oboe 1'; [oboe] 2$^{\text{d[o]}}$'; 'Flauto'; 'Fagotti'; 'Violi[no] 1°'; [Violino] 2do'; 'Viola'; 'Violoncello'; and 'Contra Bassi'. This work was dedicated, together with Symphonies No. 90 and 92, to Comte d'Ogny (cf. ill. 47) in Paris.

197 (opposite) The *Responsorium* 'Libera me' (XXIIb:1): the tenor part (with the performer's own indications for singing the traditional linking passages – 'Libera me, Domine', 'Tremens factus' etc. – in Gregorian Chant). Haydn himself wrote out all the principal parts of this work, the autograph of which was discovered in the Cathedral of St Martin, Eisenstadt, in March 1966 (before this date the work had not been known to exist). It is not certain for what occasion this 'Libera' was composed – possibly following the death in 1782 of the Dowager Princess Maria Anna Esterházy (widow of Prince Paul Anton), or after the death in 1790 of either Princess Maria Elisabeth, wife of Prince Nicolaus (March) or of the Prince himself (September).

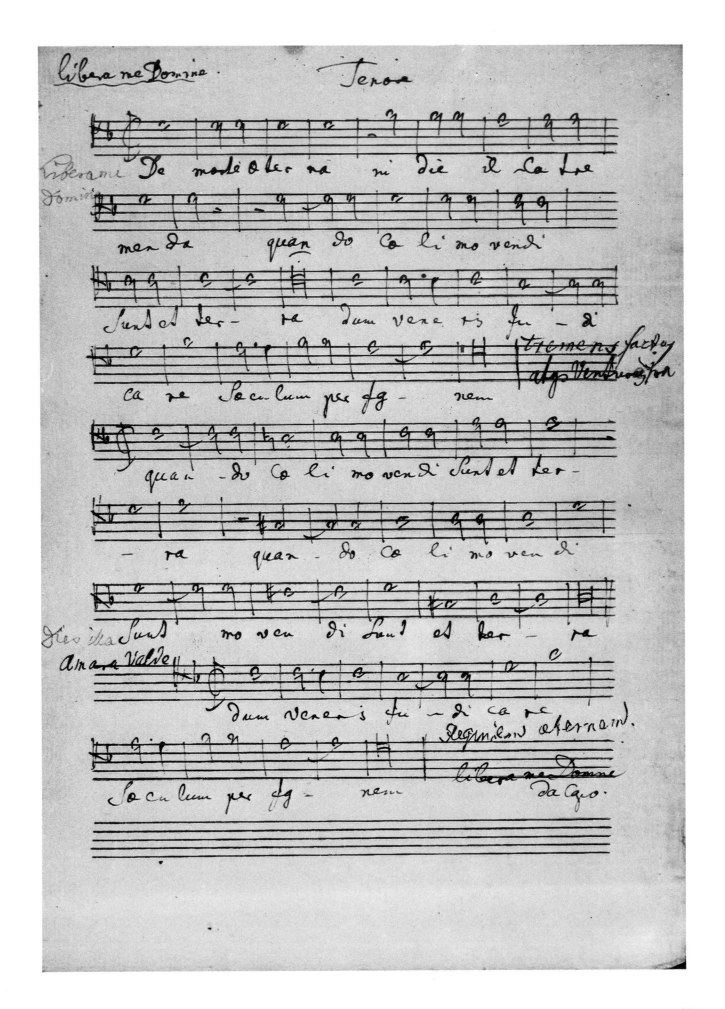

198 The 'Canon Cancrizanz' – 'Thy Voice, O Harmony'
(1791): the canon is at the bottom in two versions, one
marked 'Canone a tre. Auf Vierfache arth Cancrizanz'.
Haydn later used the canon for the First Commandment
(cf. ill. 200), and there is a pencil note (in an unknown
hand, bottom right) indicating that this is the solution to
'Du sollst an Einen Got [*sic*] glauben', the solution being
the full version written out above. Note that canon uses
both G and soprano clefs.

199 (opposite, above) Draft for the March for the Prince of
Wales, *c.* 1792; this march for wind band is scored for
trumpet, two horns, two clarinets, two bassoons and
serpent. The percussion part – following an old military
band tradition – was improvised by the players.

200 (opposite, below) Puzzle Canon, 'Du sollst an einen
Gott glauben' (First Commandment; XXVIIa:1), written
in circular fashion in four different ways, from left to right
and right to left, in black and red ink respectively.

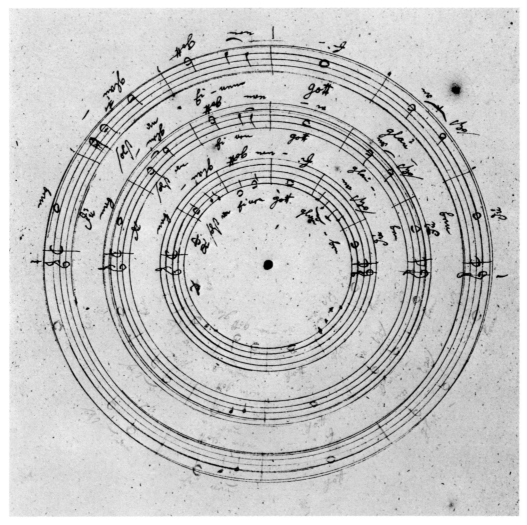

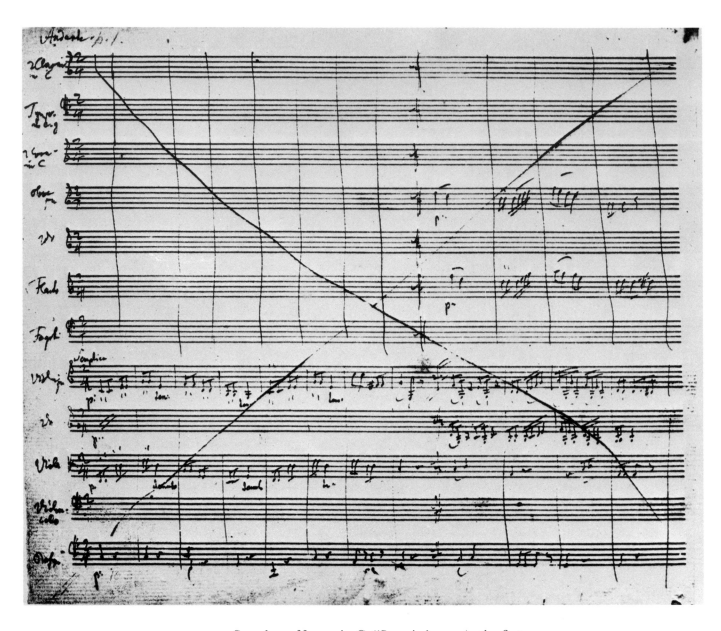

201 Symphony No. 94 in G ('Surprise'; 1791): the first page of the cancelled version of the second movement – Andante – without the surprise.

202, 203 (opposite) Symphony No. 99 (1793): *(above)* a page of sketches for this work – the first Symphony in which Haydn introduced clarinets; note, in line 6, the abbreviations 'Clar:' and 'Clarin'; and, in line 9, the entry of the timpani.

The piece for musical clock (Flötenuhrstück; XIX:32; *below*) was incorporated in a clock built in 1793 by Pater Niemecz; it was also used in the Finale of Symphony No. 99. Musical clocks were very popular in Europe in Haydn's day, and he wrote a number of pieces for this purpose, frequently adapting themes from his Quartets and Symphonies; he also adapted, for Niemecz's clock of 1793, the Minuet from Symphony No. 101 ('Clock').

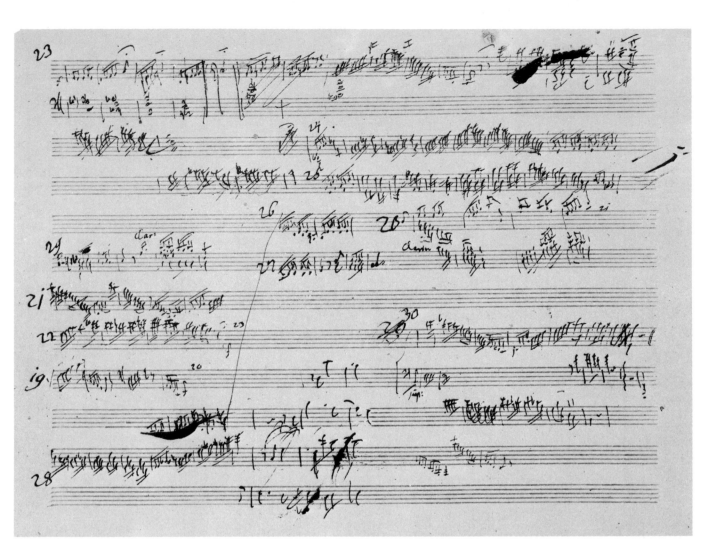

204   The opening of the *Missa in tempore belli* (1796); the
first performance of this Mass seems to have taken place in
Vienna, on 26 December 1796, at the church of the Piarists
(cf. ill. 163).

205 The first page of score (the title page is blank) of the String Quartet, Op. 77, No. 1 (1799). The two works comprising Op. 77 were dedicated to Prince Lobkowitz (cf. ill. 145).

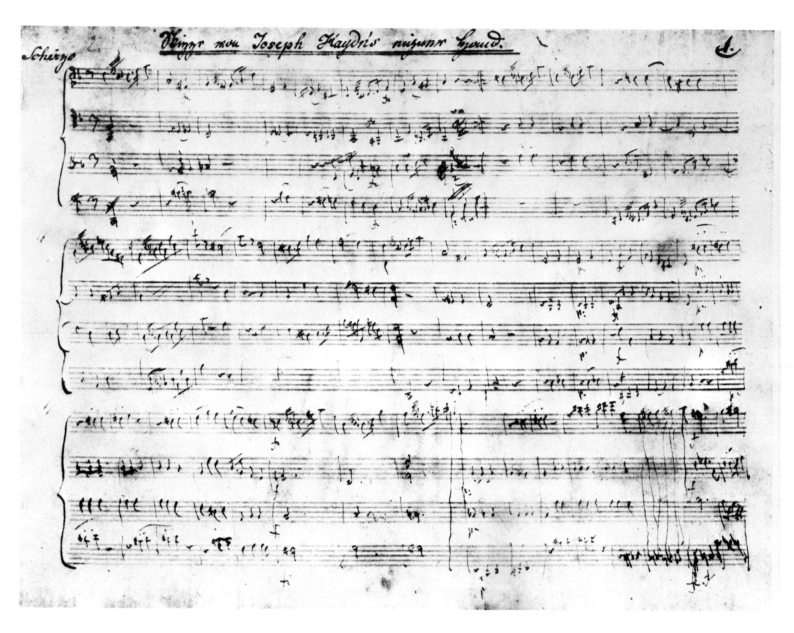

206 Haydn's sketch for the beginning of the Minuet of his unfinished String Quartet in D minor 'Op. 103' (1803); the title 'Scherzo' and note stating that this is a sketch in Haydn's own hand are later additions, not by the composer. Note, in the lower bracket, that after eight bars a full bar of rest was inserted later. This Minuet is the last known instrumental movement that Haydn composed; it was intended to be the third of four, but the Quartet's outer movements were never finished. The finished autograph of the slow movement (in a private collection) bears the date 1803.

1732 Franz Joseph Haydn born on 31 March (or 1 April?) at Rohrau and baptized there on 1 April.
1737 Having displayed musical talent by the age of five, Joseph is sent to Hainburg to attend the school run by his cousin, the town schoolmaster and choir director at the parish church, Johann Mathias Franck; there he receives his first formal musical education.
   On 14 September Johann Michael Haydn is baptized at Rohrau (he will also become a well-known composer, living for many years in Salzburg).
1738 During the celebration of the *Jubilaeum Universale* (victory 'over Turk and Heathen'), Franck organizes musical events in Hainburg in which H. takes part (he is known to have played the kettledrums on one ceremonial occasion).
1739 Georg Reutter, Jr., Chapel

Master of St Stephen's Cathedral, Vienna, visits Hainburg; after hearing H. sing, he engages him as a choir-boy.
1740 H. leaves Hainburg for Vienna to join the Cathedral choir.
   Following the death of the Emperor Charles VI, he is succeeded in Austria by his daughter, Maria Theresa.
1741 On 28 July the Cathedral *Capelle* take part in the funeral service for Antonio Vivaldi.
1743 On 23 December Johann Evangelist Haydn is baptized at Rohrau (the third, though less talented, musical brother later became an unpaid tenor in the service of the Esterházys; he dies at Eisenstadt on 16 May 1805).
1745 The Empress Maria Theresa catches H. climbing on scaffolding at Schönbrunn and has him beaten.
   Michael H. arrives in Vienna to join the Cathedral choir.

1748 Because H.'s voice is breaking, his brother Michael substitutes for him as soloist at the feast days at Klosterneuburg Abbey in honour of St Leopold; the Empress, who is present, rewards Michael with 24 ducats.
1749 In November H. is dismissed from the Cathedral choir for cutting off a fellow-chorister's pigtail.

1750 H. makes a pilgrimage to Mariazell.
1751–4(?) Now obliged to fend for himself in Vienna, H. lives in a garret of the 'Michaelerhaus' (Michaelerplatz No. 1220); the poet Pietro Metastasio – who taught H. the Italian language – and the opera composer Nicola Porpora – to whom H. attached himself as valet and assistant – also reside in this building.
   H. becomes leader of the orchestra of the Hospitallers and organist to Count Haugwitz; he studies the music and theoretical writings of C. P. E. Bach (*Versuch über die wahre Art das Clavier zu spielen*, part 1, 1753 [part 2 appeared in 1762]), Mattheson and Fux (whose *Gradus ad Parnassum* H. used for teaching purposes all his life).
1754 On 23 February H.'s mother dies at Rohrau.
1756 12 May: H.'s first love, Therese Keller, takes the veil and enters the Order of Poor Clares in Vienna; H. composes works specially for this ceremony. (In 1760 H. marries Therese's sister.)
1756–7(?) While living in the Seilerstätte in Vienna, H. is robbed of all his possessions and is helped out by friends.
   H. a guest of Carl Joseph, Edler von Fürnberg, at his Weinzierl estate near Wieselburg in Lower Austria; H.'s first

c. **1747–8**(?) A *Salve Regina* (lost) in many parts.
c. **1748–9**(?) *Missa brevis alla cappella* in G, 'Rorate coeli desuper' (XXII:3), probably composed for the Cathedral *Gnadenbildcapelle*.
1749 *Missa brevis* in F (XXII:1) for two soprano soloists (now thought to have been the Haydn brothers); the parts (at Eisenstadt) were later dated '1749' in the composer's own hand.
c. **1750–3**(?) *Motetto de Venerabili Sacramento* (nos. I–IV) composed for the Feast of Corpus Christi.
   Many string trios, harpsichord sonatas and trios, as well as organ concertos and divertimenti for various combinations of instruments; also church music and dances (including the 'Seitenstetten Minuets'; IX:1).
1752–3(?) The Opera *Der krumme Teufel* (with libretto by Felix Kurz-Bernardon); a performance – possibly the first, possibly a revival – is given at the Kärntnerthortheater on 29 May 1753.

1756 Organ Concerto in C (XVIII:1) and *Salve Regina* in E (XXIIIb:1); possibly also the Double Concerto for organ, violin and strings in F (XVIII:6).

1756–7(?)**–1760** The early string quartets, of which nine survive (Op. I, nos. 1–4 and 6; Op. II, nos. 1, 2, 4, and 6 – Hoboken III: 1–4, 6, 7, 8, 10, 12).
   Also string trios and two Divertimenti for strings and horns (II:21, 22).

string quartets written there and performed by the parish priest, the estates' manager, H. himself and one of the Albrechtsberger brothers (Johann Georg or Anton Johann).
1757–8(?) H. engaged as *Kapellmeister* by Ferdinand Maximilian Franz, Count von Morzin (1693–1763), whose summer residence was the castle at Unter-Lukavec in Bohemia (now Dolní Lukavice, Czechoslovakia).
1759 According to the composer (and his biographer Griesinger), H.'s Symphony No. 1 was composed in this year for Count Morzin's orchestra.
1760 Michael H. at Grosswardein, where he composes a series of symphonies and other works, including the Violin Concerto in B flat (20 Dec.).
   9 Nov.: H.'s marriage contract with Maria Anna Aloysia Apollonia Keller; the wedding takes place in St Stephen's Cathedral, Vienna, on 26 November.
1761 Count Morzin dismisses his *Capelle* for lack of funds.
   19 March: possible date on which H. began to reorganize the constitution of the Esterházy *Capelle*.
   Contracts for several new musicians signed 1 April, others (including Haydn's) signed in Vienna on 1 May. As *Vice-Kapellmeister* (under Gregor Werner) in Prince Paul Anton Esterházy's household, H.'s initial salary is 400 fl. p.a.
   6 Oct.: a Polish nobleman, Count Oginsky, plays the clarinet at a concert given in the Esterházy Palace in the Wallnerstraße, Vienna.
1762 Following the death of Prince Paul Anton Esterházy on 18 March, his successor, Nicolaus I, increases H.'s salary by 200 fl. on 25 June. Göttweig and Kremsmünster Abbey, begin to form collections of MS. copies of compositions by H.
1763 As part of a three-day festival at Eisenstadt after the marriage of Count Anton Esterházy and Marie Therese, Countess Erdödy, H.'s Opera *Acide* is performed on 11 January.
   Having four horn players available for the first time, H. scores two Symphonies (13 and 72) accordingly.
   The Leipzig publisher Breitkopf begins to distribute MS. copies of works by H.
   Michael H. is engaged as *Conzertmeister* to the Prince Archbishop of Salzburg, Sigismund von Schrattenbach.
1764 On 21 April H. meets his brother at Rohrau to settle their father's estate.
   During the summer H. conducts opera performances at Pressburg; *Acide* probably revived.
   Joseph Elssler engaged as music copyist at the Esterházy court.
   Quartets and Symphonies by H. printed in Paris (apparently without his knowledge) by three publishers.
1765 *Capellmeister* Werner protests to Prince Nicolaus about H. and the disorder in the *Capelle* and its music; H. is reprimanded. In this year H. probably began his *Entwurf-Katalog* (a vitally

1758 *Der neue krumme Teufel* (lost), a revival – with altered title – of H.'s opera of 1752–3(?), again performed at the Kärnterthortheater.

1757(?) or **1758–61** Symphonies Nos. 1–5, 10, 15, 18, 27, 32, 33, 37, and 'A' (? also Nos. 16, 17, 19, 20, 25 and 'B').
   Also string trios, Divertimenti for wind band, Concertini and Divertimenti for harpsichord and strings.

1761 Symphonies Nos. 6–8 ('Le Matin', 'Le Midi', 'Le Soir') composed – with many solo passages for his leading players – to inaugurate the new *Capelle*.
   The Divertimento for clarinets and horns (II:14) and that for clarinets, horns and strings (II:17; 1761?), possibly associated with the visit of Count Oginsky (the *Capelle* contained no clarinets).

1762 Symphony No. 7; the Horn Concerto in D (VIId:3) – possibly composed for Joseph Leutgeb (later a friend of Mozart).

1763 *Acide* (XXVIII:1) Symphonies Nos. 12, 13, 40, and 71; Concerto for Double Bass (Violone; VIIc:1) and Cantata, 'Vivan gl'illustri sposi' – both lost; *La Marchesa Nespola* (XXX:1), performed April–August. Cantata, 'Destatevi, o miei fidi' (XXIXa:2), performed on 6 December, Prince Nicolaus's name-day.

1764 Cantata, 'Da qual gioja' (XXIVa:3), performed on Prince Nicolaus's return from the coronation of Joseph II (27 March) as Holy Roman Emperor in Frankfurt; Symphonies Nos. 21–24; Divertimento for harpsichord and strings (XIV:4); Cantata 'Qual dubbio' (XXIVa:4), performed on Prince Nicolaus's name-day, 6 December.
1765 Symphonies Nos. 28–31 (No. 31 is scored for four horns, made possible by the replacement of two of the earlier players, one having died and one having left).

EVENTS IN HAYDN'S LIFE

important thematic catalogue of his own compositions).

Quartets by H. are published in Amsterdam and reach England by June.

On 18 August Emperor Francis Stephen dies in Innsbruck; Joseph II becomes co-regent in Austria with his mother, Maria Theresa; he is later married to Princess Maria Josepha of Bavaria.

On 12 December a son is born to Count Anton Esterházy and his wife, Marie Therese; the *Capelle* takes part in a thanksgiving service at Eisenstadt the following day. The infant will later inherit the princely title, as Nicolaus II, in 1794.

1766 Following the death at Eisenstadt of Gregor Werner (5 March), H. is appointed full *Kapellmeister*; on 2 May he buys a house (No. 82 Klostergaße) in Eisenstadt.

After the first performance of *La canterina* at Eisenstadt on 27 July, H. and the principal singers are rewarded by Prince Nicolaus.

The *Wienerisches Diarium*, referring to H. and many other Austrian composers, calls him the 'darling of our nation'.

The first phase of the construction of Eszterháza is completed.

1767 *La canterina* performed on 16 Feb. at Pressburg before Duke Albert of Sachsen-Teschen and his wife, the Archduchess Marie Christine.

In the autumn Prince Nicolaus visits Paris and Versailles; among those accompanying him is Luigi Tomasini, leader of the *Capelle*. H.'s new Symphony completed on 1 December, possibly intended for performance (along with the Cantata) on the Prince's name-day – 6 Dec. – to celebrate his safe return.

1768 In March H. conducts his *Stabat Mater* for Hasse at the Hospitallers in Vienna. On 15 May the Cantata 'Applausus' is performed at Zwettl Abbey in honour of the abbot (50th anniversary of his taking holy orders).

On 2 August, Eisenstadt is ravaged by fire and H.'s house destroyed; it is rebuilt at the Prince's expense.

Duke Albert of Sachsen-Teschen and Archduchess Marie Christine make official visit to Eszterháza, 24–29 Sept.; additional musicians from Eisenstadt and Oedenburg are required for the lavish balls and firework displays which mark the occasion. (A second visit, with similar entertainments, took place in August 1769).

1769 Strolling players are regularly engaged from now on to perform German plays at Eszterháza in summer months; H. provides incidental music.

H.'s String Quartets, Op. 9 (III: 19–24) issued by J. J. Hummel of Berlin and Amsterdam.

1770 On 21 March the Esterházy *Capelle* perform *Lo speziale* at Baron von Sumerau's palace in the Mariahilf suburb of Vienna.

On 25 July H. and the *Capelle* perform at Kittsee during a visit by Empress Maria Theresa, Joseph II and other members of the imperial family.

Le pescatrici first performed at Eszterháza to celebrate the wedding of Prince Nicolaus's niece, Countess Lamberg, and Count Pocci; other lavish entertainments are provided over a three-day period.

The painter Ludwig Guttenbrunn is engaged at Eszterháza and subsequently becomes Frau Haydn's lover.

1770–1 H. is seriously ill for a time.

1771 On 29 March in Vienna, H. conducts his *Stabat Mater* at the Basilica Maria-Treu (Piarists' Church).

COMPOSITIONS BY HAYDN

The keyboard *Capriccio* 'Acht Sauschneider' (XVII:1).

Many Baryton Trios for Prince Nicolaus – series begun before 1765, but continuing regularly thereafter.

1766 *Missa Cellensis in honorem B.V.M.* (XXII:5), composed for the Benedictine Priory of Mariazell.

Intermezzo, *La canterina* (XXVIII:2); Baryton Trio (XI:24); Piano Sonata No. 29 (XVI:45).

1767 *Stabat Mater* (XX:*bis*); Baryton Trios (XI:42, 43); Piano Sonata No. 30 (XVI:19); Horn Trio in E flat (IV:5); Symphony No. 35; Cantata, 'Al tuo arrivo felice' (XXIVa:3; lost)

1768 Cantata, 'Applausus' (XXIVa:6); Baryton Trio (XI:57); Symphony No. 49 ('La Passione').

Lo speziale, 'dramma giocoso' (XVIII:3), given on 28 Sept. to inaugurate the newly built theatre at Eszterháza.

1769 Baryton Trio (XI:79); Symphonies Nos. 41(?), 48 ('Maria Theresa'; date from MS. copy by Joseph Elssler).

Work on Opera *Le pescatrici* (XXVIII:4) begins.

1770(?) Piano Sonata No. 23 (XVI:20; lost).

1771 *Salve Regina* in G minor (XXIIIa:2); String Quartets, Op. 17 (III:25–30); Symphony No. 42; Piano Sonata No. 33 in C minor (XVI:20), in

EVENTS IN HAYDN'S LIFE

1772 The Carl Wahr troupe are engaged to perform at Eszterháza; their performances (during five seasons) include German translations of plays by Shakespeare.

The princely order that only the wives and families of H. and four leading musicians shall be allowed to come to Eszterháza gives rise to discontent among the other members of the *Capelle*, and at the end of the season (November) the 'Farewell' Symphony serves to remind Nicolaus of this fact; the hint is taken by the Prince.

On 6 December (? at Eisenstadt), H.'s new Mass performed to celebrate Nicolaus's name-day.

Sponsored by Count Ladislaus Erdődy, Ignaz Pleyel begins his studies with H. and remains until 1777.

1773 *L'infedeltà delusa* given first performance at Eszterháza on 26 July to celebrate the name-day of the Dowager Princess Maria Anna; the opera is performed again on 1 Sept. when the Empress Maria Theresa pays a formal visit, followed the next day by a performance of *Philemon und Baucis* by the marionette troupe. H. is introduced to the Empress.

1774 The Carl Wahr Troupe perform *Der Zerstreute* (the German version of Regnard's *Le Distrait*) at Eszterháza.

1775 *Il ritorno de Tobia* performed in Vienna (2 and 4 April).

The Archduke Ferdinand and his wife Maria Beatrice d'Este visit Eszterháza, 28–30 August; *L'incontro improvviso* performed for the first time on 29 August in their honour.

1776 This year sees the first full-scale operatic season at Eszterháza, with works by Haydn and other composers; this pattern will continue until 1790. Gluck's *Orfeo* is given in February, and H.'s *Dido* in March.

The town of Eisenstadt is severely damaged by fire on 17 July; H.'s house is burnt and again rebuilt at Prince Nicolaus's expense (later, in 1778, H. decides to sell the house).

1777 In July the Esterházy *Capelle* make a guest appearance at Schönbrunn, performing H.'s *Hexen-Schabbas* and Ordoñez's *Alceste*.

Prince Nicolaus's second son (also Nicolaus) marries Maria Anna, Countess von Weissenwolf, at Eszterháza on 3 August; to mark the occasion, H.'s Opera *Il mondo della luna* is performed.

1778 On 27 October H. sells his house in Eisenstadt for 2,000 gulden.

1779 The violinist Antonio Polzelli and his wife Luigia are engaged to join the *Capelle*; Luigia will shortly become H.'s mistress. He composes an Aria, 'Quando la rosa', especially for her. The operatic repertoire at Eszterháza includes twelve new productions; H.'s new marionette opera receives its first performance.

On 18 November, the theatre at Eszterháza and much of the music stored there are destroyed by fire: the opera troupe move into the adjacent marionette theatre (*L'isola disabitata*, 6 December). The cornerstone of the new theatre is laid by Prince Nicolaus on 18 December, on which occasion Symphony No. 70 is performed.

1780 H. begins a long correspondence with the Vienna publishers, Artaria & Co., who issue his Six Piano Sonatas, Nos. 48–52 and 33 in March. On 14 May H. is elected a member of the Philharmonic Society of Modena.

COMPOSITIONS BY HAYDN

which the instrument required is apparently a fortepiano, rather than a harpsichord.

1772 Symphonies Nos. 46, 47; String Quartets, Op. 20 (III:31–36); Baryton Trio (XI:106).

Symphony No. 45 ('Farewell').

Missa Sancti Nicolai (XXII:6).

1773 *Hexen-Schabbas* (marionette opera; lost); *L'infedeltà delusa* (XXVIII:5); *Acide* (revised version); *Philemon und Baucis* (marionette opera; XXIXa:1); Symphony No. 50; Piano Sonatas Nos. 36–41 (XVI:21–26), published Feb. 1774 in Vienna with dedication to Prince Nicolaus.

1774 Incidental music to Regnard's *Le Distrait*, later adapted and circulated as Symphony No. 60 ('Il distratto'); Symphonies Nos. 54–56.

Oratorio, *Il ritorno di Tobia* (XXI:1) begun.

1775 *L'incontro improvviso* (XXVIII:6); *Divertimenti a otto voci* (for baryton, 2 horns and strings; X:2, 3, 5).

1776 *Dido* (marionette opera; XXIXa:3); Symphony No. 61; Piano Sonatas Nos. 42–49 (XVI:27–32; some, e.g. No. 44, started in 1774); six Minuets for Orchestra (IX:5).

1777 Overture in D (Ia:7; for an unidentified Opera); insertion aria, 'D'una sposa meschinella' (XXIVb:2) for Giovanni Paisiello's *La Frascatana: Il mondo della luna* (XXVIII:7).

1778 *La vera costanza* begun; first performed 25 April 1779 at Eszterháza.

1779 Aria 'Quando la rosa' (XXIVb:3); marionette opera, *Die bestrafte Rachbegierde* (XXIXb:3; lost); *L'isola disabitata* (XXVIII:9); Symphonies Nos. 75 and 70; completion for publication of Piano Sonatas Nos. 48–52 and 33 (XVI:35–39, 20).

1780 The Opera *La fedeltà premiata* largely completed.

EVENTS IN HAYDN'S LIFE

The Empress Maria Theresa dies, 29 November.

1781 The rebuilt opera house at Eszterháza is inaugurated on 25 Feb. with H.'s *La fedeltà premiata*.

The first published portrait of H. (the engraving by J. E. Mansfeld) is issued in June by Artaria & Co.

H.'s first dealings with a British publisher – William Forster; Symphony No. 74 delivered to Forster on 22 August.

In September H. receives a gift of a valuable snuff-box from the Spanish Court.

1782 H. sells a collection of his Overtures to Artaria (issued as 'Sei Sinfonie opera XXXV').

Orlando Paladino performed at Eszterháza on 6 December (Prince Nicolaus's name-day).

1783 On 27 May the publisher Boßler of Speyer announces H.'s Symphonies Nos. 76–78; H. also sold these works to Forster, Torricella (Vienna) and Boyer (Paris).

On 15 September Nicolaus, grandson of Prince Nicolaus Esterházy and himself later Nicolaus II, marries Princess Marie Hermenegild Liechtenstein.

1784 On 31 January Artaria announces a collection of fourteen minuets by H. – *Raccolta de Menuetti Ballabili* (IX:7).

Armida receives its first performance, 26 Feb., at Eszterháza; H. writes 'I am told it is my best work up to now.' In June the composer Giuseppe Sarti hears a repeat performance of the opera when visiting the castle.

In March the Oratorio *Il ritorno di Tobia* is revived (with two new choruses) in Vienna.

H. commissioned by the Concert de la Loge Olympique in Paris to write six symphonies.

On 29 Dec. H. applies formally to become a Freemason.

1785 On 11 Feb. H. is admitted to the Freemasons' Lodge 'Zur wahren Eintracht' in Vienna; four days later, H. hears Mozart's six String Quartets (K. 387 etc.), formally dedicated to him by the composer in a letter on 1 Sept. for Artaria's edition of these works (as Op. X).

La fedeltà premiata performed at Pressburg in June.

1786 H. signs a contract with William Forster for a series of works to be published in London in the ensuing years.

The Eszterháza opera season comprises a total of 125 performances of seventeen different works.

1787 H. visits Graz in January; in July he writes to Sir John Gallini about a proposed visit to London (which does not materialize).

1788 The operatic season at Eszterháza comprises 108 performances.

On 28 Feb. H. writes to Forster trying to excuse the fact that Forster was not accorded exclusive rights to the 'Paris' Symphonies; their correspondence ceases. Meanwhile, Longman and Broderip import *The Seven Words* and the Quartets, Op. 50, from the Artaria editions.

1789 H. in correspondence with the Paris publisher Jean-Georges Sieber. In June H. begins corresponding with Maria Anna von Genzinger, wife of the physician-in-ordinary to Prince Nicolaus.

On 31 December H. attends a rehearsal in Vienna for Mozart's *Così fan tutte* (on 21 January H. accompanies Mozart to the first orchestral rehearsal).

1790 On 29 January H. organizes a quartet party at the house of Maria Anna von Genzinger.

COMPOSITIONS BY HAYDN

1781 String Quartets, Op. 33 (III:37–42); first series of *Lieder* (published in two sets: Dec. 1781 and 1783).

1782 *Missa Cellensis* ('Mariazellermesse'; XXII:8); Symphonies Nos. 76–78 – composed for a proposed visit to England that did not materialize; Opera, *Orlando Paladino* (XXVIII:11).

1783 Concerto for Violoncello in D (VIIb:2), composed for Anton Kraft, Esterházy's principal 'cellist; *Armida* ('dramma eroico'; XXVIII:2).

1784 Choruses 'Ah, gran Dio' and 'Svanisce in un momento' (the latter being adapted later as the Motet 'Insanae et vanae curae') added to *Il ritorno di Tobia*.

Piano Concerto in D (XVIII:11) issued by Artaria; Piano Sonatas Nos. 54–56 (XVI:40–42), dedicated to Princess Marie Hermenegild Esterházy, announced by Boßler; Flute Trios, Op. 38 (IV:6–11), for Forster; Piano Trios Nos. 17–19 (XV:2, 5, 6).

1785 Piano Trios Nos. 20–22 (XV:7–9); Symphonies Nos. 83 ('La Poule') and 87 completed for Paris; Quartet, Op. 42 (III:43) – possibly written for Spain; insertion arias for operas by Anfossi performed at Eszterháza.

1786 Five Concertos for the King of Naples (VIIh:1–5) begun; insertion arias for operas by Traetta and Gazzaniga performed at Eszterháza; Symphonies Nos. 82, 84, 86 completed for Paris; *The Seven Words* (XX:1) begun for Cádiz.

1787 Quartets, Op. 50 (III:44–49); Symphonies Nos. 88, 89; *Six Allemandes* for orchestra (IX:9) announced by Artaria; insertion arias for operas by Bianchi and Guglielmi.

1788 Quartets, Opp. 54 and 55 (III:57–62) completed; Symphonies Nos. 90, 91.

1789 Piano Sonata No. 58 (XVI:48), for Breitkopf in Leipzig; Symphony No. 92; Cantata, *Arianna a Naxos*; additional pieces for the *pasticcio* Opera, *La Circe* (performed at Eszterháza in July); pieces for musical clock (XIX:16 etc.).

1790 Insertion arias for operas by Gassmann and Cimarosa performed at Eszterháza; Piano Sonata No. 59

EVENTS IN HAYDN'S LIFE

On 20 Feb. the Emperor Joseph II dies; five days later Prince Nicolaus's wife dies at Eisenstadt.

In March H. receives a snuff-box as a gift from Prince Krafft-Ernst von Oettingen-Wallerstein, to whom H. had sent the orchestral parts of Symphonies Nos. 90–92 the previous November.

On 28 September Prince Nicolaus dies in Vienna; his successor, Prince Anton, dismisses the *Capelle*; H. takes up quarters in Vienna. There he is visited by J. P. Salomon, who arranges for H. to travel to England; they leave on 15 December, reaching Calais on 31 Dec.

1791 On 1 January H. and Salomon cross the Channel and from Dover proceed to London. H. takes lodgings at No. 18 Great Pulteney St. The first of the series of twelve Haydn-Salomon concerts is given at the Hanover Square Rooms on 11 March; the programme includes the English première of Symphony No. 92. A special benefit concert for H. is given on 16 May.

H. attends the annual Handel Festival (23 May–1 June) at Westminster Abbey. In July (at the instigation of Dr Charles Burney) H. receives an honorary doctorate at Oxford University; at a concert on 7 July, Symphony No. 92 is played (and henceforth nicknamed the 'Oxford').

From June on, H. and Rebecca Schroeter meet frequently and an intimate friendship develops.

H. attends a luncheon in honour of the Lord Mayor of London on 5 November; on 24 Nov. H. is invited by the Prince of Wales to visit Oatlands, the country house of the Duke and Duchess of York.

On 23 December H.'s former pupil Ignaz Pleyel arrives in London to act as principal composer for the rival Professional Concert series; next day the two men dine together, and a week later, they attend Guglielmi's *La pastorella nobile* at the Pantheon, accompanied by Luigia Polzelli's sister, Theresa Negri (also a singer).

1792 The first concert of Haydn-Salomon season is given on 17 February: the first performance of Symphony No. 93 is an enormous success. New works first performed at subsequent concerts: *The Storm* (24 Feb.); Symphony No. 98 (2 March); *Concertante* (9 March); Symphony No. 94 ('Surprise') rapturously received (23 March); and Symphony No. 97 (3 May – H.'s benefit concert).

On 14 June H. visits Windsor and Ascot, and also sees William Herschel's giant telescope at Slough.

In July H. returns to Vienna; he stops in Bonn, where arrangements are made for Ludwig van Beethoven to come to Vienna to study with him; Beethoven arrives there in November. H. also stops at Frankfurt, where Prince Anton Esterházy is attending the coronation of Emperor Leopold II (14 July).

On 25 November H. conducts his Redoutensaal Dances at the masked ball of the Gesellschaft bildender Künstler; Artaria afterwards publishes an arrangement (by H.) for piano. The dances are repeated at the Redoutensaal a year later.

1793 Maria Anna von Genzinger dies in Vienna on 20 January.

In London, the failure of H. to return causes much comment in the press; meanwhile, in Vienna on 15 March, H. presents three of his new 'Salomon' Symphonies at the Redoutensaal with great success.

In August H. purchases a house in the suburb of Gumpendorf (Kleine Steingasse No. 71). On 23 November H. writes a long letter about his pupil

COMPOSITIONS BY HAYDN

(XIV:49); Quartets, Op. 64 (III:63–68); Piano Variations in C (XVII:5); series of Notturni for the King of Naples (II:25–32) completed (some later re-written for London); Farewell Song, 'Trachten will ich nicht auf Erden' written (probably for Frau von Genzinger) on 14 December.

1791 *L'anima del filosofo (Orfeo ed Euridice; opera seria*; XXVIII:13), composed for the King's Theatre (Sir John Gallini) but not performed; Symphonies Nos. 96 and 95 and – for the next concert season – Nos. 93 and 94; Catch (*Maccone*) for Gallini (lost); Aria, 'Cara deh torna in pace' for Giacomo Davidde (lost); Scottish Songs, for William Napier (XXXIa:1–100 and 101–150 – last series issued in 1795).

1792 Madrigal 'The Storm' (XXIVa:8); Symphonies Nos. 98, 97 and the *Concertante* (I:105) for oboe, bassoon, violin and violoncello; March for the Prince of Wales (VIII:3); *The Ten Commandments* (XXVIIa:1–10).

The Redoutensaal Dances: Twelve Minuets (IX:11) and Twelve *Deutsche Tänze* (IX:12).

1793 Quartets, Opp. 71 and 74 (III:69–74), dedicated to Count Apponyi; Symphony No. 99; Symphony No. 101 begun; pieces for musical clock (XIX:29, 32 etc.); Piano Trio No. 31 (XV:32); *Adante con Variazioni* for piano (XVII:6).

EVENTS IN HAYDN'S LIFE	COMPOSITIONS BY HAYDN	EVENTS IN HAYDN'S LIFE	COMPOSITIONS BY HAYDN
Beethoven to the latter's patron, the Elector of Cologne. On 22/23 December H. conducts the Christmas music at charity concerts given by the Tonkünstler-Societät. **1794** On 10 January H. attends a performance of *La Principessa d'Amalfi*, an Opera by his godson, Joseph Weigl, Jr., which H. praises enthusiastically next day in a letter to Weigl. On 19 January H. departs for London (via Linz, Passau and Wiesbaden), taking his copyist Johann Elssler with him; they arrive on 4 February. Three days after H.'s departure Prince Anton Esterházy dies suddenly in Vienna. At the first Haydn-Salomon concert, H.'s Symphony No. 9 is fervently applauded at its first performance. Other new works performed: Symphony No. 101 (3 March); Symphony No. 100 (31 March). During the summer months H. visits Hampton Court, Portsmouth and the Isle of Wight (July); the Bank of England (15 July); Bath and Bristol, and Waverley Abbey (August).	**1794** Symphony No. 101 ('Clock') completed; Symphony No. 100 ('Military') completed; Six English Canzonettas (XXVIa:25–30), published 3 June. 'Dr. Harington's Compliment' (XXVIb:3) and the Canon 'Turk was a faithful dog' (XXVIIb:45) composed at Bath. Oratorio fragment *Mare Clausum* begun (two movements completed; XXIVa:9); 'London' Trios for two flutes and vc. (IV:1–4); 'Jacob's Dream', later 2nd movement of Piano Trio No. 41 (XV:31); Symphony No. 102 completed; Piano Trios Nos. 32–34 (XV:18–20), announced on 25 November (with dedication to Dowager Princess Esterházy, née Hohenfeld) by Longman and Broderip; Piano Sonatas Nos. 60–62 (XIV:50–52) for Therese Jansen; Six English Psalms (XXIII:Nachtrag), published in Rev. W. D. Tattersall's *Improved Psalmody*, 22 December; Overture to Salomon's *Windsor Castle* (Ia:3).	publishers Longman, Clementi & Co.; Rebecca Schroeter (in London) signs the document as one of the witnesses. In September H. travels to Eisenstadt: there he supplies incidental music for *Alfred* (performed on 9 Sept. – the Princess's name-day – by the visiting Stadler Troupe); in the Bergkirche on 11 Sept.(?) the *Missa Sancti Bernardi de Offida* is performed for the first time. On 26 December, before a huge congregation, H. conducts the first performance of the *Missa in tempore belli* in the Piarists' Church in Vienna; H. had begun composing this new Mass while at Eisenstadt. **1797** On the birthday of the Emperor Franz II (12 February) H.'s new anthem 'Gott erhalte' is sung throughout the Monarchy; the full orchestral version is sung at the Burgtheater in the Emperor's presence. On 24 March H. attends a concert of the Gesellschaft der Associirten at which Handel's *Acis and Galatea* is performed; here he meets the Swedish diplomat Frederik Samuel Silverstolpe (whose first-hand reports about events in Vienna and about H.'s activities are invaluable). The Empress Marie Therese visits Eszterháza on 18 August and from there proceeds to Eisenstadt. On 10 September (Princess Marie Hermenegild's name-day) a new chorus by H. – possibly the *Offertorium* 'Non nobis, Domine' (XXIIIa:1) – is given at the Bergkirche in Eisenstadt; 800 guests are present for the celebrations. On 27 September the Palatine Archduke Joseph, Viceroy of Hungary, arrives at Eisenstadt; 1,200 guests are present. On 29 Sept. H.'s *Missa in tempore belli* is performed at the Bergkirche. On 1 October Prince Nicolaus II increases H.'s annual salary to a total of 2,700 gulden (including 1,000 gulden he is already receiving as a pension under the terms of the Will of Nicolaus I). On a return visit (27 Oct.) the Archduke Joseph hears *The Seven Words* performed in the castle at Eisenstadt; 'Gott erhalte' is also sung. In Vienna on 11 December H. is unanimously elected Senior Assessor for life by the Tonkünstler-Societät, and becomes an honorary member 'with all formalities waived'. **1798** *The Seven Words* performed at the annual Easter concerts of the Tonkünstler-Societät (1 and 2 April). H. achieves the greatest success of his career with the première (29 and 30 April) of *The Creation* at the Palais Schwarzenberg; the work is repeated on 7 and 10 May. H. spends the summer months at Eisenstadt; there, the *Missa in tempore belli* is performed at the Bergkirche (12 August) and the new *Missa in angustiis* is first heard at the parish church of St Martin (23 Sept.). Meanwhile his brother Michael is visiting Vienna and the two men meet there in October. On 27 Oct. Beethoven plays his Piano Concerto No. 1 in C (Op. 15) at the Theater auf der Wieden, with Michael H. (and probably Joseph) among the audience. **1799** On 19 March *The Creation* receives its first public performance at the Burgtheater; an orchestra of 180 members (with triple woodwind, brass and timpani) perform, and the event is enormously successful. On 5 April, at a concert given by Count Fries in his Vienna palace, H. conducts his Symphony No. 102 and Beethoven plays in his Quintet, Op. 16. During April, Silverstolpe delivers to H. the membership diploma of the Royal Swedish Musical Academy. In May,	**1797** The *Volckslied*, 'Gott erhalte' (XXVIa:43); String Quartets, Op. 76 (III:75–80) begun – some of these new Quartets, including No. 3 (the 'Emperor'), are played at Eisenstadt on 27 September. *The Creation* (XXI:2) completed by H. while at Eisenstadt. **1798** *Missa in angustiis* ('Nelson' Mass; XXII:11) composed 10 July–31 August at Eisenstadt. *Aria dal 'Il Canzoniere' di Francesco Petrarca* (XXIVb:20), performed at the annual Christmas concert of the Tonkünstler-Societät by 'Demoiselle Flamm'. **1799** 'Spring' of *The Seasons* completed (April). *Missa* ('Theresienmesse'; XXII:12); String Quartets in G and F (Op. 77), played at Eisenstadt Castle on 13 October.
1795 On 12 January Salomon announces the cessation of his concerts and his merger with the Opera Concerts, at which H.'s works were performed during his last London season: first concert 2 February – first performance of Symphony No. 102; No. 103 given on 2 March. At H.'s last London benefit concert, on 4 May, the *Scena di Berenice* (with Banti as soloist) and Symphony No. 104 are performed for the first time; H. receives 4,000 gulden from the proceeds. On 1 February H. attends a musical soirée at the Duke of York's, with the King, Queen and other members of the Royal Family present. Subsequently he 'presides' at a concert given by the Prince of Wales at Carlton House on 10 April, and makes further appearances at the Prince of Wales's on 15, 17, and 19 April, and is a guest of the Queen at Buckingham House on 21 April. On 3 February H.'s friend and mentor in England, the Earl of Abingdon, is convicted for libel. On 27 May H.'s principal London publisher, Longman & Broderip, is declared bankrupt, but the firm manages to stay in business. On 15 August H. leaves England for Hamburg en route to Vienna; he takes with him the MS. libretto for an Oratorio (*The Creation*) procured for him by Salomon. On 22 November H. attends a masked ball at the Redoutensaal at which Beethoven makes his début as an orchestral composer: his Twelve Minuets (WoO7) and Twelve German Dances (WoO8) are performed. On 18 December H. gives a concert at the Redoutensaal: he introduces three of the 'Salomon' Symphonies (including No. 100) from the second series to the Viennese public, and Beethoven plays his own Piano Concerto in B flat (Op. 19). **1796** On 8 January H. and Beethoven participate again at the Redoutensaal, at a benefit concert for Maria Bolla. On 26 and 27 March H.'s choral version of *The Seven Words* is performed in Vienna at the Palais Schwarzenberg – the first of the historic Gesellschaft der Associirten performances there (cf. *The Creation* and *The Seasons*, below); the Gesellschaft was supported by members of the aristocracy and managed by Gottfried van Swieten. On 10 August H. signs a general contract with F. A. Hyde for the London	**1795** Symphonies Nos. 103 ('Drum Roll') and 104 ('London'); Piano Trios Nos. 35–37 (XV:21–23) for Preston of London, Nos. 38–40 (XV:24–26) for Longman and Broderip, and No. 41 (XX:31) probably for Therese Jansen; the Second Set of English Canzonettas (XXVIa:31–36); Marches for the Derbyshire Cavalry Regiment (VII:1, 2); *Scena di Berenice* (XXIVa:10); Song, 'O Tuneful Voice' (XXVIa:42); etc. The catalogue of music which H. composed in or for England (contained in his Fourth London Notebook) lists over 3,000 pages of MS. music, of which the 'Salomon' Symphonies occupy over one-third of the total. Revised choral version of *The Seven Words* (XX:2) begun, with text by Gottfried van Swieten. **1796** Piano Trio No. 42 (XV:30), given to Joseph Weigl Jr. on 9 Nov. to take to Breitkopf & Härtel in Leipzig; Trumpet Concerto (VIIe:1); *Mehrstimmige Gesänge* (part songs; XXVb:1–4 and XXVc:1–9) begun; Chorus, Aria and Duet (XXX:5) as incidental music to *Alfred*; *Missa Sancti Bernardi de Offida* (XXII:10); *Missa in tempore belli* (XXII:9); Piano Trios Nos. 43–45 (XX:27–29) sent to Longman and Broderip for publication; *The Creation* (XXI:2) begun.		

EVENTS IN HAYDN'S LIFE	COMPOSITIONS BY HAYDN	EVENTS IN HAYDN'S LIFE	COMPOSITIONS BY HAYDN

Georg August Griesinger arrives in Vienna to join the Saxonian Legation; he becomes the go-between in H.'s dealings with Breitkopf & Härtel in Leipzig.

In June H. announces a subscription to the full score of *The Creation* (which he will publish himself).

H.'s new Mass ('Theresienmesse') is given its first performance in the Bergkirche at Eisenstadt on 8 September, at the banquet given by Prince Nicolaus afterwards, he 'also drank Haydn's health, to general concurrence' (Rosenbaum). In October the new Quartets, Op. 77, are played at the Castle (13th) and some of the *Mehrstimmige Gesänge* at a concert given by the Provost of Eisenstadt, Andreas Seitz (16th).

On 30 October the Scottish publisher George Thomson approaches H. to have him arrange Scottish (and other British and Irish) songs; from February 1800 and in the course of the next few years H. writes/arranges several hundred songs. On 9 November Breitkopf & Härtel announce H.'s 'Oeuvres Complettes' – but this title is a misnomer.

1800 The score of *The Creation* is published on 28 February.

On 19 March H. is in Baden, where his ailing wife dies the next day; under the terms of her Will, dated 9 September 1799, H. is residuary legatee of her estate.

At a concert in the Burgtheater in Vienna on 28 March, Anton Weidinger is soloist in the Trumpet Concerto's first public performance (the work was written for him in 1796).

On 1 July H. offers to Breitkopf & Härtel *The Seasons* (still incomplete) and the choral version of *The Seven Words*; both are accepted.

On 18 August Admiral Lord Nelson, accompanied by Sir William and Lady Hamilton and Ellis Cornelia Knight, arrives in Vienna; H. dines with them. In September the party visits Eisenstadt (6–9th); during their stay the 'Nelson' Mass and the *Te Deum* for the Empress (XXIIIc:2) are performed in the Bergkirche. H. writes a Cantata for Lady Hamilton, to whom the work is dedicated.

On 11 December the Emperor, accompanied by the Empress, the Queen of Naples, the Grand Duke of Tuscany etc., pays a state visit to Eisenstadt.

At the annual Christmas concerts (22 and 23 December) given in Vienna by the Tonkünstler-Societät, *The Creation* is given for the second year in succession.

1801 On 28 March H. hears Beethoven's ballet music *Die Geschöpfe des Prometheus* at the Burgtheater, and approves.

On 20 May writes to the Paris piano builders, Érard Frères, to thank them for the gift of a grand piano in the English manner sent to him in April.

The Seasons receives its first performance at the Palais Schwarzenberg on 24 April; the work is performed at Court (with the Empress as soprano soloist) on 24 May. The first public performance is given – to a half-empty hall – at the Redoutensaal on 29 May.

H. spends the summer months in Eisenstadt; he receives a visit from Adalbert Gyrowetz in August; on 13 September his new Mass is performed in the Bergkirche. Michael Haydn visits Eisenstadt and is offered the post of *Kapellmeister* to Prince Nicolaus, but he declines.

1800 The *Te Deum* for the Empress Marie Therese (XXIIIc:2) (?); Cantata, 'Lines from the *Battle of the Nile*', with text by Ellis Cornelia Knight.

1801 *The Seasons* (XXI:3) completed; *Missa* in B flat (Schöpfungsmesse; XXII:13) composed at Eisenstadt.

In December the sculptor Anton Grassi models a bust of H. (later made in biscuit porcelain). The Tonkünstler-Societät perform *The Seasons* at their Christmas charity concerts (22, 23 Dec.).

1802 In January H. begins sending his Masses to Breitkopf & Härtel for publication; the publishers announce the works in March, beginning with the *Missa Sancti Bernardi de Offida* in full score.

In June H. begins work on his last Mass; it is performed in Eisenstadt in the Bergkirche on 8 September.

On 26 December, at a charity concert for the aged poor of St Marx (a Viennese suburb), *The Creation* is performed at the Redoutensaal; for this and other charity performances the City of Vienna awards (May 1803) H. a gold medal.

1803 H. works on his last Quartet in March. During the summer months he goes to Eisenstadt; there, on 27 August, he hears a Cantata by the new *Vice-Kapellmeister*, J. N. Fuchs, performed to celebrate the return of Prince Nicolaus from a visit to Paris.

On 26 December H. conducts *The Seven Words* at a charity concert for the poor of St Marx – his last appearance as conductor. H. retires. J. N. Hummel is engaged by Prince Nicolaus as *Konzertmeister*.

1802 *Missa* in B flat ('Harmoniemesse'; XXII:14); Hungarian National Marsch, for the wind band at Eisenstadt – H.'s last completed instrumental composition.

1803 String Quartet, 'Op. 103' (III:83), unfinished.

EVENTS IN HAYDN'S LIFE, 1804–1809

1804 On 1 April H. is accorded honorary citizenship by the City of Vienna for his charitable work. In August he is preparing the catalogue of his works (the so-called *Haydn-Verzeichnis*), which his copyist Johann Elssler drew up finally in 1805.

1805 In April the landscape painter A. C. Dies visits H. and begins his biographical record of the composer's life.

On 10 May H.'s younger brother Johann dies at Eisenstadt; the news is broken to him by Princess Marie Hermenegild Esterházy.

On 26 June the members of the Paris Conservatoire de Musique send H. a medal as a mark of their respect; Luigi Cherubini delivers the medal and accompanying letter after his arrival in Vienna in July.

On 5 November Dr Henry Reeve, a British physician, visits H. and finds him in excellent spirits.

1806 On 24 February H. presents the autograph of Symphony No. 103 to Cherubini. On 2 April Griesinger secures H.'s last, unfinished Quartet ('Op. 103') for publication by Breitkopf & Härtel.

On 10 August, Michael Haydn dies in Salzburg.

1807 On 13 April the Empress Marie Therese dies.

Because of his own frailty and failing health, H. has himself taken to the Servite Monastery on 27 April; he hopes for relief from the swelling in his legs. (The exercise is repeated the following year.)

1808 To mark H.'s 76th birthday, a special performance of *The Creation* is given at the Old University in Vienna on 27 March, with Antonio Salieri as conductor; on this, his last public appearance, H. is fêted by the distinguished company present, which includes Beethoven.

On 22 May, the Esterházy *Capelle* (63 persons) give a guest performance in Vienna; the members come in small groups to pay their respects to H. at his house in Gumpendorf. Other visitors include the actor and writer A. W. Iffland (8 Sept.) and the composer and writer J. F. Reichardt (November).

On 22 December H. writes his last surviving letter: in it he thanks Prince Nicolaus for taking care of his medical expenses.

1809 On 7 February H. signs his last Will; in it he leaves 6,000 gulden to his faithful servant and copyist Johann Elssler.

On 31 May H. dies at his home in Gumpendorf. Elssler takes a death-mask in plaster. Next day, after the funeral at the parish church, his remains are interred in the Hundsthurmer cemetery – 'Not one Viennese *Kapellmeister* was in the funeral cortège.' (Rosenbaum). On 15 June a memorial service is held in Vienna at the Schottenkirche, at which Mozart's *Requiem* is performed. The French forces, who have occupied the city, send a guard of honour; Rosenbaum records in his Diary: 'The whole of Viennese society appeared, for the most part in mourning.'

The princely Esterházy family before and during Haydn's lifetime

(names of individual princes are shown in capitals)

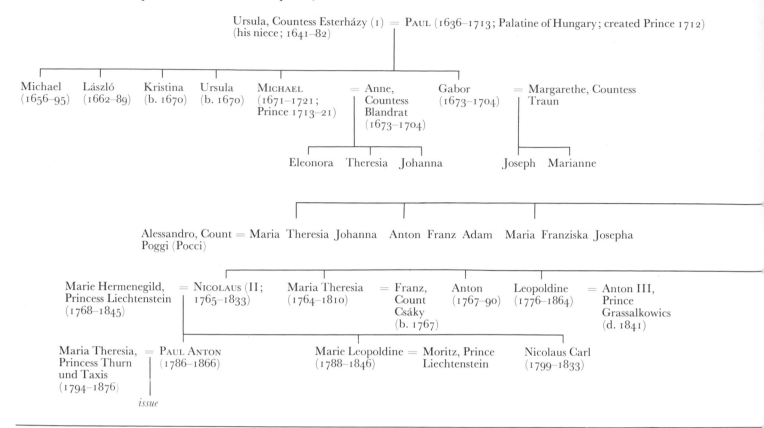

The Habsburg Dynasty (names of Holy Roman Emperors are shown in capitals)

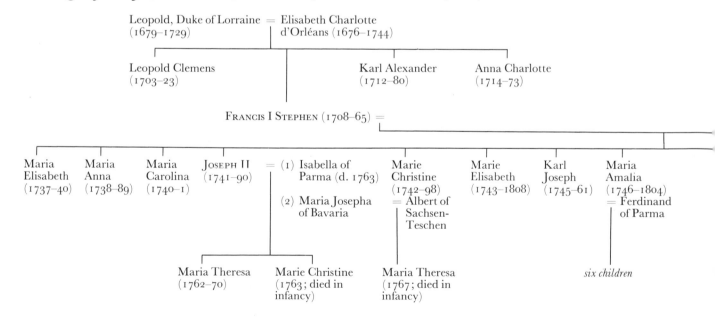

GENEALOGICAL TABLES

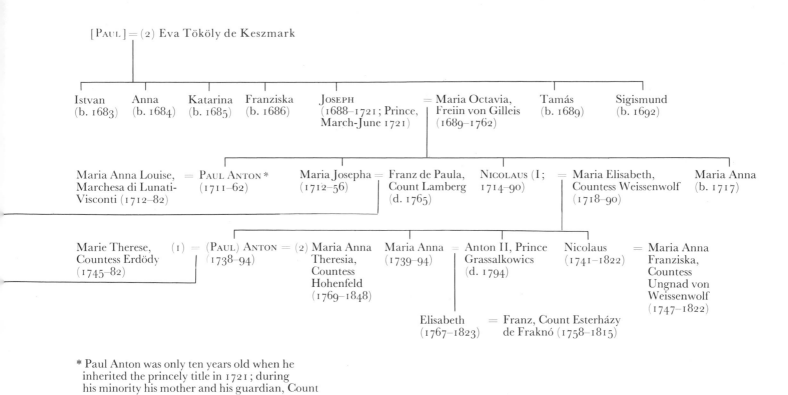

[PAUL] = (2) Eva Tököly de Keszmark

Istvan (b. 1683)   Anna (b. 1684)   Katarina (b. 1685)   Franziska (b. 1686)   JOSEPH (1688–1721; Prince, March-June 1721) = Maria Octavia, Freiin von Gilleis (1689–1762)   Tamás (b. 1689)   Sigismund (b. 1692)

Maria Anna Louise, Marchesa di Lunati-Visconti (1712–82) = PAUL ANTON * (1711–62)   Maria Josepha (1712–56) = Franz de Paula, Count Lamberg (d. 1765)   NICOLAUS (I; 1714–90) = Maria Elisabeth, Countess Weissenwolf (1718–90)   Maria Anna (b. 1717)

Marie Therese, Countess Erdödy (1745–82) (1) = (PAUL) ANTON (1738–94) = (2) Maria Anna Theresia, Countess Hohenfeld (1769–1848)   Maria Anna (1739–94) = Anton II, Prince Grassalkowics (d. 1794)   Nicolaus (1741–1822) = Maria Anna Franziska, Countess Ungnad von Weissenwolf (1747–1822)

Elisabeth (1767–1823) = Franz, Count Esterházy de Frakno (1758–1815)

* Paul Anton was only ten years old when he inherited the princely title in 1721; during his minority his mother and his guardian, Count Georg Erdödy, acted as regents.

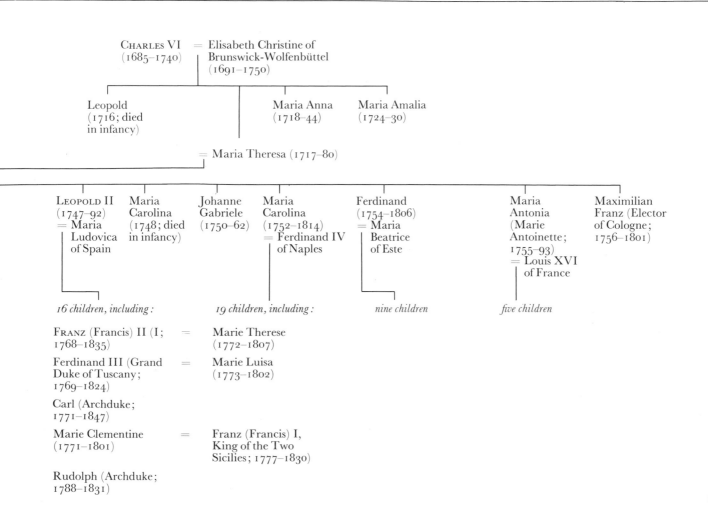

CHARLES VI (1685–1740) = Elisabeth Christine of Brunswick-Wolfenbüttel (1691–1750)

Leopold (1716; died in infancy)   Maria Anna (1718–44)   Maria Amalia (1724–30)

= Maria Theresa (1717–80)

LEOPOLD II (1747–92) = Maria Ludovica of Spain   Maria Carolina (1748; died in infancy)   Johanne Gabriele (1750–62)   Maria Carolina (1752–1814) = Ferdinand IV of Naples   Ferdinand (1754–1806) = Maria Beatrice of Este   Maria Antonia (Marie Antoinette; 1755–93) = Louis XVI of France   Maximilian Franz (Elector of Cologne; 1756–1801)

16 children, including: *19 children, including:*   *nine children*   *five children*

FRANZ (Francis) II (I; 1768–1835) = Marie Therese (1772–1807)

Ferdinand III (Grand Duke of Tuscany; 1769–1824) = Marie Luisa (1773–1802)

Carl (Archduke; 1771–1847)

Marie Clementine (1771–1801) = Franz (Francis) I, King of the Two Sicilies; 1777–1830)

Rudolph (Archduke; 1788–1831)

SELECT BIBLIOGRAPHY

Biographical

EARLY NINETEENTH-CENTURY PUBLICATIONS:
Carpani, G., *Le Haydine . . .*, Milan 1812 (2nd ed. 1823);
Dies, A. C., *Biographische Nachrichten von Joseph Haydn*, Vienna 1810 (new ed., by Horst Seeger, Berlin n.d. [1959];
Framery, N., *Notice sur Joseph Haydn*, Paris 1810;
Griesinger, G. A. von, *Biographische Notizen über Joseph Haydn*, Leipzig 1810 (new ed., by F. Grasberger, Vienna 1954).

LATE NINETEENTH-CENTURY AND MODERN PUBLICATIONS:
Geiringer, K., *Joseph Haydn*, Potsdam 1932, New York 1947, Mainz 1959, Garden City, N.Y. 1963;
Hughes, Rosemary S. M., *Haydn*, London 1950 (and later revised editions);
Landon, H. C. Robbins, *Haydn: Chronicle and Works* (5 vols.), London and Bloomington, Ind., 1976 et seq.;
Pohl, C. F., *Joseph Haydn* (vol. I, Berlin 1875; vol. II, Berlin 1882; vol. III, completed by H. Botstiber, Leipzig 1927 – all three volumes since reprinted).
Articles on Haydn in:
Grove's *Dictionary of Music and Musicians* (6th ed., 1980) by J. P. Larsen and G. Feder;
Musik in Geschichte und Gegenwart (ed. F. Blume), Kassel 1947 et seq., by H. C. Robbins Landon and J. P. Larsen.

Haydn's correspondence and other documents

Bartha, Dénes (ed.), *Joseph Haydn. Gesammelte Briefe und Aufzeichnungen*, Budapest/ Kassel 1965;
Landon, H. C. Robbins (ed.), *Collected Correspondence and London Notebooks of Joseph Haydn*, London 1959;
See also scholarly articles appearing in:
Haydn Yearbook, 1962 et seq.; and
Haydn-Studien, 1965 et seq.

Specialized monographs

Barrett-Ayres, R., *Haydn and the String Quartet*, London 1974;
Bartha, Dénes, and Somfai, László, *Haydn als Opernkapellmeister*, Budapest 1960;

Brand, C. M., *Die Messen von Joseph Haydn*, Würzburg 1941;
Brown, A. Peter, *Haydn's Piano Music* (in preparation);
Feder, G., 'Die Überlieferung und Verbreitung der handschriftlichen Quellen zu Haydns Werken' (1st series), in *Haydn-Studien* I/1 (1965); English ed., 'Manuscript sources of Haydn's works and their distribution', in *Haydn Yearbook* IV (1968); 'Haydns frühe Klaviertrios', in *Haydn-Studien* II/4 (1970); 'Apokryphe "Haydn"-Streichquartette', in *Haydn-Studien* III/2 (1974);
Finscher, L., *Studien zur Geschichte des Streichquartetts*, I, Kassel 1974;
Landon, H. C. Robbins, *The Symphonies of Joseph Haydn*, London 1955 (and *Supplement*, 1961);
Larsen, J. P., *Die Haydn-Überlieferung*, Copenhagen 1939 (reprinted 1981);
Wackernagel, Bettina, *Joseph Haydns frühe Klaviersonaten . . .*, Tutzing 1974

Critical editions of compositions by Haydn:

COLLECTED EDITIONS:
Since 1953 the Joseph Haydn-Institut, Cologne, and G. Henle Verlag, Munich/Duisburg, have to date published about half of Haydn's *oeuvre*.

ORCHESTRAL WORKS:
Symphonies: the complete Symphonies are published by Universal Edition (Haydn-Mozart Presse) and Doblinger, 1965 et seq.
Concertos: individual works are available from Bärenreiter, Breitkopf & Härtel, Doblinger, Edition Eulenburg, Edition Peters and Universal Edition.

OPERAS; INSERTION ARIAS; SECULAR VOCAL WORKS:
Individual works are published in critical/practical editions by Bärenreiter, Universal Edition (Haydn-Mozart Presse) and Schott.

ORATORIOS:
The Seven Words (choral version), *The Creation* and *The Seasons* – all in Mandyczewski's edition – are published by Breitkopf & Härtel.

MASSES:
Critical/practical editions of individual works are published by Eulenburg (Schott), Faber, Universal Edition, Schirmer, Bärenreiter and University Press, Cardiff.

[critical editions – *continued*]

SMALLER CHURCH WORKS:

Various works published by Henle, Doblinger and Universal Edition (Haydn-Mozart Presse).

CHAMBER MUSIC (complete critical editions):

The Piano Trios (ed. Landon), String Trios (ed. Landon), and String Quartets (ed. Barrett-Ayres, Landon) are published by Doblinger.

The Piano Sonatas are available from Universal Edition (ed. C. Landon) and from Henle Verlag (ed. G. Feder). The smaller works for piano are also published by Universal Edition (ed. F. Eibner) and Henle (ed. S. Gerlach).

Standard recorded editions

Symphonies: complete series (Antal Dorati), issued by Decca (in U.S.A.: London).

Operas: selected works (Antal Dorati) issued by Philips.

Oratorios: (Antal Dorati) issued by Decca.

Masses: all works available, with various artists, from Argo, Oiseau-Lyre and Decca.

Chamber music: complete Piano Trios issued by Philips (Beaux Arts Trio) and by Telefunken (Haydn Trio); complete String Quartets issued by Argo (Aeolian Quartet); complete Piano Sonatas issued by Argo (John McCabe).

SOURCES OF ILLUSTRATIONS

Apart from items in the author's and other private collections, photographs were supplied by the following (all references are to illustration numbers unless otherwise indicated).

Albertina, Vienna 6, 7, 29, 30, 31, 151; Art Institute of Chicago (Charles H. and Mary F. S. Worcester Collection) 72; Barmherzige Brüder (Hospitallers Order), Eisenstadt 26; City of Bath Museums Service: 114, 115 (Victoria Art Gallery); 116 (Pump Room); Bertarelli Collection, Milan 84, 86, 87, 122, 123, 159; Bibliothèque Nationale, Paris 47; Breitkopf & Härtel Archives 176; Trustees of the British Library 65; Trustees of the British Museum 83, 95, 97, 106, 109, 111, 124, 125, 129, 191, p. 125, p. 145; Burgenländisches Landesmuseum, Eisenstadt 22, 158, 164, 166, 167, 173, 179, 184; Peter Cannon-Brookes 39, 40; Carnegie Hall, New York City p. 93; Conservatorio di Musica, Naples 73; Conservatorio S. Cecilia, Rome 52; Conservatorio S. Pietro a Majella, Naples 12; Courtauld Institute of Art, London 94; Count Eugen Czernin Archive, Castle Jindřichův Hradec, Czechoslovakia 198; Eisenstadt: Archives of the Cathedral of St Martin 197; Esterházy Archives, Eisenstadt 44, 112; Gesellschaft der Musikfreunde, Vienna 43, 48, 64, 70, 160, 181, p. 79; Goethe-Museum, Düsseldorf 78, 88; Guy Gravett (Picture Index) 62; Harrach Archives, Vienna 190; Haydn Museum, Vienna 156; Heiligenkreuz Abbey 13; Historisches Museum der Stadt Wien 10, 16, 28, 71, 77, 141, 163, 168, 170, 186; Hluboká Castle, Czechoslovakia 113, 152; Holland Festival Press Office, Amsterdam 55, 57; Hungarian Embassy, London 36, 38; Iparmüvészeti Museum, Budapest 35; Louis Krasner, Syracuse, N.Y. 177; Kunsthistorisches Museum, Vienna 8, 9, 46, 133, 149; Erich Lessing (Magnum) 21, 27, 41, 182; Library of Congress, Washington, D.C. 201; Collections of the Ruling Prince of Liechtenstein, Vaduz 139; Galerie Liechtenstein, Vienna 172; Marc Loliée, Paris 199; Mansell Collection 107; Mellon Collection 90, 96; Metropolitan Museum of Art, New York (Bequest of George D. Pratt, 1935) 103; Mozart Gedenkstätte, Augsburg 74; National Galleries of Scotland 99; National Portrait Gallery, London 104, 120, 165; Niederösterreichische Landesbildstelle 4, 5, 42; Niederösterreichische Landesregierung 148; Olympia Publishing House, Prague 17; Orszagós Széchényi Könyvtár, Budapest 14, 37, 60, 61, 63, 143, 144, 153, 193, 194, 204, 205, p. 43; Österreichische Galerie, Vienna 137, 142; Österreichische Nationalbibliothek, Vienna 80, 85, 89, 136, 145, 154, 157, 183, 184, 187, 202, p. 138; Courtesy, the Heather Professor of Music, Oxford University 140; Trustees of the Pierpont Morgan Library, New York: 169 (gift of Reginald Allen); 196, 200 (both Mary Flagler Cary Music Collection); Countess Pilati, Schloß Riegersberg, Lower Austria 134; Preußische Staatsbibliothek, Berlin 192, 195, p. 144; Royal Acadamy of Arts, London 93; Royal Collection. By gracious permission of Her Majesty The Queen 98; Royal College of Music, London 81, 82, 100, 189; Sächsische Landesbibliothek, Dresden 206; Helga Schmidt-Glassner, Stuttgart 66, 67; Silverstolpe Collection, Näs Castle, Sweden 147; Stadtbibliothek, Vienna 155; Prof. Hans Swarowsky, Vienna 174; Universal Edition, Vienna 54, 56, 58; Victoria and Albert Museum, London 91, 108, 110; Dr Johannes Zachs, Eisenstadt 1, 18, 20, 32, 188; Stift Zwettl, Lower Austria 50

INDEX

222